ALL THINGS MADE NEW

ALL THINGS MADE NEW

John Flavel for the Christian Life

Selected and Edited by

Lewis Allen

THE BANNER OF TRUTH TRUST

THE BANNER OF TRUTH TRUST

3 Murrayfield Road, Edinburgh, EH12 6EL, UK
PO Box 621, Carlisle, Pennsylvania 17013, USA

© The Banner of Truth Trust 2017

*

ISBN
Print: 978 1 84871 733 6
EPUB: 978 1 84871 734 3
Kindle: 978 1 84871 735 0

*

Typeset in 10/13 Adobe Garamond Pro
at the Banner of Truth Trust, Edinburgh

Printed in the USA by
Versa Press, Inc., East Peoria, IL

Contents

PART THREE
LIVING THE CHRISTIAN LIFE

PART FOUR
THE CHURCH

Introduction

Old sermons, dead words?

Why read old sermons? With so many good modern Christian books to choose from, why would anyone want to invest time and energy going back to the dead voices of the past? And in a rapidly-changing modern world (not to mention, church), can we gain anything from the writings of a man who lived long before the discovery of electricity, let alone the creation of the Internet?

My own conviction is that we need John Flavel. We need him, as we need a host of other long-dead voices, to instruct us in how to know God and walk confidently with Jesus Christ. Flavel and others with him who took the name 'Puritan' have so much to teach us. If this book is your first encounter with a Puritan author, then my prayer for you is that it will ignite a fire in your soul, not so much for Puritan authors, but for the God of whom they speak so compellingly.

Don't be put off by the word 'Puritan' if it is new to you. The Puritans were godly, Bible-believing church pastors of the sixteenth and seventeenth centuries. They longed to see godliness flourish in heart, home, church, and nation, and they believed that the gospel was the power of God to transform both individuals and the nations. If they were hated then—and they met with stiff opposition—let that be a reminder to us that distinctive Christian living always brings controversy and division. John

Flavel knew this well, and the aim of his ministry was to bring people to Christ and to teach them to live in wholehearted obedience to him, especially when the going got tough.

So why read John Flavel, when there are so many other good books for us to read alongside our Bibles? Consider these three points:

1. Flavel was a man who knew Jesus Christ.

Flavel's writings are full of the Lord Jesus Christ. His mind and heart were mastered by his Saviour. Flavel knew what it was to suffer. He lost those dearest to him, was thrown out of his church and home because of his Christian beliefs, and faced danger and injustice for years on end. In all of this, Jesus Christ was his treasure and delight. It was Jesus Christ who sustained him. Flavel loved his Bible, and in the portions of his writings selected for this book he will open up to us the glory and wonder of the person of his totally trustworthy Lord and Saviour.

2. Flavel was a man who knew the human heart.

Ministry experience and qualifications mean very little if the preacher doesn't know what it feels like to have a broken heart, a tempted heart, or what it is like to live with spiritual depression. Those who shepherd the Lord's flock must be able to draw alongside and provide spiritual help and comfort where it is needed. Flavel, like his Lord, was a tender-hearted pastor. He writes with a gentleness and proven authority on issues related to the Christian life. He understood his people well, and knew how their minds worked and the kind of things that brought them sorrow and made them shed tears. When you read Flavel, you will sense his genuine concern to help others, including you!

3. Strangers sometimes become the most valued friends.

We have all been blessed by a first meeting with someone we have never known before. We have also valued a 'chance' conversation with a new acquaintance, and looked forward to further interaction. There are numerous stories from Flavel's life of how people 'happened to meet him' and came away deeply thankful, and full of resolve to walk with Christ as a result. The same is true of encounters made through Flavel's writings. Who knows, but the stranger you will meet with in the pages of this book might well become a firm friend, who will be a constant source of refreshment to you while you press on towards your heavenly home.

John Flavel: ministry in a hailstorm

John Flavel was born at Bromsgrove, Worcestershire, in 1627, the elder son of Richard Flavel, the minister of the town's parish church. After receiving his education within in the home and locally, Flavel went up to University College, Oxford, in 1646, and at some point during his two years' study there he came to a personal faith in Jesus Christ. Flavel gives us no record of how or when he was converted. In the preface to his *Treatise of the Soul of Man* he states,

> I was carried away so many years in the course of this world (like a drop with the current of the tide), wholly forgetting my best self, my invaluable soul; whilst I prodigally wasted the stores of my thoughts and time upon vanities, that long since passed away as the waters which are remembered no more … I studied to know many other things, but I knew not myself.

Jesus Christ knew Flavel, though, and brought him to himself. Flavel used his time at university to good effect, studying hard, and growing in his Christian faith. When the rector of Diptford in Devon inquired amongst his Oxford contacts of the availability of a suitable assistant, Flavel was recommended to him. So in

April 1650 Flavel began his Devon ministry, and was ordained by a presbytery at Salisbury six months later.

Flavel took to his ministry in Diptford with a zeal which would characterize his whole life. He succeeded the rector who died shortly after Flavel's arrival. His years there were devoted to pastoral ministry. He married twice, having lost his first wife and their son in childbirth. He was a well-liked man, showing a transparent kindness towards his parishioners. Nor was his popularity simply amongst his own people; Flavel was valued as a moderator in some local church matters. This gifted and respected young man was courted by the minister of Dartmouth to be his successor, and in 1656 Flavel took up that charge. By the early seventeenth century the fishing industry had brought wealth to many of the town's inhabitants, and with its deep-water harbour, Dartmouth was a base for the English navy. So began Flavel's life's work.

The next six years were a busy round of pastoral ministry, study, and writing. Flavel shared the ministry of two churches with his assistant, and together they devoted themselves to the needs of the parishes, particularly to Lord's Day and mid-week preaching, catechizing, and ministering to the sick. Nor did Flavel miss the opportunities which being in a sea-faring town afforded him. *Navigation Spiritualized: or, A New Compass for Seamen* was the first of three works which were addressed to the needs of seafarers and those in the town's related industries (the third being *A Faithful Narrative of Some Late and Wonderful Sea Deliverances*, 1679). The reception of that work encouraged him in his publication of *Husbandry Spiritualized: or, the Heavenly Use of Earthly Things* (1669), in which he sought to minister to the area's farmers.

The fruitfulness of Flavel's Dartmouth charge was cut short by the Great Ejection of 1662. The Act of Uniformity of the same year introduced a raft of measures designed to strengthen the control of the King (Charles II) and his supporters over the Church of England, as well as to end the influence of the Puritans. Some two thousand clergy refused to subscribe to the terms of the Acts, knowing that their action would lead to the end of their ministries (and livelihoods) in the Established Church. Flavel's assistant, whose health was always precarious during their shared ministry, died just four months after the Ejection. Flavel knew that his nonconformity put him in grave danger, but he continued to preach to his congregation as far as he was able, and taught in a nonconformist academy.

With the Oxford or Five Mile Act of 1665, Flavel was compelled to move away from Dartmouth. He chose to live in Slapton, which was exactly five miles from Dartmouth. Often his people and others went out to hear him preach there. Flavel also busied himself in frequent travels around the county, adopting various disguises so as to minister in secret at pre-arranged meeting places. He met members of his congregation still loyal to him in woods at night, with guards posted to warn of any approaching enemies. There are records of Flavel preaching in the vicinity of Exeter (a highly dangerous undertaking at the time), and slipping into Dartmouth by night. On occasion, he preached on horseback on Salstone Rock, an island which was exposed at low tide in the Salcombe Estuary, reasoning that, as the island belonged to no one, it wasn't subject to the King's law. The local authorities were not of the same persuasion, and once he had to plunge his horse into the rising tide to escape the soldiers sent to arrest him.

The Declaration of Indulgence of 1672 allowed Flavel to move back into Dartmouth. The Declaration, designed by King Charles II to ease persecution of Roman Catholics, was fiercely resisted by Parliament, and its revision the following year in the form of the Test Act meant that Nonconformists were again the victims of harassment which was harsher than before. Flavel's ministry had to be more circumspect, and hostility towards Nonconformists was on the increase.

It was during this time that Flavel married his second wife, who gave birth to two sons.

Amidst the turbulence of these years Flavel decided to go to London in 1682, seeing it as a place where he could work more freely and effectively. He teamed up with a London minister, and they worked together for a time. During his two years in London Flavel lost his second wife, and married again for the third time. His fellow-minister died from an infection which he caught in prison following his arrest by the authorities (Flavel had been present at the arrest but narrowly avoided capture). The congregation of the church wanted Flavel to stay with them as their pastor, but he declined and returned to Dartmouth.

There was no let-up in the trials Flavel was to face there. He had to endure house arrest and an effigy of this faithful and zealous minister was burned in the streets. During the next three years preaching opportunities were very restricted, and Flavel gave himself largely to writing. He also married for a final time.

The reversal of fortunes for the Nonconformists with the Declaration of Indulgence of 1687, and then the Glorious Revolution of 1688, brought dramatic change to Flavel's life and work. Not only was he able to preach again without restriction, but he also found his gifts and experience put to good use in the cause he so loved, that of the Reformed churches. In 1691 he was called upon to moderate the meetings between Presbyterians and Independents at Exeter, arranged for the purpose of deepening unity between the two denominations. This was to be one of his last public acts. Flavel died on 26 June that year after suffering a stroke. The loss of this good and godly man was keenly felt by many. A pastor, evangelist, theologian, educator, churchman, and disciple of Jesus Christ had at last entered into his rest and reward.

Flavel didn't live to preach the sermon he planned to deliver at Exeter. His notes, though, speak eloquently of the strain as well as the reward of ministry which his own labours so powerfully exemplified:

> How many truths we have to study! How many wiles of Satan, and mysteries of corruption, to detect! How many cases of conscience to resolve! Yea, we must fight in defence of the truths we preach, as well as study them to paleness, and preach them unto faintness; but well-spent head, heart, lungs, and all; welcome pained breasts, aching backs and trembling legs; if we can by all but approve ourselves Christ's faithful servants, and hear that joyful voice from his mouth, 'Well done, good and faithful servants.'

Words for readers

My own interest in Flavel began perhaps a dozen years ago, when an older friend in ministry urged me to buy all six volumes of the *Works of John Flavel* published by the Banner of Truth Trust. 'Read them all!' was his exhortation. And so he put me in his, as well as in Flavel's, debt. My desire now is that this book will kindle in your heart a love for the writings of John Flavel.

In *Navigation Spiritualized* Flavel says, 'Divinity … is nothing else but the art of soul-navigation, as revealed from heaven.' Perhaps no other single sentence of Flavel so fittingly summarizes his life's conviction and work. The word of God and its doctrines held the very greatest importance for Flavel. The Bible is the revelation of God. Its truth is to be studied, believed, and shared. Our never-dying souls are to be led through life's storms to Christ, and with him, to eternity. Flavel's own life of suffering bore eloquent witness to the depths of his convictions, and his multifaceted ministry showed the extent to which he endeavoured to share them with others.

Many people might hesitate to read Puritan sermons, and perhaps for good reason. A few (but thankfully not *all!*) modern readers may find reading some Puritan authors rather challenging if not difficult. Long sermons, full of complex and convoluted sentences, with numerous sub-points, asides, and exhortations, make strenuous demands on concentration and patience. Thankfully, Flavel's work is easily accessible, and speaks to all sorts of people today as it has done for more than three centuries.

As we have seen, Flavel spent almost his entire ministry in a busy town serving working people. All that he preached and wrote was prepared to meet the needs of Dartmouth's fishermen, farmers, sailors, and townspeople. Flavel insisted that he himself wanted to hear sermons that were 'hissing hot', direct and practical rather than long-winded and theoretical. His sermons have those qualities in abundance. Flavel knew that time was short, and that people needed to be led to Jesus Christ, and to be built up in him. He wasted neither time nor words.

Flavel's vision of the Christian life is panoramic. The gospel impacts and shapes every thought, every feeling, every ambition, emotion, desire, success, tragedy and joy. Christ makes all things new for the believer. He teaches us to follow him with confidence, until that day when he truly renews all things. To read Flavel is to catch and to be changed by the same vision.

Because of Flavel's direct and pastoral manner, editing his work (as well as reading it) has been a pleasure. With the exception of three chapters (two selected from *The Mystery of Providence* and one from *A Saint Indeed*), all of the works in this volume are sermons. I've done very little to shorten them, essentially because to do so would be to lose key material, with nothing gained for the reader. I want you to hear Flavel as his first hearers did, confident that as he opens up the Scriptures, you will discover the Saviour.

It is true that we are not Flavel's first readers. He preached and wrote in language that was familiar to those who first heard him and read his books when they came hot off the press. However, some words change their meaning over time, and others fall out of usage altogether. Where I've met words like 'solicitousness', 'calumniation', 'husbandman' and such like, I've looked for a modern equivalent. Even the more intelligible words such as 'hitherto', 'betwixt', 'beseech' and 'thee' and 'thou' I've put into contemporary forms. Occasionally I've reworked a sentence to bring out its meaning where it may be obscured by the original phrasing. Where Flavel quotes the Scriptures I've inserted the equivalent texts in the translation of the New International Version (1984).

Flavel was widely-read, and steeped in classical learning, with a solid grasp of biblical languages. Where he quotes a Greek or Hebrew phrase, or a comment of Cicero, or where he gives an illustration about a learned man from antiquity, I have chosen to omit them. I am confident that those features never graced his original sermon notes, and I'm pretty sure we won't lose out by their absence.

Puritan preachers were great believers in structure and order in sermons, and Flavel was no exception. Most of his sermons have the same broad outline, with introductory comments followed by a stating of the doctrine of the text, which is then explored for a little over half the sermon. After that, Flavel presses home his teaching with detailed application and exhortation. Again, like others of his time, Flavel often details his points in lists which occasionally run to a dozen. Even some of those have their own sub-points! Often these lists are called 'Directives', 'Helps', or 'Inferences', and are usually numbered. I've done away with these titles, but have usually kept Flavel's numbering where I think it helps the reader. I have added subtitles of my own.

I hope that you will find reading this edition of Flavel a pleasure and a profit. He once said, 'Labour to get the clearest and fullest knowledge of Christ and his love that is attainable in this world.' This delightful labour now awaits you.

LEWIS ALLEN
Huddersfield, Yorkshire
June 2017

PART ONE

SALVATION IS IN JESUS CHRIST

I

Love Divine

THIS is a sermon on John 3:16 from Flavel's series of forty-two sermons entitled *The Fountain of Life*, published in 1671. Each serves to build a full picture of Jesus Christ, exploring his person and work as mediator between God and men. The sermon's original title is 'The Admirable Love of God in Giving His Own Son for Us'.

The focus of the sermon is on Christ as the gift of the Father, and Flavel explores the nature of the grace of God in giving his Son. Like so many of Flavel's sermons, it displays the alluring beauty of the grace of God in Jesus Christ, and urges readers to take hold of, and enjoy, all that God offers us in his Son.

For God so loved the world that he gave his one and only Son, that whoever believes in him shall not perish but have eternal life.—John 3:16

YOU have heard of the gracious purpose and design of God, to recover poor sinners to himself by Jesus Christ, and how this design of love was laid and contrived in the covenant of redemption.

Now, according to the terms of that covenant, you shall hear from this scripture how that design was by one degree advanced towards its accomplishment in God's actual giving or parting with his own Son for us: 'God so loved the world that he gave', etc.

The whole preceding context is spent in showing the nature and necessity of regeneration, and its need in this text is urged and inferred from the peculiar respect and eye God had upon believers, in giving Christ for them. They receive all the special and saving benefits and advantages of that gift: 'God so loved the world that he gave his one and only Son, that whoever believes in him shall not perish.'

In the words are to be considered, 1. The original spring or fountain of our best mercies is the love of God. The love of God is either *benevolent*, *beneficent*, or *complacential*. His *benevolent* love is nothing else but his desire and purpose of saving, and doing us good; so his purpose and grace to Jacob is called love, 'Jacob I loved' (Rom. 9:13), but this was before Jacob was born, and so could consist in nothing else but the gracious purpose of God towards him. His *beneficent* love is his actual doing good to the persons beloved, or his bestowing the effects of his love upon us, according to that purpose. His *complacential* love is nothing else but that delight and satisfaction he finds in seeing the fruits and workings of that grace in us, which he first intended for us, and then bestowed on us.

God's beneficent love is that which this scripture speaks of. Out of this fountain Christ flowed to us, and both ran into that love of complacency. God both purposed and actually bestowed Christ on us, that he might everlastingly delight in beholding the glory and praise of all this reflected on himself, by his *redeemed* ones. This then is the fountain of our mercies.

2. The mercy flowing out of this fountain is Christ. *The mercy*, as he is emphatically called in Luke 1:72. Christ is the marrow, kernel, and substance of all other mercies. God gave his only begotten Son. This was the birth of that love, the like of which it never brought forth before, and therefore it is expressed with a double emphasis in the text: 'He *so* loved the world.' How did he love it? Why, he *so loved it*; but how much, the tongues of angels cannot declare. And moreover, to enhance the mercy, Christ is styled his *one and only* Son. To have given a Son is wonderful; but to give his one and only Son, that is love inexpressible, and beyond understanding.

3. The objects of this love, or the persons to whom the eternal Lord delivered Christ, and that is the world. This must respect the elect of God in the world, such as do, or shall actually believe, as it is expressed in the next words, 'That whoever believes in him shall not perish.' Those whom he calls the *world* in that, he styles *believers* in this expression; and the word *world* is put to signify the elect because they are scattered through all parts, and are among all ranks of men in the world; these are the objects of this love. It is not angels but men that were so loved. He is called a Lover, a Friend of men, but never the Lover or Friend of angels, or creatures of another species.

4. The manner in which this never-enough celebrated mercy flows to us, from the fountain of divine love, and that is most freely and spontaneously. He *gave*, not he *sold*, or barely parted from, but gave. The Father's giving does not imply Christ to be merely passive; for as the Father is here said to give him, so the apostle tells us that he gave himself, 'who loved me and gave himself for me' (Gal. 2:20). The Father gave him out of good will to men, and Christ willingly gave himself to that service.

Doctrine: The clear teaching of our text is that *the gift of Christ is the highest and fullest display of the love of God to sinners that was ever made from eternity to them.*

This is how this gift of God to sinners is shown: 'This is love: not that we loved God, but that he loved us and sent his Son as an atoning sacrifice for our sins' (1 John 4:10). Why does the apostle John so magnify this gift in saying, 'This is love', as if there were love in nothing else! May we not say, that to have a being, a being among the rational creatures, therein is love? To have our life carried for so many years like a taper in the hand of Providence, through so many dangers, and not yet put out in obscurity, therein is love? To have food and clothing, beds to lie on, friends and family to comfort us, in all these is love, is there not? In fact, there is almost no love in these gifts when you compare them to the love expressed in sending or giving Christ for us. These are great mercies in themselves, but compared to this mercy, they are all swallowed up, as the light of candles when brought into the sunshine. No, no, in this is love—that God gave Christ for us. And it is remarkable that when the apostle would show us what the noblest fruit is that most commends to men the root of divine love that bears it, he shows us this very fruit of it that I am now opening: 'But God demonstrates his own love for us in this: while we were still sinners, Christ died for us' (Rom. 5:8). This is the very flower of that love.

The method I will use to declare this precious point is this:
(1) To show how Jesus Christ was given by the Father; (2) to show
how that gift is the fullest and richest display of the love of God
that was ever made to the world; (3) and then to draw forth the
application of it.

Jesus, the Father's gift

(1) How was Jesus Christ given by the Father, and what is implied
therein?

You are not so to understand it, as though God parted with his
interest and property in his Son, when he is said to give him; he
was as much his own as ever. When men give, they transfer property to another; but when God had given his Son, he was still as
much his own as ever: but this giving of Christ implies,

(i) His designation and appointment to death for us. For you
read, that it was done 'by God's set purpose' (Acts 2:23). As the
Lamb under the law was separated from the flock, and set apart
for a sacrifice; though it were still living, yet it was intentionally
and preparatively given, and consecrated to the Lord. So Jesus
Christ was, by the counsel and purpose of God, thus chosen, and
set apart for his service. Therefore in Isaiah 42:1 God calls him his
Elect, or Chosen One.

(ii) His giving Christ implies a parting with him, or setting
him at some distance from himself for a time. There was a kind
of parting of the Father and the Son, when he came to tabernacle
in our flesh, as he expresses it in John 16:28, 'I came from the
Father, and entered the world; now I am leaving the world and
going back to the Father.' This distance that this incarnation and
humiliation set him at belonged to his humanity, which was really
distant from the glory into which it is now taken up. In respect of
the display of delight and love, the Lord seemed to carry it as one
at a distance from him. Oh! this was it that so deeply pierced and

wounded his soul, as is evident from that complaint, 'My God, my God, why have you forsaken me? Why are you … so far from the words of my groaning? O my God, I cry out by day, but you do not answer', etc. (Psa. 22:1-2).

(iii) God's giving of Christ implies his delivering him into the hands of justice to be punished; even as condemned persons are, by sentence of law, given or delivered into the hands of executioners, so Acts 2:23 reads, 'This man was handed over to you by God's set purpose and foreknowledge; and you, with the help of wicked men, put him to death' (Acts 2:23). In Romans 8:32 God 'gave him up for us all'. The Lord, when the time came that Christ must suffer, as it were, said, 'O all you roaring waves of my incensed justice, now swell as high as heaven, and go over his soul and body; sink him to the bottom; let him go, like Jonah, his type, into the belly of hell, down to the roots of the mountains. Come all you raging storms, that I have reserved for this day of wrath, beat upon him, beat him down, that he may not be able to look up (Psa. 40:12). Go justice, put him on the rack, torment him in every part, till all his bones are out of joint, and his heart is melted like wax within his breast' (Psa. 22:14).

(iv) God's giving of Christ implies his application of him, with all the purchase of his blood, and settling all this upon us, as an inheritance and portion: 'It is my Father who gives you the true bread from heaven. For the bread of God is he who comes down from heaven and gives life to the world' (John 6:32-33). God has given him as bread to poor starving creatures, that by faith they might eat and live. And so he told the Samaritan woman, 'If you knew the gift of God and who it is that asks you for a drink, you would have asked him, and he would have given you living water' (John 4:10). Bread and water are the two necessities for the support of natural life; God has given Christ to be all that, and more, to the spiritual life.

Jesus, the display of the Father's love

(2) This gift of Christ was the highest and fullest manifestation of the love of God that the world ever saw.

This will be evidenced by the following particulars:

(i) If you consider how near and dear Jesus Christ was to the Father; he was his Son, 'his one and only Son', as the text says, the Son of his love, the darling of his soul. He was his other self, yes, one with himself; the express image of his person; the brightness of his Father's glory. In parting with him, he parted with his own heart. What is a child, but a piece of the parent wrapt up in another skin? And yet our dearest children are but as strangers to us in comparison of the unspeakable dearness that was between the Father and Christ. Now, that he should ever be content to part with a Son, and such an only one, is such a display of love as will be admired to all eternity. And then,

(ii) Let it be considered, to what God gave Christ. He gave him to death, and that of the cross; to be made a curse for us; to be the scorn and contempt of men; and to the most unparalleled sufferings that ever were inflicted or borne by any. It melts and breaks our hearts to see our children striving in the pangs of death, but the Lord beheld his Son struggling under agonies that no one ever felt before him. He saw him falling to the ground, grovelling in the dust, sweating blood, and amidst those agonies turning himself to his Father, and, with a heart-rending cry, pleading him, 'My Father, if it is possible, may this cup be taken from me' (Matt. 26:39). Christ was delivered to wrath—to the wrath of an infinite God without mixture. Christ was delivered to the very torments of hell, and that by the hand of his own Father. Sure then that love must needs want a name, which made the Father of mercies deliver his only Son to such miseries for us.

(iii) It is a special consideration to enhance the love of God in giving Christ, that in giving him he gave the richest jewel in his cabinet, a mercy of the greatest worth, and most inestimable value. Heaven itself is not so valuable and precious as Christ is: He is the better half of heaven, and so the saints account him (Psa. 73:25) 'Whom have I in heaven but you?' Ten thousand thousand worlds, as many worlds as angels can number, and then as a new world of angels can multiply, would not all be the bulk of a balance to weigh Christ's excellency, love, and sweetness. O what a fair One! What a unique One! What an excellent, lovely, ravishing One, is Christ! Put the beauty of ten thousand paradises, like the garden of Eden, into one; put all trees, all flowers, all smells, all colours, all tastes, all joys, all sweetness, all loveliness in one; O what a fair and excellent thing would that be! And yet it should be less than that fair and dearest well-beloved Christ, than one drop of rain to the whole seas, rivers, lakes, and fountains of ten thousand earths. Christ is heaven's wonder, and earth's wonder.

Now, for God to bestow the mercy of mercies, the most precious thing in heaven or earth, upon poor sinners; and, as great, as lovely, as excellent as his Son was, yet not to account him too good to bestow upon us—what manner of love is this!

(iv) Once more, let it be considered on whom the Lord bestowed his Son. Upon angels? No, but upon men. Upon man his friend? No, but upon his enemies, This is love; and on this consideration the apostle lays a mighty weight, in Romans 5:8-10. 'But God demonstrates his love towards us in this: While we were still sinners, Christ died for us.' When we were enemies, we were reconciled to God by the death of his Son. Who would part with a son for the sake of his dearest friends? But God gave him to, and delivered him for enemies: O love unspeakable!

(v) *Lastly*, Let us consider how freely this gift came from him. It was not wrested out of his hand by our pleading for it; for we desired it as little as we deserved it. It was surprising, preventing,[1]

---

[1] preceding, going before, being or acting earlier.

eternal love that delivered him to us: 'Not that we loved God, but that he loved us … We love because he first loved us' (cf. 1 John 4:10, 19). Thus as when you weigh something, you will put on weight after weight, till the scales break; so God puts one consideration upon another to overcome our hearts, and make us cry in wonder, 'What manner of love is this!'

And thus I have shown you what God's giving of Christ is, and what matchless love is manifested in that incomparable gift.

Receiving the love of God in Jesus

(3) Next I shall apply the teaching of this verse.

(i) Learn *the exceeding preciousness of souls, and how very highly God values them, that he will give his Son, his only Son out of his bosom, as a ransom for them.* Surely this speaks of their preciousness. God would not have parted with such a Son for small matters. All the world could not redeem them. Gold and silver could not be their ransom, as the apostle says: 'You know that it was not with perishable things such as silver and gold that you were redeemed … but with the precious blood of Christ' (1 Pet. 1:18-19). God has such an esteem for them that rather than they should perish, Jesus Christ shall be made a man, yes, a curse for them. Oh then, learn to put a due value upon your own souls: do not sell *cheaply* that for which God has paid so *dearly.* Remember what a treasure you carry about you. The glory that you see in this world is not equivalent in worth to it. 'What good is it for a man to gain the whole world, yet forfeit his soul? Or what can a man give in exchange for his soul?' (Mark 8:36-37).

(ii) If God has given his own Son for the world, then it follows that *those for whom God gave his own Son may confidently expect all other temporal mercies from him.* This is the apostle's inference in Romans 8:32. 'He who did not spare his own Son, but gave him up for us all—how will he not also, along with him, graciously give us all things?'

In order to see the foundation of this most encouraging deduction, let these four things be pondered, and duly weighed in your thoughts.

(a) No other mercy you need or desire is or can be so dear to God, as Jesus Christ is: God never embraced any other thing in his arms as he did his Son. As for the world, and the comforts of it, it is the dust of his feet, he values it not; as you see by his providential disposals of it—having given it to the worst of men. 'All the Turkish empire', said Luther, 'as great and glorious as it is, is but a crumb which the master of the family throws to the dogs.' Think upon any other outward enjoyment that is valuable in your eyes, and there is not so much comparison between it and Christ, in the esteem of God, as is between your dear children and the lumber of your houses, in your esteem. If then God has parted so freely from him who was infinitely dearer to him than these, how shall he deny these, when they may promote his glory, and your good?

(b) As Jesus Christ was nearer the heart of God than all these, so Christ is, in himself, much greater and more excellent than all of them. Ten thousand worlds, and the glory of them all, is but the dust of the balance, if weighed with Christ. These things are but poor creatures, but he is God over all, for ever praised (Rom. 9:5). They are common gifts, but he is *the gift of God* (John 4:10). They are ordinary mercies, but he is *the mercy* (Luke 1:78). As one pearl or precious stone is greater in value than ten thousand ordinary ones. Now, if God has so freely given the greater, how can you suppose he should deny the lesser, mercies? Will a man give to another a large inheritance, and argue with him over a trifle? How can it be?

(c) There is no other mercy you lack that you are not entitled to by the gift of Christ; it is conveyed to you, as of right, with Christ. So, 'all things are yours', yes, 'for you of Christ' (1 Cor. 3:21-23).

'For no matter how many promises God has made, they are "Yes" in Christ' (2 Cor. 1:20); With him he has richly provided you everything for your *enjoyment* (1 Tim. 6:17). The word signifies having the sweet relish and comfort of an enjoyment—and that is what we have in all our mercies, upon the account of our title to them in Christ.

(d) Lastly, if God has given you this *nearer*, *greater*, and *all-comprehending mercy* when you were enemies to him and alienated from him, it is not imaginable he should deny you any lesser mercy, when you come into a state of reconciliation and friendship with him. So the apostle reasons in Romans 5:8-10. 'For if, when we were God's enemies, we were reconciled to him through the death of his Son, how much more, having been reconciled, shall we be saved through his life!' And thus you have the second inference with its grounds.

(iii) If the greatest love has been manifested in giving Christ to the world, then it follows, *that the greatest evil and wickedness is manifested in despising, slighting, and rejecting Christ.* It is sad to abuse the love of God revealed in the lowest gift of providence; but to slight the richest discoveries of it, even in that matchless gift, in which God commends his love in the most astonishing manner—this is sin with a witness. Blush, O heavens, and be astonished, O earth; yes, be horribly afraid! There is no guilt like this. The most wicked wretches among the barbarous nations are innocent, in comparison to these. But are there any such in the world? Dare any slight this gift of God? Indeed, if men's words might be taken, there are few or none that dare do so. But if their lives and practices may be believed, this, this is the sin of the far greater part of the Christianized world. Witness the lamentable stupidity and indifference; the contempt of the gospel; the hatred and persecution of his image, laws and people. What is the language of all this, but a vile esteem of Jesus Christ?

And now, let me reason a little with those ungrateful souls who trample underfoot the Son of God, and do not value this love that gave him forth. What is that mercy which you so despise and undervalue? Is it indeed worth no more than this in your eyes? Surely you will not be long of that opinion! Will you be of that mind when death and judgment shall have thoroughly awakened you? Oh, no: Then a thousand worlds for a Christ! It is said of King Richard III, that when he lost the field, and was in great danger from his enemies who pressed upon him: 'Oh now', he said, 'a kingdom for a horse!' Or do you think that all around you in the world are of your mind? You are deceived, if you think so: through all the world to those who believe he is precious (1 Pet. 2:7), and in the 'other world' they also are of a very different mind. Could you only hear what is said of Christ in heaven, with what language the saved of the Lord extol their Saviour! Or could you but imagine the self-revenges, the self-torments, which the damned suffer for their folly, and what a value they would set upon one offer of Christ, if it might but again be hoped for. Then you would see that such people as you are the only despisers of Christ. Beside I think it is astonishing that you should despise a mercy in which your own souls are so dearly, so deeply, so everlastingly concerned, as they are in this gift of God. If it were but the soul of another, no, less than that, the body of another, and yet even less than that, if but another's beast, whose life you could preserve, you are obliged to do it; but when it is yourself, and the best part of yourself—your own invaluable soul—that you are ruining and destroying, Oh, what a monster you are, to throw it away like this! What! will you despise your own souls? Don't you care whether they are saved, or whether they are damned? Is it indeed an indifferent thing with you which way they fall at death? Have you imagined a hell you could bear? Is it easy to perish? Are you not only turned

God's enemies, but your own enemies too? See what monsters sin can turn men and women into! Oh the stupefying, besotting, intoxicating power of sin! But perhaps you think that all these are just uncertain sounds with which we are trying to alarm you. It may be that your own heart will preach such doctrine as this to yourself—

Who can assure you of the reality of these things? Why should you trouble yourself with an invisible world, or be so concerned about what your eyes have never seen, nor have you ever had any report from anyone who has seen them? Well, though we cannot now show you these things, yet shortly they shall be shown to you, and your own eyes shall behold them. You are convinced and satisfied that many other things are real which you have never seen; be assured, that 'if the message spoken by angels was binding, and every violation and disobedience received its just punishment, how shall we escape if we ignore such a great salvation?' (Heb. 2:2-3). But if they are certain, yet they are not near. It will be a long time before they come.

Poor soul! How you cheat yourself! It may not be such a long time as you imagine for yourself. You cannot even be certain of the next moment. Besides, what are twenty or forty years when they are past? What are a thousand years compared to a vast eternity? Go trifle away a few days more, sleep out a few nights more, and then lie down in the dust. It will not be long before the trumpet of God shall awaken you, and your eyes shall behold Jesus coming in the clouds of heaven, and then you will know the price of this sin.

Please, if there is any sense of eternity upon you, any pity or love for yourselves in you, if you have any concerns more than the beasts that perish, do not despise the mercies offered to you, do not slight the richest gift that has ever been offered to the world; and a sweeter gift cannot be offered for all eternity.

2

Jesus the God-Man

IN this sermon Flavel explores the two natures of the person of Christ, the human and the divine. There are depths here, and complex points of theology. Flavel makes references to historic debates and to the participants in them, as he shows us how the church has wrestled through the ages to understand the Bible's teaching on the person of Christ. Flavel makes no apology for going into such detail. If we are to know Jesus Christ the 'God-Man' (to borrow a phrase much loved by Flavel), we must make every effort to understand something of the mysteries of our Lord's glorious person.

We cannot love God with all our mind without learning about him. The knowledge of God fuels the fire of devotion. Consider therefore not only the depths of knowledge of God in this sermon but also the heights of devotion to which it leads. Growing in our knowledge of Jesus Christ will enable us to enjoy more fully the riches of his salvation. Jesus is now in glory at the Father's right hand, where there are pleasures for evermore.

The Word became flesh and made his dwelling among us.
                                                          —John 1:14

THE work proposed by the Father, and consented to by the Son, is such as infinitely exceeds the power of any mere man to perform. He who undertakes to satisfy God by obedience for man's sin, must himself be God. And he who performs such a perfect obedience, by doing and suffering all that the law required in our place, must be man. These two natures must be united in one person, or else there could not be a concourse or co-operation of either nature in his mediatorial work. How these natures are united in the wonderful person of our *Immanuel* is the first part of the great mystery of godliness: a subject studied and adored by angels. And it is this mystery which is wrapped up in our text. Here we have, *First*, the incarnation of the Son of God plainly asserted; and *secondly*, that assertion strongly confirmed.

First, the incarnation of the Son of God is plainly asserted.

In the assertion we have three parts:

(1) The *person assuming*: the Word, i.e. the second Person or Subsistent in the most glorious Godhead, called the Word—either because he is the scope or principal matter of the prophetical and promissory word; or because he expounds and reveals the mind and will of God to men (see John 1:18). The only begotten Son who is in the bosom of the Father has declared or expounded him.

(2) The *nature assumed*: flesh, i.e. the entire human nature, consisting of a true human soul and body. For so this word *flesh* used

here rather than *man*, in order to show the amazing condescension and abasement of Christ. There is more of vileness, weakness, and opposition to spirit in this word *flesh*, as is pertinently noted by some. Hence the whole nature is shown by this word.

(3) The *assumption itself*: 'was made', not 'was', i.e. he took or assumed the true human nature (called flesh, for the reason before stated) into the unity of his divine person, with all its integral parts and essential properties, and so was made or became a true and real man by that assumption. It was the work of the whole Trinity, God the Father in the Son and by the Spirit, forming or creating that nature; as if three sisters should make a garment between them, which only one of them wears. And yet, it was the act of the Son only, as it was he only that was *made flesh*. And when it is said he was made flesh, do not think that there was a change of the Godhead into flesh; for this was performed, 'not by changing what he was, but by assuming what he was not', as Augustine expresses it so well. As when the scripture expression says, 'he was made sin' (2 Cor. 5:21), and 'made a curse' (Gal. 3:13 KJV), the meaning is not that he was turned into sin, or into a curse. We must not think here that the Godhead was turned into flesh, and lost its own being and nature, because it is said he was made flesh.

Secondly, this assertion (that the Word became flesh) is strongly confirmed.

He 'made his dwelling among us', and 'we have seen his glory'. This was no ghost, but a most real and indubitable thing. For he 'pitched his tent' or 'tabernacled' with us. And we are eye-witnesses of it. Parallel to that, consider 1 John 1:1-3. 'That which was from the beginning, which we have heard, which we have seen with our eyes, which we have looked at and our hands have touched—this we proclaim concerning the Word of life', etc.

The doctrine proposed

> **Doctrine:** *Jesus Christ did really assume the true and perfect nature of man, into a personal union with his divine nature, and still remains true God, and true man, in one person forever.*

The proposition contains one of the deepest mysteries of godliness (1 Tim. 3:16), a mystery by which understanding is overwhelmed. If ever the tongues of angels longed to explain any part of the word of God, they long to do it here. The words of this doctrine are of great significance. We walk upon the brink of danger. The least false step may engulf us in the bogs of error. Arius would have been content if the Council of Nicea would have only gratified him in a letter, *homoousios*, and *homoiousios*. The Nestorians also desired but a letter, *theotochos*, instead of *theodochos*. These seemed but small and modest requests, but, if granted, would prove no small harm to Jesus Christ and his truths.

I desire therefore the reader would, with greatest attention of mind, apply himself to these truths. It is a doctrine hard to understand, and dangerous to make mistakes in. Christ did assume a true human body, as that is plainly asserted in Scripture (Phil. 2:7-8; Heb. 2:14, 16). In one place it is called taking on himself the seed of Abraham, and in our text, *flesh*. He also assumed a true human soul; this is undeniable by its operations, passions, and expiration at last (Matt. 26:38 and 27:50). And that both these natures make but one person is evident from Romans 1:3-4: Jesus Christ 'who as to his human nature was a descendant of David, and who through the Spirit of holiness was declared with power to be the Son of God, by his resurrection from the dead'. So Romans 9:5: 'from them is traced the human ancestry of Christ, who is God over all, for ever praised! Amen.' But so that you may have a sound and clear understanding of this mystery, I will open up (1) the nature, (2) effects, and (3) the reasons or ends of this wonderful union.

(1) The nature of this union

Firstly, *negatively* considered.

(i) Do not think that when Christ assumed our nature it was united *consubstantially*, so as the three persons in the Godhead are united among themselves. They all have but one and the same nature and will; but in Christ there are two distinct natures and wills, though one person.

(ii) Nor that they are united *physically*, as soul and body are united in one person; for death actually dissolves that union, whereas this one is indissoluble. When Christ's soul expired, and his body was buried, both soul and body were still united to the second person of the Trinity as much as ever.

(iii) Nor yet is it such a *mystical union* as the one that exists between Christ and believers. Indeed that is a glorious union; but though believers are said to be in Christ, and Christ in them, yet they are not one person with him. They are not christed into Christ, or godded into God, as the blasphemous *Familists* teach.

Secondly, *positively* considered. By this assumption the second person in the Godhead took a human nature into a personal union with himself, and by virtue of that union his humanity subsists in the second person, yet without confusion, both making but one person, or *Immanuel*, God with us.

So that though we truly ascribe a twofold nature to Christ, we deny a double person. For the human nature of Christ never subsisted separately and distinctly, by any personal subsistence of its own, as it does in all other men, but from the first moment of conception, subsisted in union with the second person.

God was in Christ: five points about his nature

To explicate this mystery more particularly, let it be considered:

First, the human nature was united to the Second Person *miraculously* and extraordinarily, being supernaturally framed in the womb of the Virgin, by the overshadowing power of the Most High (Luke 1:34-35). By reason of this it may truly and properly be said to be the fruit of the womb, not of the loins of men, nor by man. And this was necessary to exempt the assumed nature from the stain and pollution of Adam's sin, which it wholly escaped. He did not receive it, as all others do, in the way of ordinary generation, by which original sin is propagated. This nature, being extraordinarily produced, was a most pure and holy thing (Luke 1:35 KJV). And indeed this perfect shining holiness, in which it was produced, was absolutely necessary, both for its union with the divine person, and for the design of that union; which was both to make satisfaction for our sin, and to sanctify us.

The two natures could not be joined in the person of Christ had there been the least taint of sin upon the human nature. For God can have no fellowship with sin, much less be united to it. Or, supposing such a union with our sinful nature, yet he being a sinner himself, would never satisfy for the sins of others, nor could any unholy thing ever make us holy. 'Such a high priest meets our need—one who is holy, blameless, pure, set apart from sinners' (Heb. 7:26). And such an one he must needs be, whom the Holy Ghost produces in such a peculiar way—'the holy one'.

Secondly, as it was produced miraculously, so it was assumed *integrally*. That is to say, Christ took a complete and perfect human soul and body, with all and every faculty and member pertaining to it. And this was necessary, that by it he might heal the whole nature of that leprosy of sin which has seized and infected every member and faculty. 'He assumed all, to sanctify all.' He designed a perfect recovery, by sanctifying us wholly in soul, body, and spirit; and therefore he assumed the whole in order to achieve it.

Thirdly, he assumed our nature, with all its integral parts, as well as with all its *sinless infirmities*. And therefore it is said of Christ, 'he had to be made like his brothers in every way in every way' (Heb. 2:17) [that is, in every natural way, not formally sinful, as is limited by the same apostle, Heb. 4:15]. But here our theologians so carefully distinguish infirmities into *personal* and *natural*. Personal infirmities are those which befall particular persons, from particular causes, such as dumbness, blindness, lameness, leprosy, and other afflictions and deformities. It was not necessary that Christ should assume these, nor did he. But he assumed the natural ones, such as hunger, thirst, weariness, sweating, bleeding, mortality, etc. which, though they are not in themselves formally and intrinsically sinful, yet are they the effects and consequents of sin. They are so many marks that sin has left of itself upon our natures. And on that account Christ is said to be sent 'in the likeness of sinful flesh' (Rom. 8:3 KJV). In this the gracious condescension of Christ for us is marvellously signalized, that he would not assume our innocent nature, as it was in Adam before the fall, while it stood in all its primitive glory and perfection, but that nature which sin had quite defaced, ruined, and spoiled.

Fourthly, Christ's human nature is so united with the divine that each nature still retains its own essential properties distinctly. This distinction is not lost by that union, nor can it be. So the two understandings, wills, powers, etc. of the divine and human are not confused, but a line of distinction runs between them still in this wonderful person. It was the heresy of the Eutychians, condemned by the Council of Chalcedon, to affirm that there was no distinction between the two natures in Christ. Against them the Council determined that the two natures of Christ were united without any change or confusion.

Fifthly, the union of the two natures in Christ form an *inseparable union*, so that from the first moment there never was, nor to eternity shall be, any separation of them.

Doubt. How did the union remain between them when Christ's human soul and body were separated from each other upon the cross? Is not death the dissolution of the union between soul and body?

Resolution. True, the natural union between his soul and body was dissolved by death for a time, but this hypostatical union remained even then as entire and firm as ever. For, though his soul and body were divided from each other, yet neither of them was divided from the divine nature. Consider this illustration: a man who holds in his hand a sword sheathed, draws forth the sword when he wishes to; but he still holds it in one hand, and the sheath in the other, and then sheaths it again, still holding the sword in his hand. Just so, when Christ died, his soul and body retained their union with the divine nature, though not (during that space) one with another.

(2) The effects or immediate results of this marvellous union of the two natures

(i) The two natures are so united in the person of the Mediator by virtue of which the properties of each nature are attributed, and do truly agree in the whole person, so that it is proper to say, the Lord of glory was crucified (1 Cor. 2:8), and the blood of God redeemed the church (Acts 20:28), and that Christ was both in heaven and on the earth at the same time (John 3:13 KJV).

Yet we do not believe that one nature imparts its properties to the other, or that it is proper to say the divine nature suffered, bled, or died. Nor do we believe that the human is omniscient, omnipotent, or omnipresent; but we do assert that the properties of both natures are so ascribed to the person that it is proper to affirm any of them of him in the concrete, though not abstractly. The right understanding of this would greatly help in teaching the true sense of the forementioned, as well as many other dark passages in the Scriptures.

(ii) Another fruit of this hypostatical union is the singular raising of the human nature in Christ, far beyond and above what it is capable of in any other person, it being hereby filled with an unparalleled measure of divine graces and excellencies. In this respect he is said to be anointed 'above or before his companions' (Psa. 45:7), and so becomes the object of adoration and divine worship (Acts 7:59). This the Socinians challenge with this argument that Christ is worshipped with a divine worship as being the Mediator, but not so worshipped as being God. But we say, that to be worshipped as Mediator as well as God are not in conflict, but the one is necessarily included in the other. And that is the ground upon which the worship of Christ is founded.

(iii) It therefore follows in the last place, as another excellent fruit of this union, *the concourse and co-operation of each nature to his mediatory works, for in them he acts according to both natures.* The human nature does what is human, suffering, sweating, bleeding, dying; and his divine nature stamps all these with infinite value. And so both natures sweetly concur to one glorious work and design of mediation. Roman Catholics generally deny that he performs any of these mediatory works as God, but only as man; and yet, how boldly do they contradict the plain teaching of Scripture (e.g. 2 Cor. 5:10; Heb. 9:14-15)!

(3) The grounds and reasons of the assumption of human nature by the Son

The divine did not assume the human nature necessarily, but voluntarily, not out of poverty, but bounty; not because it was to be perfected by it, but to perfect it, by causing it to lie as a pipe for the infinite all-filling fountain of grace and glory. And he did that to qualify and prepare himself for a full discharge of his mediatorship, in the offices of our prophet, priest, and king.

Had he not this double nature in the unity of his person, he could not have been our prophet, for as God he knows the mind and will of God (John 1:18 and 3:13), and as man he is fitted to impart it suitably to us (Deut. 18:15-18, compared with Acts 3:22).

As priest, had he not been man, he could have shed no blood, and if not God, it had been no adequate value for us (Heb. 2:17; Acts 20:28).

As king, had he not been man, he would be no fit head for us. And if not God, he could neither rule nor defend his body the church. These then are the designs and ends of Christ's taking a human nature.

These then were the designs and ends of that assumption.

Application: How to discover the blessings of the Incarnate Son

1. *Let all Christians rightly inform their minds in this truth of such great importance, and hold it fast against all subtle adversaries that could take it from them*. The learned Hooker observes that the dividing of Christ's person, which is but one, and the mixing of his natures, which are two, have been the occasion of those errors, which have so greatly disturbed the peace of the church. The Arians denied his deity, levelling him with other mere men. But you know that Christ is (i) true and very God; (ii) true and very man; and that (iii) these two natures make but one person, being united inseparably; and that (iv) they are not confounded or swallowed up one in another, but remain still distinct in the person of Christ. Hold the sound words which cannot be condemned. Great things hang upon all these truths. Do not allow a stone to be loosed out of the foundation.

2. *Adore the love of the Father, and the Son, who bid so high for your souls, and at this rate were contented you should be recovered*.

(i) The love of the Father is admirably conspicuous, who so strongly willed our salvation that he was content to degrade the darling of his soul to so vile and contemptible a state, which was for that reason a degrading of his reputation, as the apostle intimates

(Phil. 2:7). It is just as if two persons were to have a disagreement, and the superior, who also is the wronged person, begins to stoop first, and say, You have deeply wronged me, and your blood is not able to repair the wrongs you have done me: however, such is my love to you, and willingness to be at peace with you, that I will part with what is most dear to me in all the world, for the sake of peace. In fact, I stoop below myself, and seem, as it were, to forget my own relation and endearments to my own Son, I will not suffer such a breach between me and you. 'God so loved the world, that he gave his one and only Son' (John 3:16).

(ii) And how astonishing is the love of Christ that would make such a stoop as this to exalt us! Oh, it is astonishing to think that he should pass by a more excellent and noble species of creatures, refusing the nature of angels, and instead to take flesh (Heb. 2:16). And he did not seek comfort and pleasure in it, for he had no need of them, being at the fountain head of the highest joys. His aim was the very opposite, to make himself a subject capable of sorrows, wounds, and tears. It was, as Hebrews puts it, 'so that he might taste death for everyone' (Heb. 2:9), and what bitterness was in those pangs and agonies. Oh that you would get your hearts suitably impressed and affected with these deep convictions of the love both of the Father and the Son! How is the courage of some noble Romans celebrated in history, for the brave adventures they made for the commonwealth; but they could never stoop as Christ did, being so infinitely below him in personal dignity.

3. *And here infinite wisdom has also left an everlasting mark of itself, which invites and even chains the eyes of angels and men to itself.* Had there been a general council of angels, to advise upon a way of recovering poor sinners, they would all have been in an everlasting despair about it. It could not have entered their thoughts (though they are the wisest of creatures) that mercy, pardon and grace should ever find such a way as this to issue forth

from the heart of God to the hearts of sinners. Oh, how wisely is the method of our recovery set down! So that Christ may be well called, 'the power of God and the wisdom of God' (1 Cor. 1:24), forasmuch as in him the divine wisdom is more glorified than in all the other works of God, upon which he has impressed it. Hence it is that some of old have affirmed (though I confess myself unsatisfied by it), that the incarnation of Christ was in itself so glorious a demonstration of God's wisdom and power, and thereupon so desirable in itself, that if man had not sinned, yet Christ would have been made man.

4. Hence also we infer *the incomparable sweetness of Christianity, that shows poor sinners such a fair foundation to rest their trembling consciences upon.* While poor distressed souls look to themselves, they are perpetually puzzled. That is the cry of a distressed natural conscience, 'With what shall I come before the Lord?' (Mic. 6:6). Conscience sees God arming himself with wrath, to avenge himself for sin, and cries out, Oh, how shall I deal with him? If he would accept the fruit of my body for the sin of my soul, he should have them. But now we see God coming down in flesh, and so intimately united our flesh to himself, that it has no proper existence of its own, except as united with the divine person. It is easy to imagine what worth and value must be in that blood, and how eternal love, springing forth triumphantly from it, flourishes into pardon, grace, and peace. Here is a way in which the sinner may see justice and mercy kissing each other, and the latter exercised freely, without prejudice to the former. All other consciences through the world lie either in a deep sleep in the devil's arms or else are rolling (sea-sick) upon the waves of their own fears and doubts. Oh, happy are they who have dropped anchor on this ground, and not only know they have peace, but why they have it!

5. *How vitally important it is that Christ should have union with our particular persons, as well as with our common nature!* For by

this union with our nature alone, never any man was or can be saved. And let me add, that this union with our natures is utterly in vain to you, and will do you no good, unless he has union with your persons by faith also. It is indeed infinite mercy, that God has come so near you as to dwell in your flesh, and that he has fixed upon such an excellent method to save poor sinners. And has he done all this? Has he indeed come home, even to your own doors, to seek peace? Does he veil his unsupportable glory under flesh, that he might treat us with more tenderness? And yet do you refuse him, and shut your hearts against him? Then hear one word, and let your ears tingle at the sound of it: your sin is made far worse by this than the sin of devils, who never sinned against a mediator in their own nature, never despised or refused him, because indeed, they were never offered terms of mercy, as you are.

And I doubt not that the devils themselves, who now tempt you to reject, will, to all eternity, upbraid your folly for rejecting this great salvation, which in this excellent way is brought down, even to your own doors.

6. If Jesus Christ has assumed our nature, *then he is truly touched with the infirmities that attend it, and so has pity and compassion for us, under all our burdens*. And indeed this was one aim of his assuming it, that he might be able to have compassion on us: 'For this reason he had to be made like his brothers in every way, in order that he might become a merciful and faithful high priest in service to God, and that he might make atonement for the sins of the people. 18 Because he himself suffered when he was tempted, he is able to help those who are being tempted' (Heb. 2:17-18). O what a comfort is this to us, that he who is our High Priest in heaven has our nature on him, to enable him to take compassion on us!

7. Hence we see *to what a height God intends to build up the*

happiness of man, in that he has laid its foundation so deep in the incarnation of his own Son.

They that intend to build high must lay the foundation low. The happiness and glory of our bodies, as well as souls, are founded in Christ's taking our flesh upon him. For there, as in a model or pattern, God intended to show what in time he resolves to make of our bodies; for he will transform our lowly bodies, and make them one day conformable to the glorious body of Jesus Christ (Phil. 3:21). This flesh was therefore assumed by Christ, that in it might be shown, as in a pattern, how God intends to honour and exalt it. And indeed, a greater honour cannot be done to the nature of man, than what is already done, by this grace of union, nor are our persons capable of higher glory than that which consists in their conformity to this glorious head. Indeed, the flesh of Christ will always have a glory distinct from ours in heaven, by reason of this union. For being the body which the Word assumed, it is in two ways advanced singularly above the flesh and blood of all other men, *subjectively*, and *objectively*: subjectively, it is the flesh and blood of God (Acts 20:28), and so has a distinct and incommunicable glory of its own. And objectively, it is the flesh and blood which all the angels and saints adore. But though in these things it is supremely exalted, yet it is both the medium and pattern of all that glory which God designs to raise us to.

8. Lastly, *how wonderful a comfort is it, that he who dwells in our flesh is God!* What joy may even the weakest believer make out of this! God and man in one person! As man, he is full of a felt sense of our infirmities, needs, and burdens, and as God he can support and supply them all. How relieving, how reviving, and how abundantly satisfying is our faith in this wonderful person! God will never divorce the believing soul, and its comfort, after he has married our nature to his own Son, by the hypostatical union, and our persons also, by the blessed mystical union.

3

He Came for the Cross

THIS is another sermon from *The Fountain of Life*, tracing the life and work of the Lord Jesus Christ. In this sermon Flavel invites us to meditate on all that our Lord embraced in becoming man for our salvation. He sets out the hardships Jesus willingly endured in his life as he prepared for the cross. Drawing lessons directly from the things Christ suffered, Flavel gives direction and comfort to those who are following in their Lord's footsteps.

*And being found in appearance as a man, he humbled himself
and became obedient to death—even death on a cross!*
—Philippians 2:8

THIS scripture can never be enough considered: it holds forth the humbled state of the Lord Jesus during the time of his life on earth. The doctrine it teaches is that the state of Christ, from his conception to his resurrection, was a state of deep debasement and humiliation.

The humiliation of Christ is proposed to you under these three general heads or branches: his humiliation in his incarnation, his humiliation in his life, and his humiliation in his death. How he was humbled by incarnation has been opened above in an earlier sermon.[1] How he was humbled in his life is the key purpose of this sermon. Yet I do not expect that I should give you here an exact history of the life of Christ. The Scriptures say very little of the private part of his life, and it is not my design to focus upon all the memorable passages that the evangelists (those faithful narrators of the life of Christ) have preserved for us, but only to observe and improve those more observable particulars in his life, where especially he was humbled.

---

[1] Flavel refers to the previous sermon (number 18) in the series *The Fountain of Life*, entitled 'Of the Necessity of Christ's Humiliation in Order to the Execution of All These Blessed Offices for Us; and Particularly of His Humiliation by Incarnation'. *The Works of John Flavel* (Edinburgh: Banner of Truth Trust, 1997), 1:223-235.

Six stages of Christ's humiliation

1. The life of law-keeping to which he consented

The Lord Jesus was humbled in his very infancy, by his circumcision according to the law. For being of the stock of Israel, he was to undergo the ceremonies and submit to the ordinances belonging to that people, and thereby to put an end to them; for so it was necessary for him to fulfil all righteousness. 'On the eighth day, when it was time to circumcise him, he was named Jesus' (Luke 2:21). Hereby the Son of God was greatly humbled, especially in these two respects:

Firstly, he obliged himself to keep the whole law, though he was the Law-maker:[2] 'Again I declare to every man who lets himself be circumcised that he is required to obey the whole law' (Gal. 5:3). The apostle's meaning is, he is a debtor in regard to duty, because he who thinks himself bound to keep one part of the ceremonial law, thereby binds himself to keep it all. For where all the parts are inseparably united (as they are in the law of God), we pull all upon us, by engaging or meddling with any one of them. And he that is a debtor in *duty* to keep the whole law, quickly becomes a debtor in regard to its *penalty*, not being able to keep any part of it. Christ therefore comes as our surety, to pay both those debts, the debt of duty, and the debt of penalty to the law. By his circumcision Christ obliges himself to pay the whole debt of duty by fulfilling all righteousness. And though his obedience to it was so exact and perfect, that he contracted no debt of penalty for any transgression of his own, yet he obliges himself to pay the debt of

---

[2] Christ was circumcised and presented (Luke 2:22), because he became subject, not only to the eternal and moral law, but also to the ceremonial and every other divine law. [This is Flavel's own note, referencing William Ames (see *The Marrow of Theology*, Pilgrim Press, 1968, p. 139).]

penalty which he had contracted, by suffering all the pains due to transgressors. This was that unbearable yoke that none were able to bear but Christ (Acts 15:10). And it was no small measure of Christ to bind himself to the law, as a subject made under it. For he was the Law-giver, above all law: and herein that sovereignty of God (one of the choice flowers in the crown of heaven) was obscured and veiled by his subjection.

Secondly, Christ was represented to the world not only as a *subject*, but also as a *sinner*: for though he was pure and holy, yet when this ordinance passed upon him, it seemed to imply that corruption had indeed been in him, which must be cut off by mortification. For this was the mystery principally intended by circumcision: it served to mind and admonish Abraham and his seed of the natural guilt, uncleanness, and corruption of their hearts and nature. So Jeremiah 4:4 says, 'Circumcise yourselves to the Lord, circumcise your hearts, you men of Judah and people of Jerusalem', referring to their sinfulness and corruption. Thus the rebellious and unmortified are called 'stiff-necked people, with uncircumcised hearts and ears', as in Acts 7:51. And as it served to convince of natural uncleanness, so it signified and sealed 'the putting off of the sinful nature', as the apostle puts it (Col. 2:11). Now, this being the purpose of God in the institution of this ordinance for Abraham and his ordinary seed, Christ, by submitting to it in his infancy, did not only veil his sovereignty by subjection, but was also represented as a sinner to the world, though most holy and pure in himself.

2. The persecution he chose to endure

Christ was humbled by persecution, and that in the very morning of his life. He was banished almost as soon as born. As the angel said to Joseph, 'Get up, take the child and his mother and escape to Egypt. Stay there until I tell you, for Herod is going to search

for the child to kill him' (Matt. 2:13). Ungrateful Herod! Was this
the way to treat the Saviour? What, raise a country against him,
as if a *destroyer*, rather than a *Saviour*, had landed upon the coast?
What, deny him the protection of those laws, under which he
was born, and that before he had broken the least of them? The
child of a beggar may claim the benefit and protection of law,
as his birthright, and must the Son of God be denied it? But in
this Herod fulfilled the Scriptures, whilst venting his own lusts,
for it was foretold in Jeremiah 31:15. And this early persecution
was clearly hinted in the title of the twenty-second Psalm, that
psalm which looks rather like a history of the New, rather than
a prophecy of the Old Testament, as it contains a most exact
description of Christ's sufferings. The sixteenth verse says, 'Dogs
have surrounded me; a band of evil men has encircled me.' Thus
was Christ hunted out of the country he was born in. How great
a humiliation is this to the Son of God, not only to become an
infant, but in his infancy, to be harried up and down, and driven
out of his own land as a vagabond!

3. The hardship he embraced

Our Lord Jesus Christ was yet more humbled in his life, by that
poverty and outward meanness which all along attended his condition. He lived poor and low all his days, as the apostle says in
2 Corinthians 8:9: 'Though he was rich, yet for your sakes he
became poor.' So poor, that he was never owner of a house to
dwell in, but lived all his days in other men's houses, or lay in the
open air. His outward condition was more neglected and destitute than that of the birds of the air, or beasts of the earth. He
told that scribe, who professed such readiness and resolution to
follow him, but was soon cooled, when Christ told him, 'Foxes
have holes and the birds of the air have nests, but the Son of Man
has nowhere to lay his head' (Matt. 8:20). It was a common saying
among the Jews that when the Messiah came he would not find a

place to sit down on. Sometimes he feeds upon barley-bread and boiled fish, and sometimes he was hungry and had nothing to eat (Mark 11:12). As for money, he was much a stranger to it. When the tribute-money was demanded of him, he and Peter were not so well-furnished to make half-a-crown between them to pay it, but must work a miracle for it (Matt. 17:27).

He came not to be served, but to serve (Matt. 20:28), not to amass *earthly* treasures, but to bestow *heavenly* ones. His great and heavenly soul neglected and despised those things that too many of his own too much admire and run after. He spent not an anxious thought about those things that eat up thousands and ten thousands of our thoughts. Indeed, he came to be humbled, and to teach men by his example the vanity of this world, and pour contempt upon the ensnaring glory of it. Christ therefore went before us in a chosen and voluntary poverty. But he did not live a beggar's life: sometimes he was fed by ordinary, and sometimes by miraculous and extraordinary ways. He had what he needed to support that precious body of his till the time came to offer it up to God. And he would not indulge and pamper that flesh, which he purposely assumed to be humbled in.

4. The temptations he faced

Our dear Jesus was yet further humbled in his life by the horrid temptations with which Satan assaulted him, and nothing could be more grievous to his holy heart. The evangelist gives us an account of this in Luke 4, from the first to the fourteenth verse, where you find how the bold and envious spirit meets the Captain of our salvation in the field, comes up to him in the wilderness when he was alone and had not a friend with him. There he keeps him fasting forty days and forty nights, to prepare him to close with his temptation. All this while Satan was preparing and sharpening that temptation with which at last he resolves to try the breast of Christ by a home thrust. By this time he supposes Christ was hungry (as indeed he was), and now he thought it was time to make his assault, which he does in a very suitable temptation at first, and with *variety* of temptations, trying several weapons upon him afterwards. But when he had made a thrust at him with that first weapon, in which he especially trusted—'tell these stones to become bread' (verse 3)—and saw how Christ had put it by (verse 4), then he changes postures, and assaults him with temptations to blasphemy, even 'to bow down and worship the devil'. When he saw he could fasten nothing on Christ, that he was as pure fountain-water in a crystal glass, no matter how shaken that no dregs or sediment would rise, he makes a tactical retreat and leaves the field for a season (verse 13). Yet he leaves it with a resolution to return to him again.

Thus was our blessed Lord Jesus humbled by the temptations of Satan, and what can you imagine more burdensome to him who was brought up from eternity with God, delighting in the holy Father, to be now shut into a wilderness with the devil, there to be baited so many days, and have his ears *filled*, though not *defiled*, with horrid blasphemy? O how was the case altered with Christ! from what, and to what was he now come? A chaste woman would account it no common misery to be dogged up and down, and solicited by some vile man, though there were no danger of defilement. A man would account it no small unhappiness to be shut up for five or six weeks with the devil, though appearing in a human shape, and hear no language but that of all hell spoken all that time. This, I say, would be accounted no small misery for a man to undergo. How great a humiliation then must it be to the great God, to be humbled to this! to see a slave of his house, setting himself upon the Lord! His jailer coming to take him prisoner, if he can! A base apostate spirit, daring to attempt such things as these upon him! Surely this was a deep abasement to the Son of God.

5. *The concern he showed for the needy*

Our blessed Lord Jesus was yet more humbled in his life than all this, and that by his own *sympathy* with others, under all the burdens that made him groan. For he, much more than Paul, could say, who is afflicted, and I burn not? He lived all his time as it were in a hospital among the sick and wounded. And so tender was his heart, that every groan for sin, or under the effects of sin, pierced him so, that it was truly said, 'He took up our infirmities and carried our diseases' (Matt. 8:17). It was spoken on the occasion of some poor people who were possessed by the devil, and brought to him to be exorcised. It is said of him 'When Jesus saw her weeping, and the Jews who had come along with her also weeping, he was deeply moved in spirit and troubled' (John 11:33). And in verse 35, 'Jesus wept.' Yet his heart flowed with pity for those who had not one drop of pity for themselves. Witness his tears spent upon Jerusalem (Luke 19:41-42). He foresaw the misery that was coming, though they never foresaw, nor feared it. O how it pierced Christ to think of the disaster hanging over that great city! He mourned for those who could not mourn for their own sins. Therefore it is said, 'He was deeply distressed at the people's stubborn hearts' (Mark 3:5). The commendation of a good physician is that he does as it were die with every patient. This was most applicable to our tender-hearted Physician. This was one of those things that made him 'a man of sorrows, and familiar with suffering'. For the more holy a man is, the more he is grieved and afflicted for the sin of others; and the more tender a man is, the more he is pierced when he sees the miseries that lie upon others. And it is sure, there was never any heart more holy, or more sensitive, tender, and compassionate than Christ's.

6. The treatment he experienced

Lastly, that which yet helped to humble him lower was the ungrateful and most base and unworthy reception the world gave him. He was not received or treated like a Saviour, but as the vilest of men. One would think that he who came from heaven, 'to give his life a ransom for many' (Matt. 20:28); he that was 'not sent to condemn the world, but to save the world' (John 3:17); he who came 'to destroy the devil's work' (1 John 3:8), to break the chains, and open the prison-doors, and 'proclaim freedom for the captives' (Isa. 61:1); when such a Saviour arrived, O with what acclamations of joy, and demonstration of thankfulness, should he have been received! One would have thought they should even kiss the ground he trod upon. But instead of this, he was hated (John 15:18), he was despised by them (Matt. 13:55). He was so reproached, that he became 'scorned by men and despised by the people' (Psa. 22:6). He was accused of working his miracles by the power of the devil (Matt. 12:24). He was trodden upon as a worm (Psa. 22:6). They buffeted him (Matt. 26:67), struck him on the head (Matt. 27:30), decked him out as a fool (verses 28-29), spat in his face (verse 30), despised him as the lowest of men, 'this *fellow* said ...' (Matt. 26:61). One of his own followers sold him, another denied that he knew him, and all deserted him in his greatest troubles. All this was a great abasement to the Son of God, who was not thus treated for a day, or in one place, but all his days and in all places. 'He endured the hatred of sinners against himself.'

In these particulars I have pointed out to you something of the humble life Christ lived in the world. From all these particulars some useful lessons will be noted:

Seven lessons from the humiliation of Christ

1. The law's demands have been met.

From the first stage of Christ's humiliation, in submitting to be circumcised, and thereby obliging himself to fulfil the whole law, it follows *that justice itself may be set both hand and seal to the acquittances and discharges of believers.* Christ hereby obliged himself to be the law's pay-master, to pay its utmost demand, and to bear that yoke of obedience that never any before him could bear. As Christ's circumcision obliged him to keep the whole law, so he was most precise in observing it, and so exact, that the sharp eye of Divine Justice cannot see the least flaw in it, but acknowledges full payment, and stands ready to sign the believer a full acquittance: that God may 'be just and the one who justifies those who have faith in Jesus' (Rom. 3:26). Had not Christ been thus obliged, we had never been discharged. Had not his obedience been entire, complete and perfect, our justification could not have been so. He that has a precious treasure will be loath to risk it in a leaky vessel: woe to the holiest man on earth, if the safety of his precious soul were to be rested on the foundation of the best duty that ever he performed. But Christ's obedience and righteousness is firm and sound; a foundation on which we may safely trust our all.

2. The godly will suffer.

From the early flight of Christ into Egypt we infer *that the greatest innocence and piety cannot exempt from persecution and injury.* Who is more innocent than Christ? And who more persecuted? The world is the world still. 'I have given them your word, and the world has hated them' (John 17:14). The world lies in wait as a thief for those who carry this treasure. Persecution follows piety, as the shadow does the body: 'everyone who wants to live a godly life in Christ Jesus will be persecuted' (2 Tim. 3:12). Whoever resolves to live a godly life must never expect to live quietly. All who want to live a godly life, who will exert holiness in their lives, convict and anger the consciences of the ungodly. This enrages them, for there is an enmity and antipathy between them, and this enmity runs in the blood. But thus it must be, to conform us unto Christ. And O that your *spirits*, as well as your *conditions*, may better harmonize with Christ. He suffered meekly, quietly, and self-denyingly; be like him. Let it not be said of you, as it is of the hypocrite, whose lusts are only *hidden*, but not *mortified* by his duties, that he is like a *flint*, which seems cold; but if you strike him, he is all fiery. To do well, and suffer ill, is Christlike.

3. Living for God may well mean a hard life.

From the third particular of Christ's humiliation, I infer *that such as are full of grace and holiness may be destitute and empty of crea-ture-comforts*. What an overflowing fullness of grace was there in Christ! And yet to what a low ebb did his outward comforts some-times fall! As it fared with him, so it was with many others now in glory with him, whilst they were on the way to that glory: 'to this very hour we go hungry and thirsty, we are in rags, we are bru-tally treated, we are homeless' (1 Cor. 4:11). Their souls were richly clothed with robes of righteousness, their bodies naked or meanly clad. Their *souls* fed well, even on hidden manna, but their *bodies* were hungry. Let us be content (said Luther) with our hard fare; for do we not feast with angels upon that bread of life? Remember, when wants pinch hard, that these fix no marks of God's hatred upon you. He has dealt no worse with you than he did with his own Son. Nay, which of you is not better accommodated than Christ was? If you are hungry or thirsty, you have some refresh-ments and you have beds to lie on, whereas the Son of Man had nowhere to lay his head. The heir of all things had sometimes nothing to eat. And remember you are going to a plentiful coun-try, where all your needs will be supplied; 'Has not God chosen those who are poor in the eyes of the world to be rich in faith and to inherit the kingdom he promised those who love him?' (James 2:5). The meanness of your *present*, will add to the lustre of your *future* condition.

4. Satan never ignores a believer.

From the fourth particular of Christ's humiliation in his life, by Satan's temptations, we infer *that those in whom Satan has no part, may have most trouble from him in this world.* 'The prince of this world is coming. He has no hold on me' (John 14:30). Where he knows he cannot be a *conqueror*, he will not cease to be a *troubler*. This bold and daring spirit moves against Christ himself. For doubtless he was filled with envy at the sight of him, and would do what he could, though to no purpose, to obstruct the blessed design in his hand. And it was the wisdom and love of Christ to admit him to come as near him as might be, and try all his darts upon him, so that by this experience he might be filled with pity to strengthen those who are tempted. And as he set on Christ, so much more will he set upon us, and too often comes off a conqueror. Sometimes he shoots the fiery darts of blasphemies. These fall as flashes of lightning on the dry thatch, which instantly sets all into flame. And just so it is attended with a thunderclap of inward horror, that shivers the very heart, and strikes all into confusion within.

The best rule in the face of temptation is doubtless that of the apostle: 'take up the shield of faith, with which you can extinguish all the flaming arrows of the evil one' (Eph. 6:16). Act your faith, my friends, upon our tempted Saviour, who passed through temptations before you, and particularly exercise faith on three things in Christ's temptations:

1. Consider how great a variety of temptations were tried upon Christ, and of what a horrid blasphemous nature that was, 'bow down and worship me'.

2. Consider that Christ came off a perfect conqueror in the day of his trial, and beat Satan out of the field. For he saw what he attempted on Christ was as impossible as to batter the body of the sun with snow-balls.

3. Lastly, believe that the benefits of those victories and conquests of his are for you, and that for your sakes he permitted the tempter to come so near him (Heb. 2:18).

But you may well say: True, Christ was tempted as well as I (Heb. 4:15); but there is a vast difference between his temptations and mine. For the prince of this world came and found nothing in him (John 14:30). He was not internally *defiled*, though externally *assaulted*. But I am defiled by them as well as troubled.

I reply: This is a different case. True, it is so, and must be so, or else it had signified nothing to your relief: for had Christ been internally defiled, he had not been a fit mediator for you, nor could you have had any benefit, either by his temptations, or sufferings for you. But he being tempted, and yet still escaping the defilement of sin, has not only satisfied for the sins you commit when tempted, but also got an experimental sense of the misery of your condition, which is in him (though now in glory), as a spirit of pity and tender compassion to you. Remember, poor tempted Christian, 'The God of peace will soon crush Satan under your feet' (Rom. 16:20). You shall set your foot on the neck of that enemy, and as soon as both your feet are over the threshold of glory, you shall cast back a smiling look, and say, 'Now, Satan, do your worst; now I am there where you cannot come.'

Meanwhile, till you are out of his reach, let me advise you to go to Jesus Christ, and open the matter to him. Tell him how that base spirit falls and sets upon you, even in his presence. Entreat him to rebuke and call him off. Beg him to consider your case, and say, 'Lord, do you remember how your own heart was once grieved, though not defiled, by his assaults? I have grief and guilt together upon me. Ah, Lord, I expect pity and help from you; you know the heart of a stranger, the heart of a poor and tempted one.' This is singular relief in this case. O try it!

5. Learn to love like Jesus.

Was Christ more humbled by his own sympathy with others in their distresses? Hence we learn *that a compassionate spirit, towards those who labour under burdens of sin or affliction, is Christlike, and truly excellent: this was the Spirit of Christ.* O be like him! As the elect of God, clothe yourselves with compassion (Col. 3:12); 'Rejoice with those who rejoice; mourn with those who mourn' (Rom. 12:15). It was Cain who said, 'Am I my brother's keeper?' Blessed Paul was of the opposite spirit. 'Who is weak, and I do not feel weak? Who is led into sin, and I do not inwardly burn?' (2 Cor. 11:29).

Three things promote sympathy in Christians: one is the Lord's pity for them—he suffers, as it were, with them: 'In all their distress he too was distressed' (Isa. 63:9). Another is the relation we sustain to God's afflicted people: they are members with us in one body, and the members should have the same care of one another (1 Cor. 12:25). The last is we do not know how soon we may need from others what others now need from us. 'You who are spiritual should restore him gently. But watch yourself, or you also may be tempted' (Gal. 6:1).

6. Don't care about what the world says of you.

Did the world help in the humiliation of Christ by its base and vile treatment of him? Learn *that the judgment the world gives of persons and their worth is little to be regarded.* Surely it dispenses its smiles and honours very preposterously and unduly, in this respect, among others; the saints are styled persons, 'the world was not worthy of them' (Heb. 11:38). If the world gives us any help to discover the true worth and excellency of men, it is by the rule of opposites for the most part. Where it fixes its marks of hatred, we may usually find that which invites our respect and love. It should trouble us the less to be under the slights and disrespects of a blind world. 'I could be even proud of it (says Luther), that I see I have a bad name from the world.' And Jerome blessed God who counted him worthy to be hated by the world. Labour to stand right in the judgment of God, and do not trouble yourself for the rash and headlong censures of men. Let wicked men, says one, cut the throat of my credit, and do as they like best with it; when the wind of their contempt has blown away my good name from me in the way to heaven, I know Christ will take my name out of the mud, and wash it, and restore it to me again.

7. Guard your heart on the way to heaven.

From the whole of Christ's humiliation in his life, learn *to pass through all the troubles of your life with a contented, composed spirit, as Christ your forerunner did.* He was persecuted, and bore it meekly; he was poor, and never murmured; tempted, and never yielded to the temptation; and he was reviled, and reviled not again. So when you pass through any of these trials, look to Jesus and consider him. See how he passed through those things before you and how he managed himself in similar circumstances. He has not only shown the way by his life's pattern and example for you, but he has in every one of those conditions left a blessing behind him for those who follow his steps. *Thanks be to God for Jesus Christ.*

4

Jesus Reigns!

THIS is the penultimate sermon in Flavel's *The Fountain of Life*, exploring Christ's person and work. In the turmoil of the 1660s, when some 2,000 evangelical pastors were ejected from the Church of England, and then forbidden to minister to their people, Flavel seeks to comfort believers with the glories of Jesus Christ. The significance of his ascension and session at God's right hand is laid out here for us in all its beauty.

As a man who himself suffered much for his Lord, Flavel urges us to reflect on Christ's sacrifice on earth and reward in heaven. We are led to think about the depths of Christ's sufferings and the heights of his heavenly rule. We can imagine God the Father speaking to his Son, comforting and rewarding him for his obedience.

Read these passages slowly, and let the word of God dwell in you richly. After that, consider how Christ's rule opens up a world of confident hope and committed discipleship, followed by an entrance into the eternal world of rest and joy.

After he had provided purification for sins, he sat down at the right hand of the Majesty in heaven.—Hebrews 1:3

HAVING returned again to his Father, and having finished his whole work on earth, Christ is there bade by the Father to sit down in the seat of honour and rest. A seat prepared for him at God's right hand gives him honour, and all his enemies as a footstool under his feet gives him ease. How much is the state and condition of Jesus Christ changed in a few days! Here he groaned, wept, laboured, suffered, sweat, even sweat blood, and found no rest in this world; but when he comes to heaven, there he enters into rest. He sits down for ever in the highest and easiest throne, prepared by the Father for him when he had done his work. 'After he had provided purification for sins, he sat down at the right hand of the Majesty in heaven.'

The scope of this epistle is to demonstrate Christ to be the fullness of all legal types and ceremonies, and that whatever light glimmered to the world through them, yet it was but as the light of the day-star compared to the light of the sun.

Glorious, in his person, work and reward

In this chapter Christ is described, and particularly in this third verse, he is described three ways.

Firstly, by his essential glory and dignity. He is the brightness of his Father's glory, the very splendour of glory. He is the light of light, as the Nicene Creed expresses it, as a beam of light proceeding from the sun. And the secondary reason of it is with respect to men, for just as the sun communicates its light and influence to us by its beams, so God communicates his goodness, and manifests himself to us by Christ. He is the *express image* or character of his person, not as the impressed image of the seal upon the wax, but as the engraving in the seal itself. Thus he is described by his essential glory.

Secondly, he is described by the work he wrought here on earth, in his humbled state, and it was a glorious work, and that wrought out by his own single hand: 'After he had provided purification for sins.' A work that all the angels in heaven could not do, Christ did.

Thirdly, and lastly, he is described by his glory, which (as a reward of that work) he now enjoys in heaven. 'After he had provided purification for sins, he sat down at the right hand of the Majesty in heaven.' *Majesty*, i.e. the Lord clothed him with the greatest power and highest honour that heaven itself could afford.

Doctrine: *that when our Lord Jesus Christ had finished his work on earth, he was placed in the seat of the highest honour, and authority, at the right hand of God in heaven.*

This truth is transformingly glorious. Stephen had but a glimpse of Christ at his Father's right hand, and it caused 'his face to shine, as if it had been the face of an angel' (Acts 7:56; see also 6:15). Christ's high advancement was foretold and promised before the work of redemption was taken in hand: 'The LORD says to my Lord, "Sit at my right hand, until I make your enemies a footstool for your feet"' (Psa. 110:1). And this promise was punctually performed for Christ, after his resurrection and ascension, and in his supreme exaltation, far above all created beings, in heaven and earth (Eph. 1:20-22).

God's right hand

It is obvious enough that the expression 'the right hand of God' is not literal, but figurative. God has no hand, right or left. But it is a condescending expression in which God stoops to the creature's understanding, and by it he would have us understand honour, power, and nearness.

The right hand is the hand of honour, the upper hand, where we place those whom we highly esteem and honour. So Solomon placed his mother in a seat at his right hand (1 Kings 2:19). As a token or sign of honour God sets Christ at his right hand, which, on that account, in the text is called the right hand of the *Majesty*. In this God has expressed more favour, delight, and honour to Jesus Christ than ever he did to any creature. 'To which of the angels did God ever say, "Sit at my right hand"?' (Heb. 1:13).

Also, the right hand is the hand of power. We call it the *weapon hand*, and the *working hand*. And the setting of Christ there teaches us his exaltation to the highest authority, and most supreme dominion. Not that God the Father has put himself out of his authority, and advanced Christ above himself; no, 'when it says that "everything" has been put under him, it is clear that this does not include God himself, who put everything under Christ' (1 Cor. 15:27). But to sit as an enthroned king at God's right hand implies power, even the most sovereign and supreme power. And so Christ himself says, 'In the future you will see the Son of Man sitting at the right hand of the Mighty One' (Matt. 26:64).

And finally, it signifies honour and power, and nearness in place, as we use to say, *at one's elbow*, and so it is applied to Christ. 'The Lord is at your right hand; he will crush kings on the day of his wrath' (Psa. 110:5), i.e. the Lord, who is very near you, and present with you, he shall subdue your enemies. This then is what we are to understand by God's right hand—honour, power, and nearness.

And his enemies for his footstool

This expression *implies the perfecting and completing of Christ's work, for which he came into the world.* After his work was ended, then he sat down and rested from those labours. 'Day after day every priest stands and performs his religious duties; again and again he offers the same sacrifices, which can never take away sins. But when this priest had offered for all time one sacrifice for sins, he sat down at the right hand of God' (Heb. 10:11-12). Here he assigns a double difference between Christ and the Levitical priests: they stand, which is the posture of servants, but he sits, which is the posture of a Lord. They stand daily, because their sacrifices cannot take away sin; he did his work fully, by one offering, and after that, sits or rests for ever in heaven. And this was excellently shown to us in the ark, which was a type of Jesus Christ, and particularly in the rings by which it was carried, till at last it rested in Solomon's temple, with glorious and triumphal solemnity (Psa. 132:8-9; 2 Chron. 5:1-14). So Christ, while he was here on earth, being anointed with the Holy Spirit and wisdom, went about doing good (Acts 10:38). And having ceased from his works, did at last enter into his rest (Heb. 4:10), which is the heavenly temple (Rev. 11:19).

Secondly, his sitting down at God's right hand *notes the high contentment and satisfaction of God the Father in him, and in his work.* 'The LORD said to my Lord, "Sit at my right hand."' The words are brought in as the words of the Father, welcoming Christ to heaven, and (as it were) congratulating the happy accomplishment of his most difficult work. And it is as if he had said, 'O my Son, what shall be done for you this day? You have finished a great work, and in all the parts of it acquitted yourself as an able and faithful servant to me. What honours shall I now bestow upon you? The highest glory in heaven is not too high for you: come, sit at my right hand.' O how well is he pleased with Christ, and what he has done! He delighted greatly to behold him here in his work on earth, and by a voice from the excellent glory he told him so, when he spoke from heaven to him, saying, 'This is my Son, whom I love; with him I am well pleased' (2 Pet. 1:17). And Jesus himself tells us, 'The reason my Father loves me is that I lay down my life' (John 10:17). It was a work that the heart of God had been set upon from eternity: he took infinite delight in it.

Thirdly, Christ's sitting down at God's right hand in heaven *notes the advancement of Christ's human nature to the highest honour, even to be the object of adoration for angels and men.* For it is properly his human nature that is the subject of all this honour and advancement, and being advanced to the right hand of Majesty, it has become an object of worship and adoration, not simply as it is flesh and blood, but as it is personally united to the Second Person, and enthroned in the supreme glory of heaven. O here is the mystery, that flesh and blood should ever be advanced to the highest throne of Majesty, and being there installed in that glory, we may now direct our worship to him as God-Man. To this end was his humanity so advanced that it might be adored and worshipped by all. 'The Father ... has entrusted all judgment to the Son, that all may honour the Son, as they honour the Father.' And the Father will accept of no honour divided from his honour. Therefore it is added in the clause, 'He who does not honour the Son does not honour the Father, who has sent him' (John 5:22-23). Hence the apostles, in their greetings in their epistles, beg for grace, mercy, and peace, from God the Father, and our Lord Jesus Christ; and in their signing-off, they desire the grace of our Lord Jesus Christ to the churches.

Fourthly, it teaches us *the sovereignty and supremacy of Christ over all.* The investiture of Christ means his authority over the empire of both worlds. For this belongs to him who sits down upon his throne. When the Father said to him, 'Sit at my right hand', he was delivering to him the dispensation and economy of the kingdom. 'Put the awesome sceptre of government into his hand', thus the apostle interprets and understands it: 'He must reign until he has put all his enemies under his feet' (1 Cor. 15:25). And to this purpose, the writer of Hebrews applies the words of the Psalmist, 'You made him a little lower than the angels', i.e. in respect of his humbled state on earth, 'you crowned him with glory and honour, and put everything under his feet' (Heb. 2:7-8). He is over the spiritual kingdom, the church, as absolute Lord (Matt. 28:18-20). He is also Lord over the providential kingdom, the whole world (Psa. 110:2). And this providential kingdom, being subordinate to his spiritual kingdom, he orders and rules for the advantage and benefit of the church (Eph. 1:22).

Fifthly, to sit at God's right hand with his enemies for a footstool *implies Christ to be a conqueror over all his enemies*. To have his enemies under his feet notes perfect conquest and complete victory, as when Joshua set his foot upon the necks of the kings. They trampled his name, and his saints under their feet, and Christ will tread them under his feet. It is true indeed this victory is incomplete, for 'Yet at present we do not see everything subject to him. But we see Jesus … now crowned with glory and honour' (Heb. 2:8-9). And that is enough, enough to show that the power of his enemies is now broken. Although they still oppose him, yet it is to no purpose at all, for he is so infinitely above them that they must fall before him. It is not with Christ as it was with Abijah, against whom Jeroboam prevailed, because he was young and tender-hearted, and could not withstand him. His incapacity and weakness gave the watchful enemy an advantage over him. I say, it is not so with Christ: he is at God's right hand. And all the power of God stands ready bent to strike through his enemies (Psa. 110:5).

Sixthly, Christ's sitting in heaven notes to us *the great and wonderful change that is made upon the state and condition of Christ since his ascension into heaven*. Ah, it is far different with him now than it was in the days of his humiliation here on earth. What a wonderful change has heaven made upon him! It is good to compare in our thoughts the abasement of Christ, and his exaltation together. He was born in a stable, but now he reigns in his royal palace. Then he had a manger for his cradle, but now he sits on a chair of state. Then oxen and asses were his companions, now thousands of saints, and ten thousands of angels minister round about his throne. Then in contempt they called him the carpenter's son, now he obtains a more excellent name than angels. Then he was led away into the wilderness to be tempted of the devil, now it is proclaimed before him, 'Let all God's angels worship him.' Then he had no place to lay his head, now he is exalted to be heir of all things. In his state of humiliation he endured the scorn of sinners, but in his state of exaltation he is adored and admired by saints and angels. Then 'he had no beauty or majesty to attract us to him' (Isa. 53:2); now the beauty of his countenance shall send forth such glorious beams as shall dazzle the eyes of all the celestial inhabitants of heaven round about him.

O what a change is this! Here he sweated, but there he sits. Here he groaned, but there he triumphs. Here he lay upon the ground, there he sits on the throne of glory. When he came to heaven, his Father did as it were speak to him: 'My dear Son, what a hard labour you have had of it. What a world of woe you have passed through, in the strength of your love to me and my elect. You have been hungry, thirsty, weary, scourged, crucified, and reproached. Ah, what bad treatment you have had in the ungrateful world. You have not had a day's rest or comfort since you went out from me. But now your suffering days are accomplished, now your rest is come, rest for evermore. Henceforth sit at my right hand. Henceforth you shall groan, weep or bleed no more. Sit at my right hand.'

Seventhly, Christ's sitting at God's right hand implies *the advancement of believers to the highest honour*. For this session of Christ's relates to them, as he sits as our representative in which regard we are made to sit with him in heavenly places, as the apostle says (Eph. 2:6). How secure may we be, we who do now already possess the kingdom in our head, Christ. This is all my hope, and all my confidence, that we have a portion in that flesh and blood of Christ, which is so exalted, and therefore where he reigns, we shall reign. There our flesh is glorified, and we shall be glorified. Surely it is matter of exceeding joy to believe that Christ our head, and our flesh and blood, is in all this glory at his Father's right hand.

Five truths to make your heart burn

1. His present is our future.

Is this so great an honour to Christ, to sit enthroned at God's right hand? What honour then is reserved in heaven for those that are faithful to Christ now on the earth? Christ prayed, and his prayer was heard, that we may be with him to behold the glory that God has given him (see John 17:24), and what heart can conceive the joy of such a sight? It made Stephen's face shine as the face of an angel, when he had but a glimpse of Christ at his Father's right hand. 'Your eyes will see the king in his beauty' (Isa. 33:17), which referred to Hezekiah in the *type*, and to Christ in the *truth*.

But this is not all, though it is much, to be spectators of Christ in his throne of glory. We shall not only see him on his throne, but also sit with him enthroned in glory. To behold him is much, but to sit with him is more. And you know how the Queen of the South fainted at the sight of Solomon in his glory. But this sight you shall have of Christ will change you into his likeness. 'We shall be like him', says the apostle, 'for we shall see him as he is'

(1 John 3:2). He will place us as it were in his own throne with him. So runs the promise, 'To him who overcomes, I will give the right to sit with me on my throne, just as I overcame, and sat down with my Father on his throne' (Rev. 3:21), and also 'If we endure, we will also reign with him' (2 Tim. 2:12).

The Father set Christ on his right hand, and Christ will set the saints at his right hand. So you know the sheep are placed by the angels at the great day (Matt. 25), and so the church, under the figure of the daughter of Egypt whom Solomon married, is placed 'at the king's right hand ... in gold of Ophir' (Psa. 45:9). This is the honour of all the saints. O amazing love! What, we sit on thrones, while others as good as us by nature howl in flames?

These expressions indeed do not mean that the saints shall be set in higher glory than Christ, or that they shall have an equal glory with Christ, for in all things he must have the pre-eminence. They do note the great honour that Christ will put upon the saints, since his glory shall be their glory in heaven, and so it will be a shared glory. O, it is admirable to think about the free grace which has already raised up poor dust and ashes!

To think how closely related we now are to this royal, princely Jesus! And yet, how much higher are the designs of grace that are not yet come to their fullness! 'Dear friends, now we are children of God, and what we will be has not yet been made known' (1 John 3:2). What reason do you have to honour Christ on earth, who is preparing such honours for you in heaven?

2. Jesus has triumphed, and therefore so will his kingdom.

If Christ Jesus is thus enthroned in heaven then how impossible is it that ever his cause should miscarry or sink on earth! The church has many subtle and potent enemies. True, but as Haman could not prevail against the Jews whilst Esther their friend spoke for them to the king, no more can they whilst our Jesus sits at his and

our Father's right hand. Will he suffer his enemies that are under
his feet to rise up and pull out his eyes? Surely those who touch
his people touch the very apple of his eye (Zech. 2:8). 'For he must
reign until he has put all his enemies under his feet' (1 Cor. 15:25).
The enemy under his feet shall not destroy the children in his
arms. He sits in heaven on purpose to manage all to the advantage
of his church (Eph. 1:22). Our enemies are powerful, but our King
sits at the right hand of power. Heaven overlooks hell. 'The One
enthroned in heaven laughs', and derides their attempts (Psa. 2:4).
He may permit his enemies to bring them grief in one place, but
it shall be for their profit in another. For it is with the church, as
it is with the sea: what it loses in one place, it gets it another, and
so really loses nothing. He may allow them also to distress us in
outward circumstances, but we shall be repaid with inward and
better mercies, and so we shall lose nothing by that.

A footstool you know is useful to him that steps onto it, and
serves to lift him up higher. So shall Christ's enemies be to him
and his, albeit they do not think so. What singular benefits the
oppositions of his enemies bring to his people.

3. His glory must make you worship.

Is Christ seated at the right hand of the Majesty in heaven? O
with what awful reverence should we approach him in the duties
of his worship! Away with light and low thoughts of Christ. Away
with formal, irreverent, and careless frames in praying, hearing,
receiving, and in conferring and speaking of Christ. Away with
all deadness and drowsiness in duties, for he is a great King with
whom you have your dealings. He is a King, to whom the kings
of the earth are but as little bits of clay. Even the angels cover their
faces in his presence. He is an adorable Majesty. When John had
a vision of this enthroned King, such was the overpowering glory
of Christ, as the sun when it shines in its strength, that when he
saw him, he fell at his feet as though dead, and would most likely

have died, if Christ had not laid his hand on him and said, 'Do not be afraid. I am the First and the Last. I am the Living One; I was dead, and behold I am alive for ever and ever!' (Rev. 1:17-18).

When Christ appeared to Saul on the road to Damascus, it was with a glory which exceeded the glory of the sun, and which overpowered him also, and laid him as one dead upon the ground. O that you would only know what a glorious Lord you worship and serve! He makes the very place of his feet glorious, wherever he goes. Surely he is greatly to be feared in the assembly of his saints, and to be held in reverence from all who are round about him. There is indeed a boldness or free liberty of speech allowed to the saints (Eph. 3:12). We may indeed come, as the children of a king come to the father, who is both their awesome sovereign and a tender father. This double relation causes a due mixture of love and reverence in their hearts when they come before him. You may be *free*, but not *rude*, in his presence. Though he is your Father, Brother and Friend, yet the distance between him and you is *infinite*.

4. *There is no real shame in suffering for him.*

If Christ has been so gloriously advanced to the highest throne, then none need reckon themselves dishonoured by suffering the vilest things for his sake. The very chains and sufferings of Christ have glory in them. Hence Moses 'regarded disgrace for the sake of Christ as of greater value than the treasures of Egypt' (Heb. 11:26). He saw an excellence in the very worst things of Christ—his reproaches and sufferings—which made him leap out of his honours and riches into them. He did not only endure the reproaches of Christ but counted them as treasures, to be reckoned among his honours and things of value.

Disgrace itself is honourable when it is endured for the Lord of glory. And surely there is a little paradise, a young heaven, in suffering for Christ. If there were nothing else in it except that they are endured on his account, it would richly reward all we can endure for him. But if we consider how exceedingly kind Christ is to those who count it their glory to be brought low for him, that though he is always kind to his people (yet if we may so speak) he overcomes himself in kindness, when they suffer for him, it would make men love suffering reproach for Christ's sake.

5. We work hard for Christ until we rest with him.

If Christ did not sit down to rest in heaven till he had finished his work on earth, then it is in vain for us to think of rest till we have finished our work, as Christ also did his. How willing are we to find rest here, and to dream of that which Christ never found in this world, nor any ever found before us. O think not of resting till you have done working and done sinning. Your life and your labours must end together. 'Write: Blessed are the dead who die in the Lord from now on. "Yes," says the Spirit, "they will rest from their labour"' (Rev. 14:13).

Here you must have the *sweat*, and there the *sweet*. It is too much to have two heavens. Here you must be content to dwell in the tents of Kedar (see Psa. 120:5), hereafter you shall be within the curtains of Solomon. Heaven is the place of which it may be truly said, that there the weary are at rest. Do not think of sitting down on this side of heaven. There are four things which will keep the saints from sitting down on earth to rest: grace, corruption, devils, and wicked men.

First, *grace* will not allow you to rest here. Its tendencies are beyond this world. It will be looking and longing for the blessed hope. A gracious person takes himself for a pilgrim, seeking a better country, and is always suspicious of danger in every place and state. It is always beating up the sluggish heart with such language as this: 'Get up, go away! For this is not your resting place, because it is defiled' (Mic. 2:10). Its further tendencies and continual jealousies will keep you from sitting still for long in this world.

Second, your *corruptions* will keep you from rest here. They will continually exercise your spirits, and keep you upon your watch. Saints have their hands filled with work by their own hearts every day, sometimes to prevent sin, and sometimes to lament it, and always to watch and fear, to mortify and kill it. Sin will not long suffer you to be quiet (Rom. 7:21-24).

Third, there is a busy *devil* who will do it. He will find you work enough with his temptations and suggestions, and unless you can sleep quietly in his arms as the wicked do, there is no rest to be expected. 'Your enemy the devil prowls around like a roaring lion looking for someone to devour. Resist him' (1 Pet. 5:8-9).

Fourth, nor will *his servants and instruments* let you be quiet this side of heaven. 'I am in the midst of lions', says the holy man; 'I lie among ravenous beasts—men whose teeth are spears and arrows, whose tongues are sharp swords' (Psa. 57:4). Well then, be content to enter into your rest, as Christ did into his. He sweat, then sat, and so must you.

PART TWO

TRUSTING IN AND BELONGING TO CHRIST

5

The Riches of God in Christ

☞

THIS is a searching and exhilarating sermon on the apostle's great statement regarding all that God is to us in Christ. It is the opening sermon in *The Method of Grace in the Gospel Redemption* (1681). There is so much here that one may well need to read it twice, and then discuss it with others. The sermon not only deals with conversion, but also traces out the implications of being united with Christ.

One thing to notice here is Flavel's trinitarian treatment of gospel salvation. The Father's planning and power are all invested in the Son, who obeys the Father in order to accomplish salvation for the elect. Equally, Flavel insists, there is no salvation for any without the Spirit's work. He must convey the gift of the Father and the Son to the lost sinner.

The best of Puritan preachers—and Flavel ranks among them—are always clear on the responsibilities of those who hear the gospel. Flavel devotes a lengthy final section to showing us how we are to come to Christ and what we will find in him. His aim is to convince and compel us to embrace the Saviour with a living faith.

It is because of him that you are in Christ Jesus, who has become for us wisdom from God—that is, our righteousness, holiness and redemption.—1 Corinthians 1:30

HE who inquires what is the just value and worth of Christ, asks a question which puts all the men on earth, and angels in heaven, in an everlasting quandary.

The highest attainment of our knowledge in this life is to know that Christ and his love surpass knowledge (Eph. 3:19). But however excellent Christ is in himself, whatever treasures of righteousness lie in his blood, and whatever joy, peace, and comforts spring up to men out of his *incarnation*, *humiliation*, and *exaltation*, they all give their distinct benefits and comforts to them in the way of *effectual application*.

For no wound was healed by a prepared but unapplied dressing. Nobody was ever warmed by the most costly garment made, but not put on. No heart was ever refreshed and comforted by the richest tonic mixed, but not received. Nor from the beginning of the world was it ever known that a poor deceived, condemned, polluted, miserable sinner was actually delivered out of that woeful state, until Christ was made by God to him wisdom and righteousness, sanctification and redemption.

For as the condemnation of the *first* Adam passes to us because we are his through generation, just so, grace and forgiveness only pass from the *second* Adam to us because we are his through regeneration. Adam's sin hurts none but those that are in him. And Christ's blood profits none but those that are in him. How great a weight therefore hangs upon the effectual application of Christ to the souls of men! And what is there in the whole world so awfully solemn, so greatly important, as this is? Such is the strong comfort resulting from it that the apostle, in this context, offers it to the believing Corinthians as an abounding recompense for their lowly outward condition in this world, of which he had just spoken in verses 27-28, where he tells them that though the world despised them as vile, foolish, and weak, yet because of God, Christ has become for them wisdom and righteousness, sanctification and redemption.

Knowing the privileges of saving grace

In these words we have a declaration of the chief privileges of believers, and an account of the method whereby they come to be invested with them.

First, their privileges are stated, namely, *wisdom, righteousness, sanctification,* and *redemption*—mercies of inestimable value in themselves, and such as respect a fourfold misery lying upon sinful man: *ignorance, guilt, pollution,* and the whole train of miserable consequences and effects, let in upon the nature of men, even in the best and holiest of men, by sin.

Fallen man is not only deep in misery, but grossly ignorant, both that he is so, and of how to recover himself from it. Sin has left him at once senseless of his state, and at a perfect loss about the true remedy. To cure this, Christ is made to him *wisdom*, not only by *procuring* those treasures of wisdom that are in himself, for the benefit of such souls as are united to him, as a head, consulting the good of his own members; but also, by *imparting* his wisdom to them by the Spirit of illumination, whereby they come to discern both their sin and danger, as well as the true way of their recovery from both, through the application of Christ to their souls by faith.

But mere illumination only increases our burden, and aggravates our misery as long as sin in the guilt of it is either imputed to our persons to condemn us, or reflected by our consciences to accuse us.

Therefore, with the plan of remedying and healing this sore evil, Christ is made by God our complete and perfect *righteousness* whereby our just punishment is dissolved, and a solid foundation for a well-settled peace of conscience firmly established. Although the removing of guilt from our persons and consciences is an inestimable mercy, yet alone it cannot make us completely happy. For though a man should never be damned for sin, yet what is it less than hell upon earth to be under the dominion and pollution of every lust? It is misery enough to be daily defiled by sin, even if a man should never be damned for it.

To complete therefore the happiness of the redeemed, due to God, Christ is not only to us *wisdom* and *righteousness*—the one curing our ignorance, the other our guilt—but he is made *holiness* also, to relieve us from the dominion and pollutions of our corruptions. 'He comes both by water and by blood, not by blood only, but also by water' (1 John 5:6), *purging* as well as *pardoning*. How complete and perfect a cure is Christ!

But yet something is required beyond all this to make our happiness perfect and entire, and lacking nothing, and that is the removal of the effects and consequences of sin, which (notwithstanding all the fore-mentioned privileges and mercies) still lie upon the souls and bodies of illuminated, justified, and sanctified persons. For even with the best and holiest of men, what a swarm of vanity, a load of deadness, and fits of unbelief do daily appear in and oppress their souls to the embittering of all the comforts of life to them! And how many diseases, deformities, and pains oppress their bodies, which daily moulder away by them, till they fall into the grave by death, even as the bodies of other men do, who never received such privileges from Christ as they do! For, as the apostle says in Romans 8:10, 'If Christ is in you, your body is dead because of sin.' Sanctification is no exemption from mortality.

These four—wisdom, righteousness, holiness and redemption—take in all that is necessary or desirable, to make a soul truly and perfectly blessed.

Taking hold of the privileges

Next, we have here the method and way by which the elect come to be invested with these excellent privileges. Where the apostle gives us these words, 'It is because of him that you are in Christ Jesus, who has become for us …', four things are striking:

First, that *Christ and his benefits go inseparably and undividedly together.* It is Christ himself who has become all this for us. We can have no saving benefit separate and apart from the person of Christ. Many would willingly receive his *privileges* who will not receive his person, but it cannot be. If we will have one, we must take the other, too. We must accept his person first, and then his benefits. As it is in the marriage covenant, so it is here.

Secondly, Christ with his benefits must be personally and particularly applied to us, before we can receive any actual, saving privilege from him. A sum of money becomes or is made the ransom and liberty of a captive, when it is not only promised, but paid down in his name, and legally applied for that use and end. When Christ died, the ransom was prepared, and the sum laid down; but yet the elect continue still in sin and misery, notwithstanding, till by *effectual calling* it is actually *applied* to them, and then they are made free, reconciled by Christ's death, by whom 'we have now received reconciliation' (Rom. 5:10-11).

Thirdly, this application of Christ is the work of God, and not of man: 'It is because of him that you are in Christ Jesus.' The same hand that prepared it must also apply it, or else we perish, notwith-standing all that the Father has done in planning and appointing, and all that the Son has done in executing and accomplishing the design thus far. And this actual application is the work of the Spirit.

Fourthly and lastly, *this expression tells us how Christ is suited to the needs of sinners*. What they want, he is made to them; and indeed, as money answers all things, and can be turned towards meat, drink, clothes, medicine or whatever else our bodies require, so Christ is all that our souls require. He is bread to the hungry, and clothing to the naked soul. In a word, God prepared and furnished him with the purpose of answering for all our needs. This is the apostle's meaning when he says, 'who has become for us wisdom from God, that is, our righteousness, sanctification, and redemption'.

Doctrine: *that the Lord Jesus Christ, with all his precious benefits, becomes ours, by God's special and effectual application.*

There is a twofold application of our redemption, one *primary*, the other *secondary*. The first is the act of God the *Father*, apply-ing it to Christ our surety, and then to us in him. The second is the act of the *Holy Spirit*, personally and actually applying it to us in the world of conversion. What was done to the person of Christ was not only virtually done upon us, considered in him as a common public representative person, in which sense we are said to die with him, and live with him, to be crucified with him, and buried with him; but it was also intended for a platform, or idea, of what is to be done by the Spirit, actually upon our souls and bodies, in our own persons. As he died for sin, so the Spirit applying his death to us in the work of *mortification* causes us to die to sin, by the virtue of his death. And as he was given life by the Spirit, so the Spirit applying to us the life of Christ causes us to live, by spiritual *vivification*. Now this personal, secondary, and *actual application of redemption* to us by the Spirit, in his sanctifying work, is what I am engaged here to discuss.

Eight truths about coming to Christ

1. Everything changes when we come to Christ.

The application of Christ to us not only encompasses our justification, but also all these works of the Spirit which are known to us in Scripture by the names of regeneration, vocation, sanctification, and conversion.

Though all these terms have some small respective differences among themselves, yet they are all included in this general one, the applying and putting on of Christ: 'put on the Lord Jesus Christ' (Rom. 13:14).

Regeneration expresses those supernatural, divine, new qualities, infused by the Spirit into the soul, which are the principles of all holy actions.

Vocation expresses the terms from which, and to which, the soul moves, when the Spirit works savingly upon it, under the gospel call.

Sanctification notes a holy dedication of heart and life to God, as we become the temples of the living God, separate from all profane sinful practices, to the Lord's only use and service.

Conversion denotes the great change itself which the Spirit works upon the soul, turning it by a sweet irresistible efficacy from the power of sin and Satan, to God in Christ.

Now all these are imported in and done by the application of Christ to our souls. For when once the efficacy of Christ's death and the power of his resurrection come to take place upon the heart of any man, he cannot but turn from sin to God, and become a new creation, living and acting by new principles and rules. So the apostle observes, speaking of the effect of this work of the Spirit upon that people, 'our gospel came to you not simply with words, but also with power, with the Holy Spirit and with deep conviction' (1 Thess. 1:5-6). This was the effectual application of Christ to them. 'You became imitators of us, and of the Lord' (verse 6). This was their effectual call. 'You turned to God from idols to serve the living and true God' (verse 9). This was their conversion. 'You became a model to all the believers' (verse 7). This was their life of sanctification or dedication to God. All of these realities are encompassed in effectual application.

2. God appoints his servants to bring the gospel to the church.

The application of Christ to the souls of men is that great project and design of God in this world, and for its accomplishment all the ordinances and all the officers of the gospel are appointed and continued in the world.

This gospel is expressly declared to be its direct goal and the great business of all its officers. 'It was he who gave some to be apostles, some to be prophets, some to be evangelists, and some to be pastors and teachers … until we all reach unity in the faith and in the knowledge of the Son of God and become mature, attaining to the whole measure of the fulness of Christ' (Eph. 4:11, 13).

The great aim and scope of all Christ's ordinances and officers are to bring men into union with Christ, and so build them up to perfection in him, which means, to unite them to, and strengthen them in Christ. When it shall have finished this design, then the whole frame of gospel-ordinances shall be taken down, and all its officers disbanded. 'Then the end will come, when he hands over the kingdom' (1 Cor. 15:24). What are ministers, but the bridegroom's friends, ambassadors for God, to plead with men to be reconciled? When therefore all the elect are brought home in a reconciled state in Christ, when the marriage of the Lamb has come, our work and office expire together.

3. Unless the Spirit works, no one will be saved.

Such is the importance and great concern of the personal appli-cation of Christ to us by the Spirit, that whatever the Father has done in the planning, or the Son has done in the accomplishment of our redemption, is all unavailable and ineffectual to our salvation without this.

It is true that God's good pleasure in appointing us from eter-nity to salvation is, in its kind, a most full and sufficient impulsive cause of our salvation, and every way able (for so much as it is concerned) to produce its effect. And Christ's humiliation and sufferings are a most complete and sufficient meritorious cause of our salvation, to which nothing can be added to make it more ready and able to procure our salvation than it already is. Yet nei-ther the one nor the other can actually save any soul, without the *Spirit's application* of Christ to it.

For where there are different causes necessary to produce one effect, there the effect cannot be produced until the last cause has worked. So it is here: the Father has elected, and the Son has redeemed, but until the Spirit (who is the last cause) has worked his part also, we cannot be saved. For he comes in the Father's and in the Son's name and authority, to put the last hand to the work of our salvation, by bringing all the fruits of election and redemption home to our souls in this work of effective calling. So the apostle Peter notes the order of causes in their operations for the bringing about of our salvation, and writes, 'chosen according to the foreknowledge of God the Father, through the sanctifying work of the Spirit, for obedience to Jesus Christ and sprinkling by his blood' (1 Pet. 1:2). Here you find God's election and Christ's blood, the two great causes of salvation, and yet neither of these alone nor both together can save us. There must be added the sanctification of the Spirit, by which God's decree is executed, and the sprinkling (i.e. the personal application of Christ's blood) as well as the shedding of it, before we can have the saving benefit of either of the former causes.

4. The salvation of the elect is the work of the Trinity.

The application of Christ with his saving benefits is exactly of the same extent as the Father's election, and the Son's intention in dying, and cannot possibly be extended to one soul further.

'Those he predestined, he also called' (Rom. 8:30), and 'all who were appointed for eternal life believed' (Acts 13:48); 'who has saved and called us to a holy life—not because of anything we have done, but because of his own purpose and grace. This grace was given us in Christ Jesus before the beginning of time' (2 Tim. 1:9).

The Father, Son and Spirit work out their design in a perfect harmony and consent. As there was no disagreement in the planning of salvation, so there can be no disagreement in the execution of it. Those whom the Father chose before time, they and they only are the persons for whom the Son, when the fullness of time for the discharge of that decree came, died. 'I have revealed you to those whom you gave me out of the world' (John 17:6), and 'For them I sanctify myself' (i.e. consecrate, devote, or set myself apart for a sacrifice for them, verse 19). And those for whom Christ died are the people to whom the Spirit effectually applies the benefits and purchases of his blood. He comes in the name of the Father and Son. However, the 'world cannot accept him, because it neither sees him nor knows him' (John 14:17); 'but you do not believe, because you are not my sheep' (John 10:26).

Christ has indeed a fullness of saving power, but the dispensation of it is limited by the Father's will. Therefore he tells us, 'These ... belong to those for whom they have been prepared by my Father' (Matt. 20:23). In these words he in no way denies his authority to give glory as well as grace. He only shows that in the dispensation proper to him, as Mediator, he was limited by his Father's will and counsel. And so also the working of grace by the Spirit is similarly limited, both by the counsel and will of the Father and Son. For as he proceeds from them, so he acts in the administration proper to him, by commission from both. The Holy Spirit comes into the world by this joint commission (John 14:26), so his working is limited in his commission. 'He will not speak on his own; he will speak only what he hears' (John 16:13), meaning that he shall in all things act according to his commission, which the Father and Son have given him. The Son 'can do nothing by himself; he can only do what he sees the Father doing' (John 5:19). And the Spirit can do nothing of himself, but only what he hears from the Father and Son. It is impossible it should be otherwise, considering not only the unity of their nature, but also of their will and design. So that you see the application of Christ, and benefits by the Spirit, are in line with the Father's secret counsel and the Son's design in dying, which are the rule, model, and pattern of the Spirit's working.

5. New birth through the Spirit is essential.

The application of Christ to souls, by the regenerating work of the Spirit, is that which makes the first inward difference and distinction among men.

It is very true that in respect of God's foreknowledge and purpose, there was a distinction between one man and another. Before any man had a being, one was taken, another left. And with respect to the death of Christ, there is a great difference between one and another. He laid down his life for the sheep; he prayed for them, and not for the world. But all this while, as to any *relative change* of state, or *real change* of temper, they are upon a level with the rest of the wretched world. The elect themselves are 'by nature objects of wrath' (Eph. 2:3). And for the same purpose, after he has described the Corinthians as having been the most terrible wretches, men whose practices stank in the very nostrils of nature and would have made the more sober pagans blush, he writes, 'And that is what some of you were. But you were washed' (1 Cor. 6:11).

The work of the Spirit does not only show the difference which God's election has made between man and man, as the apostle says (1 Thess. 1:4-5); but it also makes a twofold difference itself, in *state* and *temper*, so believers visibly differ, not only from other men, but also from themselves. After this work, although a man is the *who* he was, yet he is not the *what* he was. This work of the Spirit makes us new creatures, namely, for quality and temper. 'Therefore, if anyone is in Christ, he is a new creation; the old has gone, the new has come!' (2 Cor. 5:17).

6. Personal knowledge of Christ the Saviour is from the Spirit.

The application of Christ by the work of regeneration is that which brings to men all the true sweetness and refreshing comforts that they have in Christ, and in all that he has done, suffered, and purchased for sinners.

An unsanctified person may enjoy the natural sweetness of the creature as much as he who is sanctified. He may also seem to enjoy and taste some sweetness in the delicious promises and discoveries of the gospel by *falsely applying* them to himself. But this is like the joy of a beggar, dreaming he is a king; he awakes and finds himself a beggar still. But for the rational, solid, and genuine delights and comforts of the gospel, no man tastes them till this work of the Spirit has first passed upon his soul. It is an enclosed pleasure, a stranger cannot stray into it. There are all those things missing in the unsanctified though elect soul that should capacitate and enable it to relish the sweetness of Christ and the gospel, namely, *propriety*, *evidence*, and *suitableness* of spirit.

Propriety or possession is the sweetest part of any excellency. Luther used to say that the sweetness of the gospel lay mostly in pronouns, as *me, my, your*, etc.—'the Son of God, who loved *me* and gave himself for *me*' (Gal. 2:20); 'Christ Jesus *my* Lord' (Phil. 3:8); 'Take heart, son, *your* sins are forgiven' (Matt. 9:2). Take away propriety, and you deflower the very gospel of its beauty and delight.

Evidence is needed for joy and comfort. It is so necessary that even interest and propriety afford no real sweetness without it. For as to comfort, it is all one not to appear, and not to be. If I am registered in the book of life and do not know it, what comfort can my name there afford me? Besides, to fit a soul for the sweetness and comfort of Christ there is also *an agreeable temper* of spirit required.

Now all these requisites being the proper effects and fruits of the Spirit's sanctifying operations upon us, it is beyond question that the comforts of Christ cannot be tasted until the application of Christ is first made.

7. Salvation in Christ is a growing experience in our lives.

Although the effectual application of Christ to the soul is achieved in the first saving work of the Spirit so as truly to unite the soul to Christ, and save it from the danger of perishing, yet it is a work gradually advancing in the believer's soul, whilst it abides on this side of heaven and glory.

It is true, indeed, that Christ is perfectly and completely applied to the soul in the first act for righteousness. 'Justification is a relative change, and properly has no degrees, but is perfected and at once, in one only act, whereas in its manifestation, sense and effects, it has various degrees.'[1] So the application of Christ to

---

[1] This definition is from William Ames (1576–1633), whose *Marrow of Theology* was a standard theological primer in Flavel's time. (see *The Marrow of Theology*, Pilgrim Press, 1968, p. 161).

us, for wisdom and sanctification, is not perfected in one single act, but rises by many and slow degrees to its just perfection.

And though we are truly said to come to Christ when we first believe (John 6:35), yet the soul after that is still coming to him by further acts of faith: 'you *come* to him, the living Stone' (1 Pet. 2:4); the verb notes a continued motion by which the soul gains ground, and still gets nearer and nearer to Christ, growing still more intimately acquainted with him. The knowledge of Christ grows upon the soul as the morning light, from its first beams to the full light of day (Prov. 4:18). Every grace of the Spirit grows, if not sensibly, yet really: for it is in discerning the growth of sanctification, as it is in discerning the growth of plants, which we perceive to have grown, rather than grow. Grace thrives in the soul as habits become more deeply rooted, and outward behaviour gets more spiritually eager. And so Christ and the soul grow increasingly close to one another, till at last the soul is wholly swallowed up in Christ's full and perfect enjoyment.

8. God's grace is all in Christ.

Lastly, although the privileges and benefits mentioned are all true and really bestowed with Christ upon believers, they are not communicated to them in one and the same way and manner, but in different ways, as their respective natures require.

These four great benefits are conveyed from Christ to us in three different ways and methods: his righteousness is made ours by *imputation*; his wisdom and holiness by *renewal*; and his redemption by our *glorification*.

In communicating his *wisdom* and *holiness*, he takes another method, for this is not *imputed*, but really *imparted* to us by the illuminating and regenerating work of the Spirit. Our righteousness comes from Christ as a *surety*, but our holiness comes from him as a life-giving *head*, sending vital influences unto all his members.

Now these gracious habits are seated in the souls of poor imperfect creatures, whose corruptions remain and work in the very same faculties where grace has its residence. It cannot be that our sanctification should be as perfect and complete as our justification is, which inheres only in Christ (see Gal. 5:17). Thus righteousness and sanctification are communicated and made ours.

Our *redemption* is the total deliverance from all the sad remains, effects and consequences of sin, both upon soul and body. This is made ours (or, to keep to the terms) *Christ is made redemption to us by glorification*. Then, and not before, are these miserable effects removed. We put these off together with the body. So just as *justification* cures the *guilt* of sin, and *sanctification* the *dominion* of sin, so *glorification* removes, together with its *existence* and being, all those *miseries* which it let in upon our whole being (Eph. 5:26-27).

And, therefore, by God Christ has been made for us wisdom and righteousness, sanctification and redemption, by imputation, regeneration, and glorification.

Seven lessons we must learn if we are to know and enjoy Christ

1. Without Christ, we are nothing.

Learn from this, what a naked, destitute and empty thing a poor sinner is, in his natural unregenerate state. He is one who naturally and inherently has neither wisdom, nor righteousness, sanctification nor redemption. All these must come from outside himself, from Christ, who is made all this to a sinner; or else he must eternally perish.

As no creature comes under more natural weakness into the world than man, naked, empty, and more helpless, so it is with his soul, but much more: all our excellencies are borrowed ones, and there is no reason therefore to be proud of any of them. 'What do you have that you did not receive? And if you did receive it, why do you boast as though you did not?' (1 Cor. 4:7). Marvel at that intolerable rudeness and vanity of a man who wears the rich and costly robe of Christ's righteousness, in which there is not one thread of his own spinning, but all made by free grace, and not by free will, as he struts proudly around the place in it as if he himself had made it, and he were indebted to no one for it? Your excellencies, whatever they are, are borrowed from Christ, and oblige you to him; but he can be no more obliged to you who wears them, than the sun is obliged to him who borrows its light, or the fountain to him who draws its water for his use and benefit.

It has always been the habit of holy men, when they have viewed their own gracious convictions and behaviour, to give themselves no credit, but to assert free grace as the source of all. The apostle Paul, viewing the principles of divine life in himself (the richest gift bestowed upon man in this world by Jesus Christ) renounces himself, and denies the least part of the praise and glory as belonging to him. 'I no longer live, but Christ lives in me' (Gal. 2:20). The same is true for the best duties that he ever performed for God (and what mere man ever did more for God?). Yet when, in a just and necessary defence, he was constrained to mention them, how careful is he to say the same: 'I worked harder than all of them—yet not I, but the grace of God that was with me' (1 Cor. 15:10).

Well then, let the sense of your own emptiness by nature humble and oblige you all the more to Christ, from whom you receive all you have.

2. A saved sinner strives to live in Christ.

Hence we are informed, that none can claim benefit by imputed righteousness, but only those who live in the power of inherent holiness. To whomever Christ was made righteousness, he was made sanctification also.

The gospel has not the least permission for impurity. It is every way as necessary to press men to their duties as to instruct them in their privileges. 'This is a trustworthy saying. And I want you to stress these things, so that those who have trusted in God may be careful to devote themselves to doing what is good' (Titus 3:8). It is a false teaching, dishonouring Christ and his gospel, that sanctification is not the evidence of our justification. Christ is as much wronged by those who separate holiness from righteousness (as if a sensual life were consistent with a justified state) as he is in the contrary extreme, by those who confuse Christ's righteousness with man's holiness in the matter of justification, or who confess no other righteousness, but what is inherent in themselves. The former opinion makes Christ a cloak for sin, the latter a needless sacrifice for sin.

It is true, our sanctification cannot justify us before God; but, what then, can it not evidence our justification before men? Is there no necessity or use for holiness, because it has no hand in our justification? Is the preparation of the soul for heaven, by altering its frame and temper, nothing? Is the glorifying of our Redeemer, by the exercises of grace in the world, nothing? Does the work of Christ render the work of the Spirit needless? God forbid: 'He did not come by water only, but by water and blood' (1 John 5:6). And when the apostle says, 'but to the man who does not work but trusts God who justifies the wicked, his faith is credited as righteousness' (Rom. 4:5), the scope of it is neither to characterize and describe the justified person as one who is lazy and slothful, and has no mind to work, nor the rebellious and stubborn, who refuses to obey the commands of God. Rather, he aims to represent him as a humbled sinner, who is convinced of his inability to work out his own righteousness by the law, and sees that all his endeavours to obey the law fall short of righteousness, and therefore fail, because he does not work so as to answer the purpose and end of the law, which accepts nothing less than perfect obedience.

3. Reject Christ and you embrace death.

How unreasonable and worse than brutish is the sin of unbelief, by which the sinner rejects Christ, and with him all those mercies and benefits which alone can relieve and cure his misery!

He is by nature blind and ignorant, and yet refuses Christ, who comes to him with heavenly light and wisdom. He is condemned by the terrible sentence of the law to eternal wrath, and yet rejects Christ, who brings to him complete and perfect righteousness. He is wholly polluted and plunged into original and actual pollution of nature and practice, yet will have none of Christ, who would become sanctification to him. He is oppressed in soul and body with the deplorable effects and miseries sin has brought upon him, and yet is so in love with his bondage that he will neither accept Christ nor the redemption he brings with him to sinners.

What monsters, what beasts has sin turned its subjects into! 'You refuse to come to me to have life' (John 5:40). Sin has stabbed the sinner to the heart, and the wounds are all fatal. Christ has prepared the only remedy that can cure his wounds, but he will not allow him to apply it. He acts like one in love with death, and judges it sweet to perish. So Christ tells us, 'all who hate me love death' (Prov. 8:36). They are loath to burn, yet willing to sin, though sin kindles those everlasting flames. In two things the unbeliever shows himself worse than brutish: he cannot think of damnation, the effect of sin, without horror, and cannot yet think of sin, the cause of damnation, without pleasure. He is loath to perish to all eternity without a remedy, and yet refuses and declines Christ as if he were an enemy, who only can and would deliver him from that eternal ruin.

How men act therefore, as if they were in love with their own ruin! Many poor wretches are now on the way to hell. Christ meets them many times in the ordinances, where they studiously shun him. Many times he checks them in their way by convictions, which they fight hard to overcome and conquer. Oh how willing are they to accept a cure and a remedy for anything but their souls! You see then that sinners cannot take a surer course to ruin themselves than by rejecting Christ in his gracious offers.

4. It is a hard heart which keeps a person outside of Christ.

What a tremendous symptom of wrath, and sad character of death, appears upon that man's soul to which no effectual application of Christ can be made by the gospel.

Christ with his benefits is frequently held out to them in the gospel. They have been pleaded with again and again to accept him. Those entreaties and persuasions have been urged by the greatest arguments, the command of God, the love of Christ, the inconceivable happiness or misery which unavoidably follows the accepting or rejecting of those offers, and yet nothing will affect them. All their arguments for unbelief have been repeatedly quashed, their reasons and consciences have stood convinced, they have been speechless, as well as Christless. Not one sound argument is found with them to defend their unbelief. They confess in general that such courses as theirs lead to destruction. They will admit that those who are in Christ are truly happy. And yet, when it comes to the point, their own closing with him, nothing will do. All arguments and all entreaties return to us without success.

What is the reason of this unaccountable obstinacy? In other things it is not so. If they are sick, they are anxious to find a doctor who offers himself, and so they will send for him and pay him too. If they are arrested for debt, and anyone will be a guarantor, and pay their debts for them, words can hardly express the sense they have of such a kindness. But although Christ would be both a physician and guarantor, and whatever else their needs require, they will rather perish for eternity, than accept him. What may we fear to be the reason for this, but that they are not Christ's sheep (John 10:26).

5. Christ is our greatest joy.

If Christ with all his benefits is made ours by God's special application, what a day of mercies then is the day of conversion! What multitudes of choice blessings visit the converted soul in that day! 'Today', says Christ to Zacchaeus, 'salvation has come to this house' (Luke 19:9). On the day Christ comes into the soul he brings with him all his treasures of wisdom and righteousness, sanctification and redemption. Troops of mercies, of the best of mercies, come with him. It is a day of great gladness and joy to the heart of Christ, when he is espoused to and received by the believing soul. It is a coronation day to a king.

Now, if the day of our being given to Christ is the day of the gladness of his heart, and he reckons himself thus honoured and glorified by us, what a day of joy and gladness should it be to our hearts, and how should we be filled with joy to see a King from heaven, with all his treasures of grace and glory, bestowing himself freely and everlastingly upon us, as our portion! No wonder Zacchaeus came down joyfully (Luke 19:6), that the eunuch went home rejoicing (Acts 8:39), that the jailer rejoiced, believing in God with all his household (Acts 16:34), that those who were converted ate with gladness, praising God (Acts 2:41, 46), and that there was great joy among those at Samaria, when Christ came among them in the preaching of the gospel (Acts 8:5, 8). It is no wonder at all that we read of such joy accompanying Christ into the soul when we consider that in one day so many blessings meet together in it, the least of which is not to be exchanged for all the kingdoms of this world and their glory. Eternity itself will scarcely be sufficient to bless God for the mercies of this one day.

6. Don't delay in coming to Christ.

If Christ is made all this to every soul to whom he is effectually applied, what reason then do those souls have, that are under the preparatory work of the Spirit, and are coming near to Christ and all his benefits, to stretch out their hands with vehement desire to Christ, and give him the most important invitation to their souls!

The whole world is distinguishable into three classes or sorts of persons—those who are far from Christ, those who are not far from Christ, and those who are in Christ. Those who are in Christ have heartily received him, whereas those who are far from Christ will not open to him, as their hearts are fast barred by ignorance, prejudice and unbelief against him. But those who have come under the initial workings of the Spirit and come near to Christ, who see their own indispensable need for him, and his fitness to their needs, in whom also encouraging hopes begin to dawn, and their souls are waiting at the foot of God for power to receive him, for a heart to close sincerely with him—oh what strong desires, what urgent pleas, what moving arguments should such people urge and plead to win Christ, and get possession of him! They are in sight of their only remedy. Christ and salvation have come to their very doors. There are but a few things to make them blessed for ever. This is the day in which their souls are exercised between hopes and fears. Now they are much alone, and deep in thought. They weep and pray for a heart to believe, and that against the great discouragements which they encounter.

Reader, if this is the case with your soul, it will not be the least bit of service I can do for you, to suggest prayers which are right for the achieving of your desire to come to Christ:

Firstly, confess your absolute need which now drives you to Christ. Tell him your hope is utterly perished in all other refuges. You come like a starving beggar to the last door of hope. Tell him you now begin to see your absolute need of Christ. Your body has not so much need of bread, water or air, as your soul has of Christ, and the wisdom and righteousness, sanctification and redemption that are in him.

Secondly, plead the Father's gracious purpose in furnishing and sending him into the world, and his own design in accepting the Father's call. 'Lord Jesus, were you not "anointed to preach good news to the poor, to bind up the broken-hearted, and to proclaim freedom for the captives, and release from darkness for the prisoners" (Isa. 61:1, 3)? Whilst I was ignorant of my condition, I had a proud rebellious heart; but conviction and self-realization have now melted it. My heart was harder than a millstone, and it was as easy to break rocks as to thaw and melt my heart for sin. But now God has made my heart soft, I feel the misery of my condition. I once thought I was perfectly free, but now I see what I thought was freedom is perfect bondage. Never did a poor prisoner sigh for deliverance more than I. Lord Jesus be, according to your name, a Jesus to me.'

Thirdly, plead the unlimited and general invitation made to such souls as you are, to come to Christ freely. 'Lord, you have made open proclamations: "Come, all you who are thirsty, come to the waters" (Isa. 55:1), and "Whoever is thirsty, let him come" (Rev. 22:17). In obedience to your call I come; had I not been invited, my coming to you, dear Lord Jesus, would be of presumption. But this invitation makes it an act of duty and obedience.'

Fourthly, plead the unprofitableness of your death to God. 'Lord, there is no profit in my blood, it will be no more advantage to you to destroy me than it will to save me. If you send me to hell (as the merit of my sin calls upon your justice to do) I shall be there dishonouring you to all eternity, and the debt I owe you will never be paid. But, if you apply your Christ to me for righteousness, then satisfaction for all that I have done will be laid down in one full, complete sum; indeed, if the honour of your justice lay as a bar to my pardon, it would silence me. But when your justice, as well as your mercy, shall both rejoice together, and be glorified and pleased in the same act, what prevents Christ being applied to my soul, since in so doing God can be no loser by it?'

Fifthly, and lastly, claim your agreement with the terms of the gospel. Tell him, 'Lord, my will complies fully and heartily to all your gracious terms. Let God offer his Christ on what terms he will, my heart is ready to comply. I have no exception against any part of the gospel. And now, Lord, I wholly give myself to your pleasure. Do with me what seems good in your eyes, only give me an interest in Jesus Christ. As to all other concerns, I lie at your feet, in full resignation of all to your pleasure.'

7. True contentment is found in Christ.

Lastly, if Christ with all his benefits is made ours, then how contented, thankful, comfortable, and hopeful should believers be in every condition which God casts them into in this world!

After such a mercy as this, let them never open their mouths any more to grumble at the outward inconveniences of their condition in this world. What are the things you want, compared with the things you enjoy? What is a little money, health or liberty, to wisdom, righteousness, sanctification, and redemption? All the crowns and sceptres in the world, sold at their full value, are no price for the least of these mercies. But I will not insist here, your duty lies much higher than contentment.

Be thankful, as well as content, in every state. Says the apostle, 'Praise be to the God and Father of our Lord Jesus Christ, who has blessed us in the heavenly realms with every spiritual blessing in Christ' (Eph. 1:3). O think what men are when compared with angels, that Christ should pass by them to become a Saviour to men! And what are you among men, that you should be taken, and others left! And among all the mercies of God, what mercies are comparable to these conferred upon you! O bless God even when outward comforts are few for such privileges as these.

And yet you will not come up to your duty in all this, except you be joyful in the Lord, and rejoice evermore after the receiving such mercies as these. 'Rejoice in the Lord always. I will say it again: Rejoice' (Phil. 4:4). For has not the poor captive reason to rejoice, when he has regained his liberty, and the debtor rejoice when all scores are cleared, and he owes nothing? Shall not the weary traveller rejoice, even if he doesn't own a shilling, when he has almost come home, where all his needs shall be supplied? Why, this is our case, when Christ once becomes ours. You are the Lord's freeman, your debts to justice are all satisfied by Christ, and you are within sight of complete redemption from all the troubles and inconveniences of your present state.

Thanks be to God for Jesus Christ!

6

United to Jesus

THIS sermon is the second in the thirty-five-sermon series *The Method of Grace in the Gospel Redemption* (1681), and Flavel probes further into the glories and necessities of union with Christ. His focus is on what he calls the 'mystical union', which is the believer's union with Christ by faith through the Holy Spirit. This union, as Flavel explains, is the goal of our redemption, and itself depends upon the union of Father and Son.

Flavel is concerned that we receive these truths, not as interesting theories, but as life-changing realities. He urges us to explore our identity as believers united to Christ, so that we find comfort as well as motivation for Christian living. Note how Flavel shows us that this union, far from being just a personal enjoyment of Christ, is also a *de facto* joining of believers to one another. If we grasp union with Christ, then discipleship will become what it always should be, a shared life in Christ.

I in them, and you in me. May they be brought to complete unity to let the world know that you sent me and have loved them even as you have loved me.—John 17:23.

Introduction: three types of union, one aim

THE design and purpose of the application of Christ to sinners is the communication of his benefits to them. But seeing all communications of benefits necessarily imply communion, and all communion necessarily presupposes union with his person, I shall therefore from this scripture explore the mystical union between Christ and believers. This union is the principal act wherein the Spirit's application of Christ consists.

In this verse we find a threefold union, one between the Father and Christ, a second between Christ and believers, a third between believers themselves.

First, 'You in me'. This is a glorious union, and is fundamental to the other two. The Father is not only in Christ, in respect of dear affections, as one dear friend is in another, who is as his own soul, nor only in respect of the identity and oneness of nature and attributes, in which respect Christ is the express image of his person (Heb. 1:3); but he is in Christ also as Mediator, by communicating the fullness of the Godhead which dwells in him as God-man, in a transcendent and singular manner which never dwelt nor can dwell in any other (Col. 2:9).

Secondly, 'I in them'. There is the mystical union between Christ and the saints. You and I are one essentially, they and I are one mystically. You and I are one by communication at the Godhead, and singular fullness of the Spirit to me as Mediator, and they and I are one by my communication of the Spirit to them.

Thirdly, from here results a third union between believers themselves, 'that they be brought to complete unity'. Just as the same Spirit dwells in them all, and equally unites them all to me, as living members to their head, so there must be a dear and intimate union between themselves, as fellow-members of the same body.

Now my business here is to trace namely the union between Christ and believers. I shall gather up the substance of it into this doctrinal proposition:

> **Doctrine:** *There is an exact and dear union between Christ and all true believers.*

Four pictures of union which don't quite work

The Scriptures have borrowed from the book of nature four metaphors to help us to understand the nature of this mystical union: pieces of timber united by glue; a graft taking hold of its stock, and making one tree; a husband and wife, by the marriage-covenant, becoming one flesh; and the limbs and head directed by one soul, and so becoming one natural body. Every one of these is more lively and full than the other, and what is defective in one, is supplied in the other. Yet none of these, apart or together, can give us a full and complete account of this mystery.

Take the two pieces united by glue: 'he who unites himself with the Lord is one with him in spirit' (1 Cor. 6:17), glued to the Lord. For though this cements and strongly joins them as one, yet this is but a faint and imperfect shadow of our union with Christ. Although this union by glue is intimate, it has no life, unlike that of the soul with Christ.

What about the union of graft and stock, mentioned in Romans 6:5? Although it says there that believers are implanted or ingrafted by way of incision, and this union between it and the stock is living, for it partakes of the sap and juice of it, yet here the image is also inadequate, for the graft is of a more excellent kind and nature than the stock, and, upon that account, the tree receives its identity from it, as from the more noble and excellent part. But Christ, into whom believers are ingrafted, is infinitely more excellent than they, and they derive their identity from him.

Then there is the union of husband and wife by marriage-covenant. Although it is exceedingly dear and intimate, so that a man leaves father and mother, and cleaves to his wife, and they two become one flesh, yet this union is not unbreakable, but may and must be broken by death. Then the bereaved partner lives alone without any relationship with the person who was once so dear. But the union of Christ and the soul can never be dissolved by death; it lasts for all eternity.

Finally, there is the union of the head and limbs, united by one living spirit, and so making one physical body (mentioned in Eph. 4:15-16). Although one soul animates every member, yet it does not knit every limb alike near to the head, but some are nearer, and others removed further from it. Here every limb is alike closely united with Christ the head: the weak are as near to him as the strong.

Union with Christ: real and precious

It is a real union.

Firstly, there is a real communion which is between Christ and believers, and in this the apostle is explicit: 'our fellowship is with the Father and with his Son Jesus Christ' (1 John 1:3). This signifies such a fellowship or partnership as persons have by a joint interest in one and the same enjoyment, which is shared between them. So Hebrews 3:14 says that we are partakers of Christ. In Psalm 45:7 the saints are called the companions of Christ, and that not only in respect of his assumption of our mortality, and investing us with his immortality, but it has a special reference and respect to the anointing of the Holy Ghost, or graces of the Spirit, of which believers are partakers with him and through him.

Now this communion of the saints with Christ is entirely and necessarily dependent upon their union with him, even as the branch's participation of the sap and juice depends upon its union with the stock. Take away union, and there can be no communion or life, which is clear from 1 Corinthians 3:22-23: 'all are yours, and you are of Christ, and Christ is of God'. And so, you see how all our participation in Christ's benefits is built upon our union with Christ's person.

Secondly, the reality of the believer's union with Christ is evident from the imputation of Christ's righteousness to him for his justification. That a believer is justified before God by a righteousness apart from himself is undeniable from Romans 3:24: 'justified freely by his grace through the redemption that came by Christ Jesus'. And that Christ's righteousness becomes ours by imputation is equally clear from Romans 4:23-24. But it can never be imputed to us unless we are united to him, and become one with him, which is also plainly asserted in 1 Corinthians 1:30: 'it is because of him that you are in Christ Jesus, who has become for us wisdom from God—that is, our righteousness, holiness and redemption'. He communicates his merits to none except those who are in him.

Thirdly, the sympathy that is between Christ and believers, proves a union between them. Christ and the saints smile and sigh together. Paul in Colossians 1:24 tells us, that he did 'fill up in my flesh what is still lacking in regard to Christ's afflictions'. It is not as if Christ's sufferings were imperfect ('by one sacrifice he has made perfect for ever those who are being made holy', Heb. 10:14), but in these two scriptures Christ is considered in a two-fold capacity. He suffered once in his own person, as Mediator, and these sufferings are complete and full. In that sense he suffers no more. He suffers also in his church and members, and thus he still suffers in the sufferings of every saint for his sake. These sufferings in his mystical body are not equal to the other, either in their weight and value, nor yet designed for the same use and purpose to satisfy, by their proper merit, offended justice. Nevertheless they are truly reckoned the sufferings of Christ, because the head suffers when the members do. Without this perspective, Acts 9:4 cannot be understood, when Christ, the head in heaven, cries out, 'Saul, Saul, why are you persecuting me?' How does Christ sensibly feel our sufferings, or we his, if there is not a mystical union between him and us?

Fourthly, and lastly, the way and manner in which the saints shall be raised at the last day proves this mystical union between Christ and them. For they are not to be raised as others, by the naked power of God without them, but by the virtue of Christ's resurrection as their head, sending forth life-giving power into their dead bodies, which are united to him as well as their souls. For so we find: 'if the Spirit of him who raised Jesus from the dead is living in you, he who raised Christ from the dead will also give life to your mortal bodies through his Spirit, who lives in you' (Rom. 8:11).

Now it is impossible the saints should be raised in the last resurrection by the Spirit of Christ dwelling in them, if that Spirit did not knit and unite them to Christ, as members to their head. So then by all this, it is proved, that there is a real union of the saints with Christ.

It is a precious union.

Next, I shall endeavour to open the quality and nature of this union, and show you what it is, according to the weak apprehensions we have of so sublime a mystery.

This union is an intimate joining of believers to Christ by the imparting of his Spirit to them, whereby they are enabled to believe and live in him.

All divine and spiritual life is originally in the Father, and comes not to us, but by and through the Son (John 5:26). To him the Father has given a life-giving power in himself. But the Son communicates this life which is in him to none but by and through the Spirit: 'through Christ Jesus the law of the Spirit of life set me free from the law of sin and death' (Rom. 8:2).

The Spirit must therefore first take hold of us before we can live in Christ. When he does so, then we are enabled to exert that vital act of faith, whereby we receive Christ. All this lies plain in that one scripture, John 6:57: 'Just as the living Father sent me, and I live because of the Father, so the one who feeds on me [that is, by faith applies to me] will live because of me.' So these two, namely, the Spirit on Christ's part, and faith, his work on our part, are the two ligaments by which we are knitted to Christ.

More particularly, we shall consider the properties of this union, that so we may the better understand the nature of it. The saints' union with Christ is not a mere mental union only in conceit or notion, but really exists, whether we realize it or not. I know the godless world scoffs at all these things as fancies and idle imaginations, but believers know the reality of them. 'On that day you will realize that I am in my Father, and you in me, and I am in you' (John 14:20).

Equally, the saints' union with Christ is not a physical union, such as is between the members of a natural body and the head. Our nature indeed is assumed into union with the person of Christ, but it is the singular honour of that blessed and holy flesh of Christ to be so united as to make one person with him. That union is hypostatical, whilst ours with Christ is only mystical.

It is not an essential union with the divine nature, so that our beings are swallowed up and lost in the divine being. There are those who foolishly talk of being 'godded' into God, and 'christed' into Christ. But there is an infinite distance between us and Christ, in respect of nature and excellency, notwithstanding this union.

The union is not a union by covenant only. There is a covenant union between Christ and believers, but that is a consequence of and wholly depends upon this.

Finally, it is not a mere moral union by love and affection. We may say, one soul is in two bodies, a friend is another self, or the lover is in the person beloved. Such a union of hearts and affections there is also between Christ and the saints, but this is of another nature. There we are talking about what is referred to as a moral union, which only knits our affections; but with Christ we mean a mystical union, which unites our persons to Christ.

Ten characteristics of this precious union

1. Though this union neither makes us one person nor essence with Christ, yet it *knits our persons most intimately to the person of Christ.* The church is Christ's body (Col. 1:24), not his natural, but his mystical body. The saints stand to Christ in the same relation that the natural members of the body stand to the head, and he stands in the same relation to them, as the head stands in to the natural members. Consequently they stand related to one another, as the members of a natural body do to each other. Christ and the saints are not one, as the oak and the ivy that clasps it are one, but as the graft and stock are one. Neither husband and wife nor soul and body are so near as Christ and the believing soul are near to each other.

2. The mystical union is *wholly supernatural*, wrought alone by the power of God. So it is said, 'it is because of him that you are in Christ Jesus' (1 Cor. 1:30). We can no more unite

ourselves to Christ, than a branch can incorporate itself into another stock.

There are only two ligaments, or bonds of union, between Christ and the soul, the Spirit on his part, and faith on ours. But when we say faith is the band of union on our part, the meaning is not, that it is our own act, as that it springs naturally from us, or is achieved from the power of our own wills; no, for the apostle expressly contradicts it, 'and this not from yourselves, it is the gift of God' (Eph. 2:8). But we are the subjects of it, and though the act on that account is ours, yet the power enabling us to believe is God's (Eph. 1:19-20).

3. The mystical union is an *immediate union*. Immediate, I say, not because it excludes means and instruments; in fact several means and many instruments are employed for the effecting of it; but immediate, in the sense of excluding degrees of nearness to Christ among the members of his mystical body.

Every member in the natural body stands not as near to the head as another, but so do all the mystical members of Christ's body to him. Every member, the smallest as well as the greatest, has an immediate coalition with Christ: 'To the church of God in Corinth, to those sanctified in Christ Jesus and called to be holy, together with all those everywhere who call on the name of our Lord Jesus Christ—their Lord and ours' (1 Cor. 1:2).

4. The saints' mystical union with Christ is a *fundamental union*. It is life-bringing, and all our fruits of obedience depend upon it. 'No branch can bear fruit by itself; it must remain in the vine. Neither can you bear fruit unless you remain in me' (John 15:4). It is fundamental to all our privileges and comforts (1 Cor. 3:23): 'all are yours, and you are of Christ' (1 Cor. 3:22-23). And it is fundamental to all our hopes and expectations of glory, for it is 'Christ in you, the hope of glory' (Col. 1:27). So then, destroy this union, and with it you destroy all our fruits, privileges, and eternal hopes, at one stroke.

5. The mystical union is a *most effective union*, for through this union the divine power flows into our souls, both to quicken us with the life of Christ, and to conserve and secure that life in us after it is so infused.

6. The mystical union is an *unbreakable union*. There is an everlasting bond between Christ and the believer. It is beyond all other unions in the world: death dissolves the dear union between husband and wife, friend and friend, and even between soul and body, but not between Christ and the soul. The bands of this union will never rot in the grave. 'Who shall separate us from the love of Christ?' asks the apostle (Rom. 8:35). He bids defiance to all his enemies, and triumphs in the firmness of his union over all hazards that seem to threaten it. It is with Christ and us, in respect of the mystical union, as it is with Christ himself, in respect of the hypostatic union. That was not dissolved by his death, when the natural union between his soul and body was, nor can this mystical union of our souls and bodies with Christ be dissolved when the union between us and our dearest relations, even between the soul and body, is dissolved by death. God calls himself the God of Abraham, long after his body was turned into dust.

7. It is an *honourable union*, the highest honour that can be given to men. The greatest honour that was ever done to our common nature was in its assumption into union with the second person hypostatically, and the highest honour that was ever done to our single persons was their union with Christ hypostatically. To be a servant of Christ is a dignity far beyond the highest advancement among men. How matchless and singular is the glory of being a member of Christ! And yet all the saints enjoy such an honour: 'we are members of his body', of his flesh, and of his bones (see Eph. 5:30).

8. It is a union which *brings great comfort*. It is the ground of all solid comfort, both in life and death. Whatever troubles, needs, or distresses befall us, there is abundant relief and support

in knowing that Christ is mine, and I am his. If I am Christ's, then let him take care of me, and indeed, in so doing, he is only taking care of his own. He is my head, and to him it belongs to consult the safety and welfare of his own members (Eph. 1:22-23). He is not only an head to his own by way of influence, but to all things else, by way of dominion, for their good. How comfortably may we rest under that cheering consideration upon him at all times and in all difficult cases!

9. It is a *fruitful union*, as the immediate end of it is fruit: We are married to Christ, that we should bring forth fruit to God (see Rom. 7:4). All the fruit we bear before our being ingrafted into Christ is worse than none. Until a person is in Christ, the work cannot be truly good and acceptable to God. Christ is a fruitful root, and makes all the branches that live in him fruitful too (John 15:8).

10. Lastly, it is an *enriching union*, for, by our union with his person, we immediately share in all his riches (see 1 Cor. 1:30). How rich and great a person do the little arms of faith clasp and embrace! 'All are yours' (1 Cor. 3:22). All that Christ has, becomes ours, either by communication to us, or improvement for us: his Father (John 20:17), his promises (2 Cor. 1:20), his providence (Rom. 8:28), his glory (John 17:24). It is all ours by virtue of our union with him.

Nine ways to take enjoyment and profit from union with Christ

1. Glory in the status God gives you in Christ.

If there is such a union between Christ and believers, *then what transcendent dignity has God put upon believers!*

Well might Constantine prefer the honour of being a member of the church before that of being head of the empire. For it is not only above all earthly dignities and honours, but, in some respect, above that honour which God has put upon the angels of glory.

Great is the dignity of the angels. For the angels are the highest and most honourable species of creatures. They also have the honour continually to behold the face of God in heaven, and yet, in this one respect the saints are preferred to them, since they have a mystical union with Christ, as their head of influence, by whom they are quickened with spiritual life, which the angels do not have.

It is true, there is a gathering together of all in heaven and earth under Christ as a common head (Eph. 1:10). He is the head of angels as well as saints, but in different respects. To angels he is the head of dominion and government, but to saints he is both a head of dominion and of life-giving influence, too. Angels are as the barons and nobles in his kingdom, but the saints as the dear spouse and wife of his heart. This dignifies the believer above the greatest angel. And as the nobles of the kingdom think it a preferment and honour to serve the queen, so the glorious angels think it no degradation or dishonour to them to serve the saints, for to this honourable office they are appointed to be ministering spirits for the good of them who shall be heirs of salvation (Heb. 1:14). The greatest servant disdains not to honour and serve the heir.

2. Be confident—our union with Christ is unbreakable.

If there is such a strict and inseparable union between Christ and believers, *then the grace of believers can never totally fail*. Immortality is the privilege of grace, because sanctified persons are inseparably united to Christ the fountain of life: 'Your life is now hidden with Christ in God' (Col. 3:3). Whilst the sap of life is in the root, the branches live by it. Thus it is between Christ and believers: 'Because I live, you also will live' (John 14:19). See how Christ binds up their life in one bundle with his own, plainly teaching that it is as impossible for them to die as it is for himself; he cannot live without them.

It is true, the spiritual life of believers is encountered by many strong and fierce oppositions. It is also brought to a low ebb in some, but we are always to remember that there are some things which pertain to the essence of that life in which the very being of it lies, and some things that pertain only to its well-being. All those things which belong to the well-being of the new creature, as manifestations of grace, joys, spiritual comforts, etc, may for a time fail, and grace itself may suffer great losses in its degrees, notwithstanding our union with Christ. But still the essence of it is immortal, which is no small relief to gracious souls. When the means of grace fail, as it is threatened (Amos 8:11), when temporary formal professors drop away from Christ like withered leaves from the trees in a windy day (2 Tim. 2:18), and when the natural union of their souls and bodies is suffering, a dissolution from each other by death, when that silver cord is loosed, then this golden chain holds firm (1 Cor. 3:23).

3. Serve the saints, because you are then serving Christ.

Is the union so intimate between Christ and believers? *How great and powerful a motive then is this, to make us open-handed and liberal in relieving the necessities and wants of every gracious person!* For in relieving them, we relieve Christ himself.

Christ *personal* is not the object of our pity and charity. He is as the fountain-head of all the riches in glory (Eph. 4:10). Christ *mystical*, however, is exposed to necessities and wants; he feels hunger and thirst, cold and pains, in his body the church; and he is refreshed, relieved, and comforted, in their refreshments and comforts. Christ the Lord of heaven and earth, in this consideration is sometimes in need of a penny. He tells us his wants and poverty, and how he is relieved (Matt. 25:35-40). This text is believed and understood by very few: "'I was hungry, and you gave me something to eat, I was thirsty, and you gave me something to drink, I was a stranger, and you invited me in." … Then the righteous will answer him, "Lord, when did we see you hungry …?" The King will reply, "I tell you the truth, whatever you did for one of the least of these brothers of mine, you did for me."'

It is incredible that a Christian can be hard-hearted and close-fisted to a Christian in need, if in refreshing and relieving of him he truly believes that he ministers refreshment to Christ himself.

Here you see believers' near relation to Christ. They are mystically one person: what you did to them, you did to me. Here you see also how kindly Christ takes it at our hands, acknowledging all those kindnesses that were bestowed upon him, even to a bit of bread. He is, you see, content to take it as a courtesy, when he might demand it by authority.

So you see that one single branch or act of obedience (our charity to the saints) is singled out from among all the duties of obedience, and made the test and evidence of our sincerity in that great day, and men blessed or cursed according to the love they have manifested this way to the saints.

O then, let none that understand the relation the saints have to Christ, as the members to the head, or the relation they have to each other thereby, as fellow-members of the same body, allow Christ to hunger, if they have bread to relieve him, or Christ to be thirsty, if they have the resources to refresh him. This union between Christ and the saints affords an argument beyond all other arguments in the world to prevail with us. A little rhetoric might persuade a Christian to part with anything he has for Christ, who parted with the glory of heaven and his own blood for his sake.

4. Be honest: coldness to Jesus is treachery.

Do Christ and believers make but one mystical person? *How unnatural and absurd then are all those acts of unkindness, whereby believers wound and grieve Jesus Christ!* This is as if the hand should wound its own head, from which it receives life, sense, motion, and strength.

Now the evil of such sins is to be measured not only by the near relation Christ enjoys with believers as their head, but more particularly from the several benefits they receive from him as such. For in wounding Christ by their sins,

First, they wound their head of influence, through whom they live, and without whom they would still remain in the state of sin and death (Eph. 4:16). Shall Christ send life to us, and we return that which is death to him?

Secondly, they wound their head of government. Christ is a guiding, as well as a life-giving head (Col. 1:18). He is your wisdom, he guides you by his counsels to glory. But must he be thus responded to for all his faithful conduct? What do you, when you sin, but rebel against his government, refuse to follow his counsels, and obey instead a deceiver, rather than him?

Thirdly, they wound their consulting head, who cares, provides, and projects, for the welfare and safety of the body. Christians, you know your affairs below have not been steered and managed by your own wisdom, but that orders have been given from heaven for your security and supply from day to day. 'I know, O Lord', says the prophet, 'that a man's life is not his own; it is not for a man to direct his steps' (Jer. 10:23).

It is true, Christ is out of your sight, and you do not see him. He sees you, however, and orders everything that concerns you. And is this a due response for all that care he has taken for you? Do you thus requite the Lord for all his benefits? What recompense is evil for good? O let shame cover you.

Fourthly, and lastly, they wound their head of honour. Christ your head is the fountain of honour to you. This is your glory that you are related to him as your head. You are, on this account, exalted above angels. Now then consider how vile a thing it is to reflect the least dishonour upon him, from whom you derive all your glory. Consider and bewail it.

5. Know that you will always have your daily bread.

Is there so close and intimate a relation and union between Christ and the saints, *then surely they can never lack what is good for their souls or bodies.*

Everyone naturally cares and provides for his own, especially for his own body; yet we can more easily violate the law of nature, and be cruel to our own flesh, than Christ can be so to his mystical body. I know it is hard to rest upon, and rejoice in a promise, when needs harass, and we do not see where relief should arise from; but oh what sweet satisfaction and comfort might a believer find in these considerations, if he were to keep them upon his heart in such a day of trouble.

First, whatever my distresses are for quality, number, or degree, they are all known even to the smallest detail, by Christ my head. He looks down from heaven upon all my afflictions, and understands them more fully than even I who feel them: 'All my longings lies open before you, O Lord; my sighing is not hidden from you' (Psa. 38:9).

Secondly, he not only knows them, but feels them as well as knows them. 'For we do not have a high priest who is unable to sympathize with our weaknesses' (Heb. 4:15). In all your afflictions he is afflicted, and tender sympathy cannot but flow from such intimate union. Therefore in Matthew 25:35 he says, *I* was hungry, and *I* was thirsty, and *I* was naked.

Thirdly, he not only knows and feels for me in my needs, but has enough in his hand, and much more than enough to supply them all. For all things are delivered to him by the Father (Luke 10:22). All the storehouses in heaven and earth are his (Phil. 4:19).

Fourthly, he bestows an abundance of all good earthly things upon his very enemies. He is bountiful to strangers to his grace, and he loads his very enemies with these things, and can it be supposed he will in the meantime starve his own, and neglect those whom he loves as his own flesh? It cannot be!

Moreover, *fifthly*, thus far he has not allowed me to perish in any former troubles to this day. When and where was it that he forsook me? This is not the first plunge of trouble I have been in; have I not found him a God at hand? How often have I seen him in the middle of all my difficulties!

Sixthly, and lastly, I have his promise that he will never leave me nor forsake me (Heb. 13:5; John 14:18), a promise which has never failed since the hour it was first made. If then the Lord Jesus knows and feels all my needs, and has enough and more than enough to supply them, if he gives copiously to his enemies, has not forsaken me to this day, and has promised he never will—why then is my soul so troubled in me? Surely there is no cause it should be so.

6. Remember that persecution is a great sin.

If the saints are so nearly united to Christ, as the members to the head, then, *how great a sin, and full of danger is it for any to wrong and persecute the saints!* For in so doing, they actually persecute Christ himself. 'Saul, Saul', says Christ, 'why do you persecute me?' (Acts 9:4). The righteous God holds himself obliged to vindicate oppressed innocence, even when it is in the persons of wicked men; how much more when it is in a member of Christ? 'Whoever touches you touches the apple of his eye' (Zech. 2:8). And is it to be imagined that Christ will sit still, and suffer his enemies to hurt or injure the very apples of his eyes? No, 'He has prepared his deadly weapons' (Psa. 7:13). O it would be better that your hand should wither and your arm fall from your shoulder, than ever it should be lifted up against Christ, in the poorest of his members. Believe it, sirs, not only your violent actions but your bitter words are all set down upon your Doom's-day book; and you shall be brought to an account for them in the great day (Jude 15). Beware the arrows you shoot, and be sure of your mark before you shoot them.

7. Rejoice in your certain salvation in the face of death.

If there is such a union between Christ and the saints as has been described, *upon what comforting terms then may believers part with their bodies at death!* Christ your head is risen, therefore you cannot be lost. No, he is not only risen from the dead himself, but has also become 'the firstfruits of those who have fallen asleep' (1 Cor. 15:20). Believers are his members, his fullness, he cannot therefore be complete without you. A part of Christ cannot perish in the grave, much less burn in hell. Remember, when you feel the natural union dissolving, that this mystical union can never be dissolved. The pains of death cannot break this bond. And as there is a peculiar excellency in the believer's life, so there is a singular support and peculiar comfort in his death. 'For to me, to live is Christ and to die is gain' (Phil. 1:21).

8. Make sure that you truly know this union.

If there is such a union between Christ and believers, *how does it concern every man to try and examine his state, whether he is really united with Christ or not, by the natural and proper effects which always flow from this union!*

Firstly, the real communication of Christ's holiness is to the soul. We cannot be united with this root and not partake of the vital sap of sanctification from him. All that are planted into him, are planted into the likeness of his death, and of his resurrection, by mortification and vivification (Rom. 6:5-6).

Secondly, they who are united to him as members to the head, cannot but love him and value him above their own lives. As we see in nature, the hand and arm will interpose to save the head. The nearer the union, the stronger always is the affection.

Thirdly, the members are subject to the head. Dominion in the head needs subjection in the members (Eph. 5:24). In vain do we claim union with Christ as our head whilst we are governed by our own sins, and our lusts give us law.

Fourthly, all that are united to Christ bear fruit to God (Rom. 7:4). Fruitfulness is the next end of our union, and there are no barren branches growing upon this fruitful root.

9. If you know him through union, you will walk with him.

Lastly, *believers are engaged to walk as the members of Christ, in the visible exercises of all those graces and duties.*

Firstly, how contented and well pleased should we be with our outward lot, however providence has cast it for us in this world! Oh do not complain, when God has dealt bountifully with you. He has bestowed the good things of this world upon others, but upon you, he has given himself in Christ.

Secondly, how humble and lowly in spirit should you be under your great advancement! It is true, God has magnified you greatly by this union, but yet do not swell with pride. You shine, but you shine like the moon, with a borrowed light.

Thirdly, how zealous should you be to honour Christ, who has put so much honour on you! Be willing to give glory to Christ, though his glory should rise out of your shame. Never reckon that glory that goes to Christ, to be lost to you. When you lie at his feet, in the most heart-breaking confessions of sin, yet let this please you, that therein you have given him glory.

Fourthly, how exact and careful you should be in all your ways, remembering whose you are, and who you represent! Shall it be said, that a member of Christ was convicted of unrighteousness and unholy actions? God forbid. 'If we claim to have fellowship with him yet walk in the darkness, we lie and do not live by the truth' (1 John 1:6). 'Whoever claims to live in him must walk as Jesus did' (1 John 2:6).

Fifthly, how careful you should be to live at peace among yourselves, who are so closely united to such a head, and thereby are made fellow-members of the same body! The heathen world has never come close to such an argument as the apostle urges for unity, in Ephesians 4:3-4.

Sixthly, and lastly, how joyful and comforted you should be, to whom Christ, with all his treasures and benefits, is effectually applied in this blessed union of your souls with him! This brings him into your possession. O how great and how glorious a person do these little weak arms of your faith embrace! *Thanks be to God for Jesus Christ.*

7

Salvation Belongs to the Trinity

ENGLAND'S DUTY is a series of eleven sermons based on Revelation 3:20, and this one is the ninth in the series. The work is aimed at a nation experiencing upheavals, as well as opportunities. With the Revolution of 1688, and King William's Toleration Act of 1689, Nonconformists found themselves enjoying new freedoms. Flavel wanted to lose no time in pressing the claims of Christ upon his hearers. In the introduction to the sermon, addressed to fellow-pastors, Flavel says, 'Let it not seem much to us to spend a little sweat for the sake of those souls for which Christ so willingly and plentifully poured out his most precious blood. If we hide the Lord's talent in a napkin, where shall we find a napkin to dry up our tears of blood for so base a crime?' The whole series is a fine example of urgent evangelistic preaching.

This sermon explores the place of faith in salvation. Faith is a gift of God, and we cannot exercise it apart from receiving it as a gift. Flavel explains that, once received, our placing this faith in Christ is the only right response to hearing his voice. Salvation is a work of each of the persons of the Trinity, and brings us into an experience of triune love.

If anyone hears my voice and opens the door ...
—Revelation 3:20

THE powerful voice of Christ is the key that opens the door of the soul to receive him. The opening of the heart to receive Christ is the main design aimed at in all the external and internal administrations of the gospel and Spirit.

The gospel has two great designs and intentions. One is to open the heart of God to men, and to show them the everlasting counsels of grace and peace which were hidden in God from ages and generations past, so that all men may now see what God has been designing and contriving for their happiness in Christ before the world was: 'to make plain to everyone the administration of this mystery, which for ages past was kept hidden in God, who created all things. His intent was that now, through the church, the manifold wisdom of God should be made known to the rulers and authorities in the heavenly realms' (Eph. 3:9, 10). The next intention and aim of the gospel is to set open the hearts of man to receive Jesus Christ, without which all the glorious discoveries of the eternal counsels and gracious contrivances of God for and about us, would signify nothing to our real advantage. Christ's standing, knocking, and speaking by his Spirit receive their success, and attain their end, when the heart opens itself by faith to receive him, and not till then.

Doctrine: The doctrine of our text is that *the opening of the heart to receive Christ, by faith, is the great design and aim of the gospel.*

This is the mark to which all the arrows in the gospel-quiver are aimed, the centre into which those blessed lines are drawn: 'these are written that you may believe that Jesus is the Christ, the Son of God, and that by believing you may have life in his name' (John 20:31). All those precious truths that are written in the Scriptures are to bring you to faith. The great aim of the Spirit in his illuminations, convictions, and humiliations is the very same thing: 'The work of God is this: to believe in the one he has sent' (John 6:29). It is not only a work worthy of such an author, but it is that on which God's eye is fixed in his workings upon us, and is the end and aim of his work.

Great persons have great designs. This is the glorious project of the great God, and every person in the Godhead is engaged and concerned in it. The Father has his hand in this work, and such a hand as without it no heart could ever open or move in the least towards Christ: 'No-one can come to me', says Christ, 'unless the Father who sent me draws him' (John 6:44). None but he who raised up Christ from the dead can raise up a dead heart to saving faith in him. The Son's hand is in this work. He is not only the object, but the author of our faith: 'We know also that the Son of God has come and has given us understanding, so that we may know him who is true. ... He is the true God and eternal life' (1 John 5:20). And then for the Spirit, he comes from heaven designedly and expressly to convince sinners of their need of Christ, and to beget faith in them (John 16:9). This is the great purpose of heaven, and of both the word and works of God.

Four aspects of God's salvation plan

1. The greatness of the plan of God

We scarcely understand what a marvellous thing is done on earth when the heart of a sinner is brought to close with Christ by faith.

It would transport us with admiration, if we thoroughly considered it. Well may the apostle place it in the first rank of all the glorious and wonderful works of God, as he does: 'Beyond all question, the mystery of godliness is great: He appeared in a body, was vindicated by the Spirit, was seen by angels, was preached among the nations, was believed on in the world' (1 Tim. 3:16). Observe with what works of wonder faith is here ranked and associated. It is an astonishing work of God that ever God should be manifested in the flesh; that he that thunders in the clouds should be heard crying in a cradle; that he who is over all God blessed for ever, should become a man. It is astonishing, that when he was taken down dead from the cross, laid in the tomb, and the stone sealed upon it, he should rise on the third day from the dead by his own power, and that ever the gospel should be preached to such a miserable and forlorn people as the Gentiles were, the scorn and contempt of the Jews. And no less marvellous is it to see the hearts of such poor creatures, glued so fast to idolatry, so perfectly dead in sin, to open to Christ upon such self-denying terms, as to let go all they had in the world for a blessed inheritance which they never saw.

And were not this a marvellous work of God indeed, there would never be such joy and triumph in heaven among the holy angels, as there is upon the opening of every sinner's heart to Christ (Luke 15:7). The whole city of God is moved with it. Heaven rings again with the joyful tidings. As soon as ever the will begins to bow and open to Christ, the news is quickly in heaven, and all the angels of God rejoice at the tidings. As when a young prince is born, the fountains run with wine, so there is joy in every city throughout the kingdom. So also there is in heaven, when Christ has got a new dwelling-place in the soul of any sinner upon earth.

Moreover, the greatness of this design appears from the great rewards promised by the Lord to every servant of his, who has but the least hand to help it on. God would never reward the instruments so richly, if the success of the work were not of great value in his eyes. The ministers of Christ may be ill-rewarded by men, persecuted and reproached for their labour, but God will bountifully repay their pains and faithfulness: 'Those who are wise will shine like the brightness of the heavens, and those who lead many to righteousness, like the stars for ever and ever' (Dan. 12:3). All these things show that it is a very great and important design upon which the heart of God is much set.

2. The difficulty of it

As it is an exceeding great and important design and work of God, so it is a very hard and difficult work in itself, a work whose difficulties surmount the ability of angels. It is certainly a work carried on by the mighty power of God, through the greatest oppositions imaginable. And therefore it is noted that it is the peculiar prerogative of Jesus Christ, who alone holds the key of the house of David, to open the heart of a sinner by faith (Rev. 3:7). Men think it is an easy thing to believe; but if you consult the Scriptures, you will quickly be informed how grossly you mistake the nature of this work. In Colossians 2:12 the believing soul is said to be 'raised with Christ, through faith in the power of God, who raised him from the dead'. In the resurrection of Christ there was a glorious operation of the power of God! You know it astonished the world to hear of it. The very same power that wrought *that*, must also be put forth to work *this*, or else it would never be wrought. So again, 'it is by grace you have been saved, through faith—and this not from yourselves, it is the gift of God' (Eph. 2:8)—'not from yourselves'—you are no more able to believe in Christ, than you were to raise him from the dead; no more able in your own power to come one step towards him by faith, than Lazarus was able to unbind himself in the grave, and come forth. In Ephesians 1:18-20 the work of believing is ascribed to the exceeding greatness of the power of God. Nothing but power can do it, and no other power but the almighty power of God can do it. It exceeds the power of ministers, and even of angels. Three things will teach us the difficulty of this work:

1. The *nature* of the work of faith, which is wholly supernatural. It is no less than gaining over the hearty and full consent of the will to take Jesus Christ with his yoke of obedience (Matt. 11:29) and with his cross of sufferings (Matt. 16:24). And who can tell how far these will carry a man into outward dangers, losses, torments, and sufferings? And all this is upon the account of an unseen happiness and glory. Dearest lusts and corruptions must be mortified, sweetest pleasures and profits in the world abandoned and forsaken, all reproaches, losses, pains, and penalties the devil and the world can lay upon us for Christ's sake must be embraced and welcomed. And can it be supposed that any power beneath the almighty power of the Lord, any voice except the effective voice of Christ, can prevail with the will to give its firm explicit consent to such difficult and self-denying terms as these?

2. Consider the *subject* wrought upon—the dead, hard, obstinate heart of a blind, perverse sinner, a heart harder by nature than the lower mill-stone. It is as easy to melt the hardest rock into a sweet syrup, as it is to melt the heart of a sinner into penitential sorrows for sin. What, to bring a dead heart to life! To make that man bitterly bewail the sins that were his pleasure and delight, more than ever he bewailed the death of his nearest and dearest relation in the world! To make a proud heart renounce its own self-righteousness, which it dotes upon, and take all shame and reproach to itself upon the account of sin! This is wonderful. You would think it a strange thing to see the course of the tide stopped with the breath of a man; but oh, what a marvellous thing is here, that at the preaching of the gospel by a poor worm, the Lord

should turn the tide of the will, and thus work about the soul to a ready compliance with his most self-denying terms and proposals!

3. And that which further increases the difficulty of believing is the *fierce and obstinate opposition* made by the enemies of faith. All the powers of hell and earth, devils and men *without* us, are in league with the corruptions *within* us, to resist and hinder this work of believing. Never is the devil more busy than when Christ and the soul are treating about union. Oh, the discouragements, objections, and difficulties that are rolled into the way of faith! One says it is the highest presumption, and another, that it is impossible, and far too late. Sometimes blasphemous injections, like fiery darts, are shot reeking hot out of hell into the soul; whilst at other times the invincible difficulties of religion are objected, and all losses and torments are opposed to this work. The tempter casts himself into a thousand shapes to hinder the soul's passage out of nature to Christ, sometimes objecting the greatness of sin, and sometimes the lapse and loss of the proper season and opportunity of mercy, together with the lack of due qualifications to come to Christ. Thus, and many other ways, he endeavours to peel off the fingers of faith from taking hold of Christ. And as every devil in hell opposes this work, so every carnal interest we have in the world, is an enemy to faith. We have enemies enough within us, as well as without us, both conspiring together to obstruct this work. All things increase the difficulty of believing.

3. *The two key instruments employed in this great plan*

(i) *God the Holy Spirit.* The primary instrument, by whose effectiveness the heart is opened, is the Spirit of God, without whom it is impossible the design should ever prosper. Neither ordinances, providences, or ministers can successfully manage it without him. If the Lord will make use of any man for the conversion and salvation of another's soul, he may rejoice in it; but we must say, as Peter to the Jews, 'Why do you stare at us as if by our own power or godliness we had made this man walk?' (Acts 3:12). So may the ablest minister in the world say, when God blesses his labours to the conversion of any soul, do not look at me as though by the strength of my reason, or power of my gifts, I had opened your soul to Christ: this is the work of God's Spirit, in whose hand I am an instrument. 'So neither he who plants nor he who waters is anything' (1 Cor. 3:7). The very first stroke of conviction, which begins the whole work of conversion, is justly ascribed to the Spirit: 'when the Spirit comes, he will convict the world of guilt in regard to sin' (John 16:8). He is the Lord of all sanctifying and gracious influences. Ordinances are but as the sails of a ship. Ministers are like the seamen that manage those sails: the anchor may be weighed, the sails spread, but when all this is done, there is no sailing till a strong wind comes. We preach and pray, and you hear; but there is no motion Christward until the Spirit of God (compared to the wind, John 3:8) blows upon them. Until he illuminates the understanding with divine light, and bows the will by an almighty power, there can be no spiritual motion heavenward. Now the Spirit of the Lord is a free agent, not tied to means, time, or instruments; but as at a certain time an angel came down upon the waters of Bethesda, and put a healing virtue into them, so it is here. Therefore never come to any gospel ordinance without an eye to the Spirit, on whom all their blessing and efficacy depend. O lift up your hearts for his blessing upon the means, as ever you expect saving benefits from them.

(ii) *The ministry of the gospel.* The secondary instrument by which this blessed design is effectually managed in the world, is the gospel-ministry. 'What, after all, is Apollos? And what is Paul? Only servants, through whom you came to believe' (1 Cor. 3:5). This is the ordinary stated method of begetting faith. Although God has not tied himself to this or that minister, time or place, yet he has tied us to a diligent and constant attendance upon them. 'How, then, can they call on the one they have not believed in? And how can they believe in the one of whom they have not heard? And how can they hear without someone preaching to them?' (Rom. 10:14). I confess, it seems a very unlikely means, a weak and foolish method, according to the dictate of corrupt human wisdom. Yet by the foolishness of preaching it pleases God to save those who believe (1 Cor. 1:21 KJV). That which the wisdom of man derides, God makes effective to salvation. And oh, how many are there that will have cause to bless God for all eternity, for equipping and sending such ministers among them, whose doctrine the Lord blessed for the conversion of their souls!

4. The great purpose for which these instruments are employed

Now there are two things in the eye and intention of this design, which are worthy of it.

(i) *The exaltation of God's own grace, and the riches of his goodness before angels and men to all eternity.* The name of God is never made so glorious in this world, as it is by bringing over the hearts of men and women to believe. God reaps more glory from the faith of a poor creature that comes to Christ empty and weary, than he does from the other works of his hands. He has not the same glory from the sun, moon, and stars as he has from such poor creatures whose hearts open to Jesus Christ under the gospel call. Thus they are fitted to display the glory of his grace ('to the praise of his glorious grace', Eph. 1:5-6). God will have his rich and glorious grace praised and admired by angels and men for evermore, and every converted soul is as it were a monument erected to the praise of his grace. Heaven will ring with praises for ever, that the great God would humble himself to come into the heart of a vile sinner, and live in it. O this is amazing, that the high and lofty one, who inhabits eternity, will take up his dwelling-place in a poor contrite sinner who trembles at his word (Isa. 57:15).

(ii) *The eternal salvation and blessedness of the soul so opened to Christ* is also the design and aim of this work of opening the heart. When the soul of Zacchaeus was opened by faith, 'Today', says Christ, 'salvation has come to this house' (Luke 19:9). You do not only believe to the glory of God, but to the salvation of your own souls (Heb. 10:39). The opening of our hearts to Christ now is in order to the opening of heaven to us hereafter. This is both the goal of the work and the intention of the worker. 'God was pleased through the foolishness of what was preached to save those who believe' (1 Cor. 1:21). It presently puts them into a state of salvation, though they are not yet actually and completely saved. There is a necessary connection between conversion and salvation, though between conversion and complete salvation there may be many groaning hours, sick and sad days and nights; but full deliverance from sin and misery is secured to the soul in the work of faith: 'Christ in you, the hope of glory' (Col. 1:27).

Thus you see this great and glorious design projected and managed. And this very scope, aim and intention of the whole gospel, even the opening the hearts of sinners unto Christ by faith, will evidently appear by considering the several parts of the gospel which have a direct aspect upon this design, and the declared end of the Spirit, who is sent forth to make it effectual to this very end and purpose.

To this the *commands* of the gospel look. 'And this is his command: to believe in the name of his Son, Jesus Christ' (1 John 3:23). And it is a very great encouragement (if rightly considered) that faith is constituted a duty by a plain gospel-command; for this cuts off that vain pretence and plea of presumption. What! Such a vile wretch as you, says Satan, presume to believe in Christ? But this cuts off the plea; here is a command from the highest sovereignty, and men shall answer at their utmost peril if they despise it.

This also is the declared end and scope of the gospel *promises and threatenings*, whereby the souls of sinners are assaulted on both sides. As for promises, how are all the sacred pages of the Bible adorned with them as the heavens with radiant stars! Amongst which this promise in the text seems to excel in glory: 'If any man open to me, I will come in to him.' This promise brings us to John 6:35, 37: 'I am the bread of life. He who comes to me will never go hungry, and he who believes in me will never be thirsty ... and whoever comes to me I will never drive away.' Such rich and excellent encouragements to faith had never been put into the promises, but for faith's sake. And then for gospel-threatenings, though they have a dreadful sound, yet they have a gracious design. What a terrible thunder-clap are the words 'whoever rejects the Son will not see life, for God's wrath remains on him' (John 3:36). There are dreadful things, you see, threatened in the gospel against unbelievers. But what is the intention of those threatenings but to scare men out of their unbelief and carnal security to Christ? And thus both the promises and the threatenings, though of far different natures, conspire and meet in the self-same design, even to open the heart to Christ by faith.

For the sake of this design all *gospel-ordinances and officers* are instituted and appointed, maintained and continued in the world, right to this day. Why did Christ at his triumphant ascension shed forth such variety of gifts upon men, but that God might dwell among them? 'When you ascended on high, you led captives in your train; you received gifts from men, even from the rebellious—that you, O Lord God, might dwell there' (Psa. 68:18). The whole frame of gospel-ordinances is declaredly set up for this purpose to bring men to Christ, and build them up in Christ (Eph. 4:12).

All the scripture-records of converted sinners, whose hearts God has in any age opened, were made for this very purpose to encourage other souls *by their examples* to believe in, or open to Christ, as they did. For this purpose that famous and memorable conversion of Paul was graciously recorded: 'But for that very reason I was shown mercy so that in me, the worst of sinners, Christ Jesus might display his unlimited patience as an example for those who would believe on him and receive eternal life' (1 Tim. 1:16). Never was any man's heart bolted and made fast with stronger prejudices against Christ than this man's was; yet the Spirit of the Lord opened it. O how flexible was his will! 'Lord, what will you have me to do?' This gives great encouragement to other sinners to come in to Christ as he did; and therefore when men shall see other sinners receiving Christ, and themselves continue still obstinate and unbelieving, those very examples which God has set before their eyes put a dreadful aggravation upon their unbelief! 'For John came to you to show you the way of righteousness, and you did not believe him, but the tax collectors and the prostitutes did. And even after you saw this, you did not repent and believe him' (Matt. 21:32). Though you saw tax collectors, reputed the worst of men, and prostitutes the worst of women, convicted, humbled, and brought to faith, yet these sights in no way affected your souls. You never had one such reflection so as to say, 'Lord! have not I as much need to flee from the wrath to come, and mind the salvation of my own soul as these? Will it not be a dreadful aggravation of my misery, that such as these should obtain Christ and heaven, and I be shut out?'

To conclude: the opening of the heart to Christ is the very *goal and business of the Spirit of God*, upon whose working and blessing the success of all ordinances depends. He is sent expressly from heaven for the purpose of opening the understanding and consciences of sinners by conviction (John 16:8). For it is not in the power of the word alone to produce this effect. Thousands of excellent sermons may be preached, and not one heart opened by conviction. He is expressly set to this end and purpose. What remains is the application of this point.

Four important lessons to learn

1. Don't settle for less.

If the opening of the heart to Christ is the great and direct intention and end of the gospel, how deceived are those who bless themselves in the attainment of some lesser goal and intentions of the gospel, whilst the great goal (the effective persuasion of the will to Christ) is not at all effected upon them! There are some by-effects as I may call them, which the gospel has upon men. It would pity a wise consider-ate man to see how poor souls hug themselves with a conceited happiness in these lesser things, whilst they still stick fast in the state of unregeneracy. I would show the truth to such mistaken wretches who bow down under the power of self-deceit, and that in so great and important a point, in which their eternal salvation is concerned.

There are two things which are exceeding apt to deceive men in this matter:

(i) *Partial convictions on the understanding.* This seems to be the effectual opening of the understanding to Christ, though alas, to this day they never saw sin in its vileness, much less their own special sin, nor Christ in his suitableness and necessity. People who live under the gospel can hardly avoid the improvement of their understanding by the light that shines upon them. Knowl-edge grows, parts thrive, and these enable them to discourse and defend the points of religion excellently. Yes, it may be from the strength of these gifts, they can pray with commendable expres-siveness: these things bring applause from men, and confidence in yourselves, whilst all the while no saving influences are shed down to enliven, change, and spiritualize the heart.

(ii) *Fleeting influences upon the affections.* There are fleeting motions and touches of the gospel upon the affections, which give some men their melting pangs and moods now and then under the word, though it never settles into a spiritual frame, an habitual heavenliness of temper. The apostle speaks of this in Hebrews 6:5. And this is the more dangerous, because they now seem to have attained all that is essential to religion, or necessary to salvation. For when unto the light of their understandings there shall be added melting feelings, a man now seems to be complete in all that the gospel requires to the being and constitution of a Christian. Poor souls are apt to reason, If I had only light in my mind, and never found any meltings of my affections, I might suspect myself justly to be an hypocrite; but there are times when my *affections*, as well as my *understanding*, seem to feel the power of the gospel. And yet these things may be where the heart never effectually opens to Christ. All this may be but a morning dew, an early cloud, that vanishes away. This is plain in John's hearers (John 5:35) and in Paul's hearers (Gal. 1:6; 3:1). For unless the convictions upon the understanding are particular and effective, and the motions upon the affections settled to a heavenly habit and temper, the man is but where he was before as to the real state and condition of his soul. If your understanding were so convinced of the evil nature and dreadful consequences of sin, and your affections and will so strongly determined to choose and embrace the Lord Jesus upon a considerate and thorough examination of his own terms and articles propounded in the gospel, then you might conclude the great design of it were accomplished upon your soul. But to rest in general convictions and passing affections without this is but to mock and deceive your own soul.

2. Hard hearts stubbornly resist the gospel.

Learn from this *the incredible stubbornness and hardness of the hearts of men living daily under the gospel, who still resist it, though it bears upon them in part of it.*

You have heard how all its *commands*, *promises*, *threatenings*, and *examples* bear directly and jointly upon the hearts of sinners to get open the will to Christ. Yet how few there are, comparatively, that obey and answer this great design of it! All these are like heaven's great artillery planted against the unbelief and stubbornness of the hearts of men, to batter down their carnal reasonings, overthrow their vain hopes, and open a fair passage for Christ into their souls. 'The weapons we fight with are not the weapons of the world. On the contrary, they have divine power to demolish strongholds. We demolish arguments and every pretension that sets itself up against the knowledge of God, and we take captive every thought to make it obedient to Christ' (2 Cor. 10:4-5). If a mound is raised, and many cannons planted on it, and all set against the wall of a fort, and thousands of shots made, but there is yet no breach, and not one stone moved out of its place, you will say that is a strong wall indeed. Beloved, God has, as I may say, raised a mound in the gospel, planted the great artillery of heaven upon it, and discharged many dreadful volleys of threatenings. He has, as it were, come under the walls of the unbelieving soul with terms of grace and mercy, and yet there is no opening. O incredible stubbornness! 'We played the flute for you, and you did not dance; we sang a dirge, and you did not mourn' (Matt. 11:17). Neither the sweet songs of gospel-grace, nor the dreadful thunders of the law, make any impression upon you. O what a hard rock is the heart by nature! Certainly, every Christian may see enough in others, and find enough in himself, without the help of other books to confute the Arminian doctrine, which so extols and flatters the nature of man. It is as possible to make an impression with your finger upon a wall of brass as it is for the best sermon in the world, in its own strength, to make an effective saving impression upon a sinner's will.

3. Satan opposes true gospel ministry.

If it is the great design of the gospel to open the hearts of men to Christ, then do not be amazed that it meets with such strong and fierce opposition from Satan, wherever it is sincerely and powerfully preached.

As for general and formal preaching, which brings no life, the devil is not so much concerned about it, as he knows it will do him no great damage. In fact, it fastens and secures his interests in the souls of men. But wherever the gospel comes with Spirit and power, laying the axe to the root, showing men the vanity of their ungrounded hopes, pressing the necessity of regeneration and faith, this preaching quickly gives an alarm to hell, and raises all manner of opposition against it. 'What is it to preach the gospel', says Luther, 'but to drive the rage and fury of the whole world upon us?' Satan is the god of this world, and all men by nature are his born subjects. No prince on earth is more jealous of the revolt of his subjects than he is, and it is time for him to stir himself, when the gospel comes to dethrone him, as it does in the faithful preaching of it. 'Now is the time for judgment on this world; now the prince of this world will be driven out' (John 12:31). Now he falls as lightning from heaven (Luke 10:18). Now sinners are made alive of the cruel tyranny and bondage of Satan's government, and to the glorious liberty offered to them by Jesus Christ. Satan, suspecting the issue of these things, stirs himself to purpose. O what showers of slander and storms of persecution he pours upon the names and persons of Christ's faithful ambassadors! Certainly, he owes Christ's ministers a spite, and they shall know and feel it, if ever he gets them within the compass of his chain. But let this not discourage anyone employed in this glorious design: the Lord is with them to protect their persons and reward their diligence.

4. Christ and faith are the heart of gospel preaching.

If the opening of the heart is the main design of the gospel, Christ and faith ought to be the principal subjects that ministers should insist on among their people.

There are many other useful doctrines which may and ought to be opened and pressed in their time and place. Moral duties have their excellencies, but Christ and faith are the great things we are to preach. Let men be once brought to Christ, and the rest will follow. But to begin and end with morality will never make men gospel Christians. Grace teaches morality (Titus 2:11), but morality without grace saves no man. I doubt not that it has been a grand scheme of the devil, to confuse grace with morality, and make men believe that nothing is more required for their salvation except a civil sober life in the world, and so pass by the principal part of the gospel, which opens and presses the necessity of regeneration, repentance, and faith in the blood of Christ. Such preaching as this does not answer the end and design of Christ in the conversion of souls. This kind of preaching does not disturb the consciences of men. May the Lord help all his ambassadors to mind the example and charge of their Redeemer, and laying aside all earthly interest, to apply themselves faithfully to the souls and consciences of their hearers, not as men-pleasers, but as the servants of Christ.

Convince yourselves of these three things

In the next place, this doctrine is of excellent use *to convince men of the dreadful damning nature of the sin of unbelief,* a sin which defeats and frustrates the main design of the blessed gospel of Christ on the unbeliever's soul.

This is the sin that keeps the heart fast shut against him. As faith is the radical grace, so unbelief is the radical sin. What shall I say of it? It is the traitor's gate, through which those souls pass that are to perish forever. The gospel can do you no good, the blood of Christ can yield no saving benefit, whilst your souls remain under the dominion and power of this sin. When we consider the mighty arguments of the gospel, we may wonder how all who hear them are not immediately persuaded to come to Christ by them. And, on the other side, when we consider the mighty power of unbelief, how strongly it holds the soul in bondage to sin, we may be amazed that any soul is brought over to Christ by the gospel. It was not without cause that the apostle puts faith in Christ among the great mysteries and wonders of the gospel (1 Tim. 3:16). Now the intrinsic evil and fearful consequences of this sin of unbelief will appear in these following particulars:

1. Unbelief fixes the guilt of all other sins on the person of the unbeliever.

It binds them all fast upon his soul, 'if you do not believe that I am the one I claim to be, you will indeed die in your sins' (John 8:24). *Die in your sins!* It would be better for you to die any other death. What more terrible thing can God threaten, or man feel? This is the sin that makes the death of Christ of no effect for us (Gal. 5:4). There is indeed a sovereign virtue in the blood of Christ to pardon sin, but your soul cannot have the benefit of it while it remains under the dominion of this sin. As it was said of the miraculous works of Christ, 'And he did not do many miracles there because of their lack of faith' (Matt. 13:58), so none of his spiritual works and no ordinances can do your soul good, until the Lord breaks the power of this sin; 'the message they heard was of no value to them, because those who heard did not combine it with faith' (Heb. 4:2). If a man were dangerously sick or wounded, the best medicine in the world can never help him, unless taken by him. Unbelief spills the most sovereign remedy of the gospel as water upon the ground. The greatest sins that you ever committed might be pardoned, if this sin did not lie in the way. If this were gone, all the rest were gone too: but whilst unbelief remains, they also remain upon you.

2. *Of all the sins that are upon the souls of men, unbelief is the most difficult sin to be removed and cured.*

Other sins lie more open to conviction, but unbelief is the most plausible in supporting and defending them. Men commit this sin out of a fear of sin. They will not believe, lest they should presume, whilst they dare not believe, because they are not qualified. The strength of other sins meets in this sin of unbelief: it is the strongest fort where Satan puts his trust. Take an adulterer, or a profane swearer, and you have a fair open way to convince him of his sin. Show him the command he has violated, and he has nothing to say in his own defence. But the unbeliever has a thousand plausible defences.

3. *This is the great damning sin of the world.*

I do not say but all other sins deserve damnation (for the wages of sin is death), but this is the sin by which other sins damn and ruin the soul. This is the condemnation (John 3:19). And as it is a damning sin, so it is a sin which damns with aggravated damnation (2 Thess. 1:8). O then, let us mourn over and tremble at this dreadful sin which opposes and so often frustrates the great design and main end of the whole gospel.

Ten encouragements to believe

Is it the main scope of the gospel to bring men to Christ by faith? *Then be persuaded heartily to comply with this great design of the Father, Son, and Spirit, ministers, ordinances, and providences, in opening your hearts to receive Christ this day by genuine faith.*

And, O that I could suitably press this great point, which falls in so directly with the main stream and scope of the whole gospel:

and O that while I am pressing it, you would lift up a hearty cry to heaven, 'Lord, give me faith, whatever else you do to me, open my heart to Christ under the gospel calls.' I do not only press you to a general and common assent to the truths of the gospel, that Christ is come in the flesh, and laid down his life for sinners, but to a full consent to receive him upon gospel terms; to close with him in all his offices, subjecting heart and life to his authority, living entirely upon him for righteousness, and to him by holiness.

The value of such a faith as this is above all estimation.

1. Faith is the grace which God has dignified and crowned with glory and honour above all its fellow-graces.

Its singular praises are in all the scriptures. This is called *precious faith* (2 Pet. 1:1), and *rich faith* (James 2:5). That is a miserable poor soul indeed that is destitute of it, whatever the gifts of providence have been to him. And he is truly rich to whom God has given faith, whatever he has denied him of the comforts of this life. This Christ calls the work of God: 'The work of God is this: to believe in the one he has sent' (John 6:29). Why, so are all other things that your eyes behold; they are the works of God. The earth, the sea, the sun, moon, and stars, are all his handiwork. True, they are so; but this is the work, the most eminent, glorious, and admirable work of God, excelling all his other works which your eyes behold.

2. God has singled out the grace of faith from among all the other graces, to be the instrument of receiving and applying the right-eousness of Christ for the justification of a guilty soul (Rom. 5:1).

You are never said to be justified by love, hope, or desire, but by faith. It is true, all other graces are supposed in the person justi-fied; but none apprehends and applies the righteousness of Christ for justification, but this only. And the justifying act of faith being a receiving act, the glory of God is secured by it; therefore it is of faith that it might be by grace.

3. The grace of faith, which I am recommending to you this day, is not only the instrument of your justification, but it is also the bond of your union with Christ, 'that Christ may dwell in your hearts through faith' (Eph. 3:17).

It is the uniting grace, the marriage-knot. It is that which gives interest in and title to the person and benefits of Christ. It is the great thing upon which the eyes of all the awakened world are intently fixed. Whatever apprehensions you have of an interest in Christ, and whatever his benefits are worth in your eyes, neither he nor they can ever be obtained without faith. O brothers, there is a day coming when those who now slight and neglect this interest and concern of their souls would gladly part with ten thousand worlds for a good title to Christ, could it be purchased. But it is faith, and nothing without faith, that entitles you to Christ and to his benefits.

4. That which should yet more endear this grace of faith to you is this, that it is the hand which receives your pardon from the hand of Christ, the messenger that brings a sealed pardon to a trembling sinner.

'Through him everyone who believes is justified from everything you could not be justified from by the law of Moses' (Acts 13:39). They are cleared of all those sins from which the law could never clear them, nor any repentance, restitution, nor obedience of their own without faith. O what a welcome messenger is faith, and what joyful tidings it brings! You would say so if ever you had felt the power of the law upon your consciences; if ever you had lain, as some sinners have, with a cold sweating horror upon your panting breast, under the apprehensions of the wrath of God. This fruit of faith is rather to be admired than expressed (Psa. 32:1).

5. Faith is not only the messenger that brings you a pardon from heaven; it is, as I may say, that heavenly herald that publishes peace in the soul of a sinner.

O peace, how sweet a word you are! How welcome to a poor condemned sinner! ' How beautiful on the mountains are the feet of those who bring good news, who proclaim peace' (Isa. 52:7). Now it is faith that brings this blessed news and announces it to the soul, without which all the bringers of peace without us, can administer but little support (Rom. 5:1). Faith brings the soul out of the storms and tempests with which it was tossed, into a sweet rest and calm. 'Now we who have believed enter into that rest' (Heb. 4:3). Is the quiet harbour welcome to poor weather-beaten seamen, after they have endured furious storms and many fears upon the raging sea? O how welcome then must peace be to that soul that has been tossed on the tempestuous ocean of its own fears and terrors, blown up and incensed by the terrible blasts of the law and conscience! It was a comforting sight to Noah and his family to see an olive-leaf in the mouth of the dove, by which they knew the waters were receding. But, oh! what is it to hear such a voice as this from the mouth of faith: fury is not in me, says the Lord. His anger is turned away, and he comforts you. Do not be afraid, poor storm-tossed soul, the God of peace is your God.

6. Faith not only brings the storm-tossed soul into a calm, but it is the grace also which opens to the soul a door of access into the gracious presence of God.

Without it there is no coming to him acceptably. 'Anyone who comes to God must believe' (Heb. 11:6). This liberty and access to God is indeed the purchase of the blood of Christ, procured at a great price. But faith is the grace that brings the soul into the actual presence of God, and there helps it to open and ease its griefs, and, with liberty of speech, to bring all its grievances, fears, and burdens to the Lord. And truly, this world were not worth the living in without such a blessed opening to our troubles as this is. Only the believer has the key that opens the door of access to God. If he has any sins, wants, burdens, afflictions, temptations, etc., here he can ease them. Ah Christian, the time may come when your heart may be filled with sorrows to the brim, and there may not be found a person of your acquaintance in all the world to whom you can turn to ease your sorrows, or give vent to your troubles. Now, blessed be God for faith. O the ease one act of faith gives a troubled soul, which is like bottles full of new wine, and must either vent or break! Well may it be said, the just shall live by faith. How can we imagine we should live without it? Certainly our afflictions and temptations would swallow us up, were it not for the sweet reliefs that come in by faith.

7. And yet further to enflame your desires after faith, this is the grace that gives you the soul-reviving sights of the invisible world, without which this world would be a dungeon to us.

'Now faith is being sure of what we hope for and certain of what we do not see' (Heb. 11:1). O it is a precious eye! How transporting are those visions of faith: 'Though you have not seen him, you love him; and even though you do not see him now, you believe in him and are filled with an inexpressible and glorious joy' (1 Pet. 1:8). We who preach heaven to you cannot show you the glorious person of Christ there, nor the thrones, crowns, and palms that are above; but faith can make these things visible. That is an eye that can penetrate the clouds, and show you to him who is invisible (Heb. 11:27).

8. The grace of faith, which I am recommending to you this day, is instrumentally the livelihood of your souls in this world: 'the righteous will live by his faith' (Hab. 2:4).

When God gives a soul faith, he gives it him for a livelihood, and expects he should keep house upon it while he lives in this world; and God reckons he has made plentiful provision for your souls, when he has given them faith, and furnished out such variety of precious promises for your faith to feed upon. Abraham, Moses, David, and all the saints, kept house upon no other provision but what faith brought in. And at what a high and excellent rate did they live. Here man eats angels' food. It is a storehouse of provision, and a shop of cordials. A believer lives the best life of all men upon earth. And as the believer's soul is daily fed by faith, so all the other graces in his soul are maintained and daily supported by the provision faith brings in to them. The other graces, like the young birds in the nest, live upon that provision the grace of faith gathers for them, and puts into their mouths. Take away faith, and you quickly starve the soul of a Christian. Will not all this engage your desires after faith?

9. Why then, consider this is the grace whereby we die safely as well as live with comfort.

As you cannot live comfortably without it in this world, so neither can you die safely or comfortably without it when you go out of this world. 'All these people were still living by faith when they died. They did not receive the things promised; they only saw them and welcomed them from a distance' (Heb. 11:13). Notice how these excellent persons died: they all died embracing the promises in the arms of their faith. O precious promises, says the dying believer, what unspeakable use and benefit have you been to me all the days of my pilgrimage! You are they to whom I have turned in all my troubles and distresses. But I am now going into the life of immediate vision. Farewell blessed promises, scriptures, ordinances, and communion of imperfect saints. I shall walk no more by faith, but by sight.

10. In a word, and that a great word too, this is the grace that saves you: 'For it is by grace you have been saved, through faith' (Eph. 2:8).

Your salvation is the fruit of free-grace. But grace itself will not save you in any other method but that of believing. The grace of God runs down through the channel of faith. Faith is the grace that espouses your soul to Christ here, and accompanies it every step of the way until it comes to its full enjoyment in heaven, and then is swallowed up in vision. It embarks you with Christ, and pilots you through the dangerous seas, till you drop anchor in the haven of everlasting rest and safety, where you receive the goal of your faith, the salvation of your souls. O then, in consideration of the incomparable worth and absolute necessity of this precious grace, make it your great study, make it your constant cry to heaven, night and day, *Lord, give me a believing heart, an opening heart to Jesus Christ*. If you fail in this, you come short of the great end and design of the whole gospel, which is to bring you to faith, and by faith to heaven.

8

True Freedom

IN 1681 Flavel published *The Method of Grace in the Gospel Redemption*, a book of thirty-five sermons tracing the work of God's grace in a sinner through effectual calling, and intended as a sequel to *The Fountain of Life*.

This sermon from that book has a deeply pastoral tone to it. Flavel is writing primarily to Christians, and wants them to explore and appreciate the various aspects of freedom in Christ. The reader will discover a healthy biblical realism here: Christians will suffer and struggle all the way to glory, even as free people in Christ. Notice, too, how Flavel handles the law of God, explaining how we have been not only redeemed from its curse but set free in order to obey the law as the rule for godly living. Whilst Flavel urges us to live out the Christian life with thankfulness and joy, there is very little mention of the Spirit of God as our help in doing so. Omission this may be, but the overall force of the sermon will stimulate appreciation for the work of Christ for sinners, and renew zeal for godly living.

If the Son sets you free, you will be free indeed.—John 8:36

Jesus alone brings freedom.

FROM the 30th verse of John 8 you have an account of the different effects which the words of Christ had upon the hearts of his hearers: many believed (verse 30); these he encourages to continue in his word, giving them this encouragement, 'you will know the truth, and the truth will set you free' (verse 32). At this the unbelieving Jews take offence, and start a quarrel with Jesus: 'We are Abraham's descendants and have never been slaves of anyone' (verse 33). We are no slaves; the blood of Abraham runs in our veins. Christ challenges this scornful boast of the proud Jews. He distinguishes a twofold bondage, one to men, another to sin; one civil, another spiritual. 'Everyone who sins is a slave to sin', he then tells them (verse 34). 'Now a slave has no permanent place in the family, but a son belongs to it forever' (verse 35). In this he points to two great truths, the first being that the servants and slaves of sin may for a time enjoy the external privileges of the house or church of God, but it would not be long before the master of the house would turn them out of doors. The second truth is that if they were once the adopted children of God, then they should remain in the house for ever. This privilege is only to be had by their believing in and being united to the natural Son of God, Jesus Christ. This brings us to the text: 'If the Son sets you free, you will be free indeed.' The womb of nature cast you forth into the world in a state of bondage. In that state you have lived all your days, servants to sin, and slaves to your lusts. And yet, freedom is to be obtained. And this freedom is the prerogative belonging to the Son of God to bestow: 'If the Son sets you free.'

After this Christ says, 'Then will you be free indeed', i.e. you shall have a real freedom, an excellent and everlasting freedom. If ever therefore you will be free men, believe in me.

> **Doctrine:** *This statement teaches, that interest in Christ sets the soul at liberty from all the bondage it was subjected to in its natural state.*

Believers are the children of the new covenant, the inhabitants of Jerusalem which is above, which is free, and the mother of them all (Gal. 4:26). The glorious liberty which is spiritual and eternal, is the liberty of the children of God (Rom. 8:21). Christ, and none but Christ, delivers his people out of the hand of their enemies (Luke 1:74).

In the doctrinal part of this point, I must show you *firstly*, what believers are not freed from by Jesus Christ in this world, and *secondly*, what that bondage is from which every believer is freed by Christ. I will show you *thirdly*, what kind of freedom that is which commences with believing, and *fourthly*, I will show you the excellency of this state of spiritual freedom.

In Christ, freedom comes with boundaries.

Set free, but not from everything.

First, we look at those things which believers are not made free from in this world. We must not think that our spiritual liberty by Christ brings us into an absolute liberty in all respects. Christ does not free believers from obedience to the moral law. It is true we are not under it as a covenant for our justification, but we are and must still be under it as a rule for our direction. The matter of the moral law is unchangeable, as the nature of good and evil is, and cannot be abolished except that distinction could be destroyed (Matt. 5:17-18). The precepts of the law are still urged under the gospel to enforce duties upon us (Eph. 6:12). It is therefore a vain distinction, invented by libertines, to say it binds us as creatures but not as Christians, or that it binds the unregenerate part but not the regenerate. It is a sure truth, that they who are freed from the penalties of the law are still under its precepts. Though believers are no more under its curse, yet they are still under its conduct. The law sends us to Christ to be justified, and Christ sends us to the law to be regulated. Let the heart of every Christian join therefore with David's in that holy wish, 'You have laid down precepts that are to be fully obeyed. Oh, that my ways were steadfast in obeying your decrees!' (Psa. 119:4, 5). It is excellent when Christians begin to obey the law *from* life, which others obey *for* life, and because they are justified, not that they may be justified. It is also excellent when duties are done in the strength and for the honour of Christ, and not in our own strength, and for our own ends, which is servile and legal obedience.

Set free, but not from the attacks of the devil.

Secondly, Christ has not freed believers in this world from the temptations and assaults of Satan; even those that are freed from his dominion are not free from his assaults. It is said indeed, 'God will soon crush Satan under your feet' (Rom. 16:20), but in the meantime he has power to bruise and buffet us (2 Cor. 12:7). He now strikes Christ's heel (Gen. 3:15). i.e. strikes him in his tempted and afflicted believers. Although he cannot kill them, he can and does afflict and frighten them by shooting his flaming arrows of temptation at them (Eph. 6:16). It is true that when the saints have got safely to heaven they are out of gunshot and there is perfect freedom from all temptation. A believer may then say, 'O my enemy, temptations have come to a final end. I have now arrived

here, where none of your fiery darts can reach me.' But this freedom is not yet.

Set free, but not from indwelling sin.

Thirdly, Christ has not yet freed believers in this world from the
power of indwelling sin. This is continually acting, and infesting
the holiest of men (Rom. 7:21, 23, 24). Corruptions, like Canaanites, are still left in the land to be thorns in your eyes and goads in
your sides. Those that boast most of freedom from the power of
sin, have most cause to suspect themselves still under the dominion of sin. All Christ's freemen are troubled with the same complaint. Who among them does not complain as the apostle did,
'What a wretched man I am! Who will rescue me from this body
of death?' (Rom. 7:24).

Set free, but not from the inward sting of sin.

Fourthly, Jesus Christ does not free believers in this world from
inward troubles and exercises of soul upon the account of sin.
God may let loose Satan, and conscience too, in the way of terrible accusations, which may greatly distress the soul of a believer,
and woefully eclipse the light of God's countenance, and break the
peace of their souls. Job, Heman, and David were all made free by
Christ, yet each of them has left upon record his bitter complaint
upon this account (Job 7:19-20; Psa. 88:14-16; 38:1-11).

Set free, but not from suffering.

Fifthly, Christ has not freed believers in this world from the rods
of affliction. God, in giving us our liberty, does not remove his
own liberty (Psa. 89:32). All the children of God are made free,
yet what son is there whom the father does not chasten (Heb.
12:8)? Exemption from affliction is so far from being the mark
of a free man, that the apostle there makes it the mark of a slave.
Illegitimate children, not sons, lack the discipline and blessing of

the rod. To be free from affliction would be no benefit to believers, who receive so many benefits by it.

Set free, but not from death.

Sixthly, no believer is freed by Christ from the stroke of death, though they are all freed from the sting of death (Rom. 8:10). The bodies of believers are under the same law of mortality as other men (Heb. 9:27). We must come to the grave just as others. We must come to it through the same agonies, pangs and griefs that other men do. The foot of death treads as heavy upon the bodies of the redeemed as of other men. Believers, indeed, are distinguished by mercy from others, but the distinguishing mercy lies not here. Thus you see what believers are not freed from in this world.

What does freedom in Christ look like, then?

Set free from the oppression of the law of God.

If you shall now say, what advantage does a believer have, or what profit is there in regeneration? I answer, that believers are freed from many great and sad miseries and evils by Jesus Christ, notwithstanding all that has been said. For, firstly, all believers are freed from the rigour and curse of the law. The rigorous yoke of the law is broken off from their necks, and the sweet and easy yoke of Jesus Christ put on (Matt. 11:28-30). The law required perfect obedience, under the pain of a curse (Gal. 3:10). The law accepted no half-measures, permitted no repentance, and gave no strength. It is not so now. The strength we need is given (Phil. 4:13), and gospel faith is reckoned perfection (Job 1:1). Transgression does not bring us under condemnation (Rom. 8:1). Blessed freedom, when duty becomes light and failings do not hinder acceptance! This is one part of the blessed freedom of believers.

Set free from the guilt of sin

Secondly, all believers are freed from the guilt of sin. It may trouble us, but it cannot condemn us (Rom. 8:33). The handwriting which was against us is cancelled by Christ, nailed to his cross (Col. 2:14). When the seal and handwriting are torn off from the bond, the debtor is made free. Believers are totally freed, and finally freed (Acts 13:39; John 5:24). 'They shall never come into condemnation.' O blessed freedom! How sweet is it to lie down in our beds, and then in our graves, when guilt shall neither be our bed-fellow, nor grave-fellow!

Set free from sin's mastery

Thirdly, Jesus Christ frees all believers from the dominion as well as the guilt of sin. 'For sin shall not be your master, because you are not under law, but under grace' (Rom. 6:14). 'Through Christ Jesus the law of the Spirit of life set me free from the law of sin and death' (Rom. 8:2). Now, who can estimate such a liberty as this? What slavery, what an intolerable drudgery is the service of our lusts, from all which believers are freed by Christ, not from the residence, but from the reign of sin.

Set free from Satan's mastery

Fourthly, Jesus Christ sets all believers free from the power of Satan, in whose right they were by nature (Col. 1:13). They are translated from the power of darkness into the kingdom of Christ. Satan had the possession of them, as a man of his own goods; but Christ overcomes that strong man armed, takes the property, and recovers them out of his hand (Luke 11:21, 22). There are two ways by which Christ frees believers out of Satan's power and possession: by price, and by power.

Firstly, we are set free by price. The blood of Christ purchases believers out of the hands of justice, by satisfying the law for them, which being done, Satan's authority over them falls of course, as the power of a jailer over the prisoner does, when he has a legal discharge. 'Since therefore the children share in flesh and blood, he himself likewise partook of the same things, that through death he might destroy the one who has the power of death, that is, the devil' (Heb. 2:14). The cruel tyrant beats and burdens the poor captive no more after the ransom is once paid, and he actually freed.

Secondly, Christ delivers us by his power. Satan is exceeding unwilling to let go of his prey: he is a strong and malicious enemy. Every rescue and deliverance out of his hand is a glorious effect of the almighty power of Christ (Acts 26:18; 2 Cor. 10:5). How did our Lord Jesus Christ grapple with Satan at his death, and triumph over him (Col. 2:15)! Glorious salvation! Blessed liberty of the children of God!

Set free from the sting of death

Fifthly, Christ frees believers from the poisonous sting and hurt of death. Death can kill us, but it cannot hurt us. '"Where, O death, is your victory? Where, O death, is your sting?" The sting of death is sin, and the power of sin is the law. But thanks be to God! He gives us the victory through our Lord Jesus Christ.' (1 Cor. 15:55-57). If there is no hurt, there should be no horror in death. It is guilt that arms death, both with its hurting and terrifying power. To die in our sins (John 8:24), to have our bones full of the sins of our youth, which shall lie down with us in the dust (Job 20:11), to have death, like a dragon, pulling a poor guilty creature as a prey into its dreadful den (Psa. 49:14)—in this lie the danger and horror of death. But from death as a curse, and from the grave as a prison, Christ has set believers at liberty, by submitting to death in their place. And by his victorious resurrection from the grave, as the firstborn of the dead, death is disarmed of its hurting power. The death of believers is but a sleep in Jesus.

Enjoying our freedom in Christ: six aspects

The next thing to be spoken about is the kind and nature of that freedom and liberty purchased and procured by Christ for believers. Now liberty may be considered two ways, as civil and as holy liberty.

As to civil freedom or liberty, it belongs not to our present business. Believers, as to their civil capacity, are not freed from the duties they owe to their superiors. Servants, though believers, are still to be subject to their masters, according to the flesh, with fear and trembling (Eph. 6:5). Nor are we free from obedience to lawful magistrates, whom we are to obey in the Lord (Rom. 13:1, 4). Religion does not loosen the bonds of civil relations, nor is it to be used as a pretext for indulging the sinful nature (1 Pet. 2:16). It is not a carnal but a spiritual freedom Christ has purchased for us. The liberty believers have at present is but a beginning liberty; they are freed but in part from their spiritual enemies; but it is a growing liberty every day, and will one day be complete. Believers are not only freed from many miseries, burdens, and dangers, but also invested by Jesus Christ with many royal privileges and invaluable protection.

What are the properties of this blessed freedom which the saints enjoy by Jesus Christ?

1. They are, firstly, a wonderful liberty, never enough to be admired.

Remember who we are: we are those who owed to God more than we could ever pay by our own eternal sufferings, and who were under the dreadful curse and condemnation of the law, in the power and possession of Satan, the strong man armed. We are those who were bound with so many chains in our spiritual prison. Our understanding was bound with ignorance, our wills with obstinacy, our hearts with impenetrable hardness, and our affections with a thousand bewitching vanities. That God should set such people as us at liberty, notwithstanding all this, is the wonder of wonders, and will be deservedly marvellous in the eyes of believers for ever.

2. The freedom of believers is a particular freedom, a liberty which few obtain.

The most part remain in bondage to Satan, who, from the multitude of his subjects, is called the god of this world (2 Cor. 4:4). In Scripture believers are often called a remnant, which is but a small part of the whole piece. The people of God therefore have all the more reason to admire distinguishing mercy. How many nobles and great ones of the world are but royal slaves to Satan, and their own lusts!

3. The liberty of believers is a liberty dearly purchased by the blood of Christ.

That captain said, 'I had to pay a big price for my citizenship' (Acts 22:28), and this may be much more said of the believers' freedom: it was not silver or gold, but the precious blood of Christ that purchased it (1 Pet. 1:18).

4. The freedom and liberty of believers is a growing liberty.

They get more and more out of the power of sin, and nearer still to their complete salvation every day (Rom. 13:11). The body of sin dies daily in them, they are said to be crucified with Christ, the strength of sin abates continually in them, in the manner of crucified persons, who die a slow but sure death. And see in what degree the power of sin abates, in proportion to their spiritual liberty increasing in them.

5. The freedom of believers is a freedom full of comforts.

The apostle comforts Christians of the lowest rank, poor servants, with this consideration: 'he who was a slave when he was called by the Lord is the Lord's freedman' (1 Cor. 7:22). Let not the lowliness of your outward condition, which is a state of subjection and dependence, a state of poverty and contempt, at all trouble you. You are the Lord's freemen, of precious account in his eyes. O it is a comforting liberty!

6. Lastly, it is a perpetual and final freedom.

They that are once freed by Christ, have their freedom and final discharge from that state of bondage they were in before. Sin shall never have dominion over them anymore. It may tempt them and trouble them, but shall never more rule and govern them (Acts 26:18). And thus you see what a glorious liberty the liberty of believers is.

Concluding thoughts

1. All joy is here!

How rational is the joy of Christians, above the joy of all others in the world! Shall not the captive rejoice in his recovered liberty? The very birds of the air would rather be at liberty in the woods, though lean and hungry, than in a golden cage with the richest fare. Every creature naturally prizes its liberty, none more than believers, who have felt the burden and bondage of corruption, who in the days of their first illumination and conviction have poured out many groans and tears for this mercy. What was said of the captive people of God in Babylon excellently shadows forth the state of God's people under spiritual bondage, with the way and manner of their deliverance from it: 'because of the blood of my covenant with you, I will free your prisoners from the waterless pit' (Zech. 9:11). Believers are delivered by the blood of Christ out of a worse pit than that of Babylon. And look at how the tribes in their return from exile were overwhelmed with joy and astonishment: 'When the LORD restored the fortunes of Zion, we were like those who dream. 2 Then our mouth was filled with laughter, and our tongue with shouts of joy' (Psa. 126:1-2). They were overwhelmed with the sense of the mercy. So should it be with the people of God. When the prodigal son (there made the emblem of a returning, converting sinner) was returned again to his father's house, there was music and dancing, joy and feasting in that house (Luke 15:24). The angels in heaven rejoice when a soul is brought back from the power of Satan; and shall not the recovered soul, immediately concerned in the mercy, greatly rejoice? Yes, let them rejoice in the Lord, and let no earthly trouble or affliction ever have power to interrupt their joy for a moment, after such a deliverance as this.

2. Backsliding must be unthinkable.

How unreasonable and wholly inexcusable is the sin of apostasy from Jesus Christ! What is it but for a delivered captive to put his feet again into the shackles, his hands into the manacles, and his neck into the iron yoke, all of which he has been delivered from! 'When the unclean spirit has gone out of a person, it passes through waterless places seeking rest, but finds none. Then it says, "I will return to my house from which I came." And when it comes, it finds the house empty, swept, and put in order. Then it goes and brings with it seven other spirits more evil than itself, and they enter and dwell there, and the last state of that person is worse than the first.' (Matt. 12:43-45).

As a prisoner that has escaped and caught is loaded with double irons, let the people of God be content to face any danger, and endure any difficulties in the way of religion, rather than return again into their former bondage, to sin and Satan. O Christian! if ever God gave you a sight and a sense of the misery and danger of your natural state, if ever you have felt the pangs of a labouring and distressed conscience, and, after all this, tasted the unspeakable sweetness of the peace and rest that are in Christ, you will rather choose to die ten thousand deaths than to forsake Christ and go back again into that sad condition.

3. Live with your new free heart.

How fitting and attractive is a free spirit in believers for their state of liberty and freedom. Christ has made your condition free. O let the life of your hearts be free also. Do all that you do for God with a spirit of freedom, not by constraint, but willingly. The new nature that is in you should stand for a command, and be instead of all arguments that use to work upon the hopes and fears of other men. See how all creatures work according to the principle of their natures. You need not command a mother to draw forth her breasts to her infant child; nature itself teaches and prompts to that. You need not bid the sea ebb and flow at the stated hours. So why should your heart need any other argument, than its own spiritual inclination, to keep its stated times and seasons of communion with God? Let none of God's commandments be grievous to you. Let not your heart need dragging and forcing to its own benefit and advantage. Whatever you do for God, do it cheerfully, and whatever you suffer for God, suffer it cheerfully. It was a brave spirit which moved holy Paul when he said, 'I am ready not only to be imprisoned but even to die in Jerusalem for the name of the Lord Jesus' (Acts 21:13).

4. Do not be surprised that Satan opposes this freedom.

Do not wonder at the hatred and opposition of Satan to the preaching of the gospel. It is by the gospel that souls are recovered out of his power. It is the express work of ministers 'to turn [men] from darkness to light, and from the power of Satan to God' (Acts 26:18). Satan is a great and jealous prince: he will never endure to have liberty proclaimed by the ministers of Christ within his dominions. And, indeed, what is it less, when the gospel is preached in power, but as it were by beat of drum, and sound of trumpet, to proclaim liberty, spiritual, sweet, and everlasting liberty, to every soul aware of the bondage of corruption and the cruel servitude of Satan, and who will now come over to Jesus Christ? What numbers and multitudes of prisoners have broken loose from Satan at one proclamation of Christ (Acts 2:41)! Satan owes the servants of Christ a spite for this, and will be sure to pay them if ever they come within his reach. Persecution is the evil genius of the gospel, and follows it as the shadow does the body.

5. Guard your freedom in Christ.

How careful should Christians be to maintain their spiritual liberty in all and every point thereof! 'It is for freedom that Christ has set us free', says Paul. 'Stand firm, then, and do not let yourselves be burdened again by a yoke of slavery' (Gal. 5:1). And again, 'You were bought at a price; do not become slaves of men' (1 Cor. 7:23). It is Christ's prerogative to prescribe the rules of his own house. He has given no man dominion over your faith (2 Cor. 1:24 KJV). One man is no rule to another, but the word of Christ is a rule to all. Do not follow the holiest men one step further than they follow Christ (1 Cor. 11:1). Man is an ambitious creature, naturally wanting power. To give law to others feeds pride in himself; so far as any man brings the word of Christ to warrant his commands, so far we are to obey, and no farther. Christ is your Lord and Lawgiver.

6. Offer Christ's freedom to others.

Lastly, let this encourage and persuade sinners to come to Christ. For with him is sweet liberty to poor captives. Oh that you did but know what a blessed state Jesus Christ would bring you into! 'Come to me, all you who are weary and burdened' (Matt. 11:28). And what encouragement does he give to comers? Why this: 'For my yoke is easy and my burden is light.' The devil persuades you that the ways of obedience and strict godliness are a perfect bond-age. But if ever God regenerate you, you will find that his ways are 'ways of pleasantness, and all his paths peace' (Prov. 3:17 KJV): you will 'rejoice in following his statutes as one rejoices in great riches' (Psa. 119:14). You will find the worst work Christ puts you about, even suffering work, sweeter than all the pleasures that ever you found in sin. O therefore open your hearts at the call of the gospel: come to Christ, then you will be free indeed.

PART THREE

LIVING THE CHRISTIAN LIFE

9

Guard Your Heart

☞

FLAVEL published *A Saint Indeed or, The Great Work of a Christian, Opened and Pressed, from Proverbs 4:23*, in 1667. The work is a treatise on the verse, and unlike a number of Flavel's well-known works, gives no obvious evidence of having been a series of sermons. And yet, its direct, pastoral, and practical style has made it one of the most appreciated of Flavel's writings. The excerpts here are a portion from the original work which runs to nearly 50,000 words. It's all great—let this selection whet your appetite for the whole piece!

A Saint Indeed speaks to our busy age, where our great temptation—one for every period, but maybe more so for our times—is to be too much focused on activity and appearance. This work calls us back to first things. Flavel shows us our hearts, and what it means to guard them, especially in those periods when living for Christ is especially difficult. He also brings a remarkable balance of incentives which both warn and encourage us to guard our hearts. The goal is to encourage us to be more serious, as well as satisfied, disciples of the Lord Jesus Christ.

Above all else, guard your heart, for it is the wellspring of life.
—Proverbs 4:23

THE heart of man is his worst part before it is regenerate, and the best afterwards. It is the seat of principles and the wellspring of actions. The eye of God is, and the eye of a Christian ought to be, principally fixed upon it. The greatest difficulty in conversion is to win the heart *to* God; and the greatest difficulty after conversion is to keep the heart *with* God. Direction and help in this great work are the scope and sum of this text.

Hearing the text

1. You have a heart to keep.

By 'heart' the Scriptures sometimes understand some particular noble faculty of the soul. In Romans 1:21 it means the understanding part—'their foolish hearts', i.e. their foolish understanding, 'were darkened'. And in Psalm 119:11, it is put for the memory—'I have hidden your word in my heart'; and in 1 John 3:20 it is put for the conscience, which has it in both the light of the understanding, and the recognitions of the memory: 'whenever our hearts condemn us', i.e. whenever our conscience, whose proper office it is to condemn. But here we are to take it more generally for the whole soul, or inner man. For what the heart is to the body, that the soul is to the man; and what health is to the heart, that holiness is to the soul. The state of the whole body depends upon the soundness and vigour of the heart, and the everlasting state of the whole man upon the good or ill condition of the soul. And by keeping the heart, I mean the diligent and constant use and improvement of all holy means and duties, to preserve the soul from sin, and maintain its sweet and free communion with God.

The expression 'guard your heart' seems to put it upon us as our work, yet it does not imply a sufficiency or ability in us to do it. We are as able to stop the sun in its course, or make the rivers run backwards, as by our own skill and power to rule and order our hearts. We may as well be our own saviours, as our own keepers. And yet Solomon speaks properly enough when he says 'guard your heart', because the *duty* is ours, though the *power* is God's. A natural man has no power, gracious man has some, though not sufficient. And the power he has depends upon the energizing and assisting strength of Christ. 'Apart from me you can do nothing' (John 15:5).

2. Keeping your heart is serious work.

The Hebrew is very emphatic: 'keep with all keeping', or 'keep, keep'; set double guards, your hearts will be gone, if not. And this vehemency of expression with which the duty is urged, plainly implies how difficult it is to keep our hearts, and how dangerous to let them go.

As the text says, 'for it is the wellspring of life'. That is, it is the source and wellspring of all vital actions and operations. It is the wellspring of both good and evil, says Jerome. It is the spring both of good and evil, as the spring in a watch that sets all the wheels in motion. The heart is the treasury, the hand and tongue but the shops. The hand and tongue always begin where the heart ends. The heart contrives, and the members execute (Luke 6:45). A good man out of the good treasury of his heart brings forth good things, and an evil man out of the evil treasury of his heart brings forth evil things. For out of the abundance of his heart his mouth speaks. So then, if the heart errs in its work, these will fail in theirs; for heart-errors are like the errors of the first order, which cannot be put right afterwards, or like the misplacing, and inverting of the stamps and letters in the press, which must cause so many errors in all the copies that are printed off. O then how important a duty is that which is contained in the following proposition: *the keeping and right managing of the heart in every condition is the great business of a Christian's life.*

What the philosopher says of waters can be equally applied to hearts: it is hard to keep them within any bounds. God has set bounds and limits to them, yet how frequently do they transgress, not only the bounds of grace and religion, but even of reason and common honesty! This is the great task which affords the Christian matter of labour, fear and trembling to his dying day. It is not the cleansing of the hand that makes a Christian, for many a hypocrite can show as fair a hand as he, but the purifying, watching, and right ordering of the heart. This is the thing that provokes so many sad complaints, and costs so many deep groans and bitter tears. It was the pride of Hezekiah's heart that made him lie in the dust mourning before the Lord (2 Chron. 32:26). It was the fear of hypocrisy invading the heart that made David cry, 'May my heart be blameless toward your decrees, that I may not be put to shame' (Psa. 119:80). It was the sad experience he had of the divisions and distractions of his own heart in the service of God, that made him pour out that prayer, 'give me an undivided heart, that I may fear your name' (Psa. 86:11).

Going deeper

What it means to keep the heart.

To keep the heart necessarily supposes a previous work of sanctification, which has set the heart right, by giving it a new spiritual bent and inclination. For as long as the heart is not set right by grace as to its habitual frame, no duties or means can keep it right with God. Self is the poise of the unsanctified heart, which biases and moves it in all its designs and actions, and, as long as it is so, it is impossible that any external means should keep it with God. Man, by creation, was of one constant, uniform frame and tenor of spirit, held one straight and even course. His mind had a perfect illumination to understand and know the will of God, his will a perfect obedience in it, and his appetite and other inferior powers stood in a most obedient subordination.

Due to the fall, man has become a most disordered and rebellious creature, contesting with and opposing his Maker. His first cause is now self-dependence, his chief good is self-love, and his highest Lord is self-will. His illuminated understanding is clouded with ignorance, and his once-obedient will is now full of rebellion and stubbornness, and his subordinate powers cast off the dominion and government of the superior faculties. But by regeneration this disordered soul is set right again. Sanctification is the renovation of the soul after the image of God (Eph. 4:24) in which self-dependence is removed by faith, self-love by the love of God, self-will by subjection and obedience to the will of God, and self-seeking by self-denial. The darkened understanding is again illuminated (Eph. 1:18), the stubborn will sweetly subdued (Psa. 110:3), the rebellious appetite gradually conquered (Rom. 6:6-7). And thus the soul, which sin had universally depraved, is again by grace restored.

In the light of this it will not be difficult to understand what it is to keep the heart, which is nothing else but the constant care and diligence of a renewed man, to preserve his soul in that holy frame to which grace has brought it, and daily strives to hold it. For, though grace has in great measure restored the soul, and given it an habitual heavenly temper, yet sin often actually disturbs it again, so that even a gracious heart is like a musical instrument, which, though it is ever so carefully tuned, a small matter places it out of tune again. This is the case with gracious hearts. If they are in frame in one duty, yet how dull, dead and disordered when they come to another! And therefore every duty needs a particular preparation of the heart.

Six ways to keep the heart

To keep the heart is to preserve it carefully from sin which disorders it, and maintain that spiritual and gracious frame which fits it for a life of communion with God. And this includes these six acts in it:

1. Study the heart.

Worldly and formal people pay no attention to this, and cannot be brought to confer with their own hearts. There are some men and women that have lived forty or fifty years in the world, and have scarcely had one hour's discourse with their own hearts all that while. It is a hard thing to bring a man and himself together upon such an account; but saints know that these times are of excellent use and advantage. The heathen could say that the soul is made wise by sitting still in quietness. Though bankrupts care not to look into their account books, yet upright hearts will know whether they make progress or not. The heart can never be kept, until its case is examined and understood.

2. Grieve over sin.

Hezekiah humbled himself for the pride of his heart (2 Chron. 32:26), and the people were ordered to spread forth their hands to God in prayer, aware of the plague of their own hearts (1 Kings 8:38). Many an upright heart has been laid low before God. O what a heart I have! They have in their confessions pointed at the heart as the place of real pain. 'Lord, here is the wound, here is the plague-sore.' It is with the heart well-kept as it is with the eye, which is a fitting emblem of it, that if a small bit of dust gets into the eye, it won't stop watering until it has been wept out. Just so, the upright heart cannot be at rest till it has wept out its troubles, and poured out its complaints before the Lord.

3. Pray for grace to deal with indwelling sin.

As Psalm 19:12 says, 'Forgive my hidden faults'; and Psalm 86:11 says, 'give me an undivided heart, that I may fear your name.' Saints have always many such prayers before the throne of God's grace, and this is what is most pleaded by them with God. When they are praying for outward mercies, their spirits may be more remiss, but when it comes to the heart's case, then they extend their spirits to the utmost, fill their mouths with arguments, weep and make supplication: oh, for a better heart! 'Oh for a heart to love God more, to hate sin more, to walk more closely with God. Lord, deny not to me such a heart, whatever else you deny me; give me a heart to fear, love, and delight in you, even if I have to beg my bread in desolate places.'

4. Put in place strategies to help the heart.

This will include the imposing of strong engagements and bonds upon ourselves to walk more closely with God, and avoid the occasions whereby the heart may be induced to sin. Well composed, advised, and deliberate vows are, in some cases, of excellent use to guard the heart against some special sin; so Job 31:1, 'I made a covenant with my eyes not to look lustfully at a girl.' By this means, holy ones have overcome their souls, and preserved themselves from defilement from some special heart-corruption.

5. Be on constant alert.

Exercise a constant holy jealousy over your own heart. Quick-sighted self-jealousy is an excellent preservative from sin. He who will keep his heart must have the eyes of his soul awake and open to all the disorderly and tumultuous stirrings of his affections. If the affections break loose, and the passions are stirred, the soul must discover and suppress them before they get to a height. As we fear the Lord we depart from evil, shake off false security, and preserve ourselves from sin. He who will keep his heart must eat with fear, rejoice with fear, and pass the whole time of his sojourning here in reverent fear. And all of this is scarcely enough to keep the heart from sin.

6. Above all, keep in mind the all-seeing eye of God.

And lastly, to add no more, it includes the realizing of God's presence with us, and setting the Lord always before us. In this way the people of God have found a singular means to keep their hearts upright, and awe them from sin. When the eye of our faith is fixed upon the eye of God's omniscience, we dare not let our thoughts and desires go to worthless things. Job didn't dare allow his heart to yield to an impure, vain thought, and what was it that moved him to such great carefulness? Why, he tells you: 'Does he not see my ways, and count my every step?' (Job 31:4). 'Walk before me', says God to Abraham, 'and be blameless' (Gen. 17:1). Even as parents use to set their children in the congregation before them, knowing that otherwise they will be playing with their toys, so would the heart of the best man too, were it not for the eye of God.

True Christians express the care they have for their hearts in such ways as these. They are as careful to prevent the breaking loose of their spiritual corruptions in times of temptation as seamen are to bind fast the guns, so that they don't break loose in a storm; and as careful to preserve the sweetness and comfort they have received from God in any duty, as one who comes out of a hot bath, or a great sweat, is of catching a cold by going forth into the chill air.

Warning: hard work ahead!

This is the work we face to guard our hearts, and of all works in religion it is the most difficult, constant, and important.

1. It is the hardest work.

Heart-work is hard work indeed. To shuffle over religious duties with a loose and heedless spirit, will cost no great pains; but to set yourself before the Lord, and tie up your loose and vain thoughts to a constant and serious attendance upon him will cost you something. To attain a skill and fluency in prayer, and put your meaning into apt and decent expressions, is easy; but to get your heart broken for sin while you are confessing it, and melted with free grace, whilst you are blessing God for it, is a different matter altogether. To be really ashamed and humbled through a sight of God's infinite holiness, and to keep your heart in this frame, not only during but after duty, will surely cost you some groans and travailing pains of soul. To repress the outward acts of sin, and compose the external part of your life in a laudable and comely manner, is no great matter. Even worldly people can do this by some well-chosen habits. But to kill the root of corruption within, to set and keep up a holy government over your thoughts, to have all things lie straight and orderly in the heart, this is not easy.

2. It is a work that ends only at death.

The keeping of the heart is such a work as is never done till life is over. This labour and our life end together. It is with a Christian in this business as it is with seamen that have sprung a leak at sea: if they do not constantly work at the pump, the water increases upon them, and will quickly sink them. It is in vain for them to say, the work is hard, and we are weary. And there is no time or condition in the life of a Christian which will allow a letting-up in this work. It is in the keeping watch over our hearts, as it was in the keeping up of Moses' hands, whilst Israel and Amalek were fighting below (Exod. 17:12). No sooner do Moses' hands grow heavy and sink down, but Amalek prevails. You know it cost David and Peter many a sad day and night for giving up the watch over their own hearts for just a few minutes.

3. It is the most important business of a Christian's life.

Without this we are but formalists in religion. All our professions, gifts, and duties signify nothing: 'My son, give me your heart' (Prov. 23:26). God is pleased to call that a gift which is indeed a debt. He will put this honour upon the creature to receive it from him in the way of a gift. But, if it is not given to God, he sets no value on whatever else you bring to him. There is so much only of worth and value in what we do as there is of heart in it. Concerning the heart, God seems to say, as Joseph of Benjamin, 'You will not see my face again unless your brother is with you' (Gen. 43:3). Among the heathens, when the beast was cut up for sacrifice, the first thing the priest looked upon was the heart, and, if that were unsound, the sacrifice was rejected. God rejects all duties (however glorious in other respects) offered him without a heart. He who performs duty without a heart is no more accepted with God than he who performs it with a double heart, as a hypocrite (Isa. 66:3).

How to keep the heart in hard times.

When providence frowns upon you, and destroys your outward comforts, then look to your hearts, keep them with all diligence from complaining against God, or fainting under his hand. For troubles, though sanctified, are troubles still. Jonah was a good man, and yet how stubborn was his heart under affliction! Job was the mirror of patience, yet how was his heart harassed by trouble! You will find it as hard to get a composed spirit under great afflictions, as it is to fix quicksilver. O the hurries and tumults which they occasion even in the best hearts!

Eight directions for keeping the heart from complaining or being downcast under the hand of God in hard times

1. Remember that God is in control and is working out his great purpose of his grace.

Remember that, by these difficult providences, God is faithfully pursuing the great design of electing love upon the souls of his people, and orders all these afflictions as means sanctified to that end.

Afflictions come not by chance, but by counsel (Job 5:6; Eph. 1:11). By this counsel of God they are ordained as means of much spiritual good to saints (Isa. 27:9). Our sufferings are God's work-men upon our hearts, to pull down pride and carnal security, and as they are, their nature is changed as they are turned into blessings and benefits. 'It was good for me to be afflicted' (Psa. 119:71). With this perspective, you have every reason not to quarrel with but rather to admire that God should concern himself so much with your good as to use any means for the accomplishing of it. Paul could bless God, if by any means he might attain to the resurrection of the dead (Phil. 3:11). 'Consider it pure joy, my brothers', says James, 'whenever you face trials of many kinds' (James 1:2). Is my God about a design of love upon my soul, and am I right to be angry with him? All that he does is in pursuit of an eternal glorious purpose for my soul. O, it is my ignorance of God's design, that makes me quarrel with him. He says to you in this case, as to Peter, 'You do not realize now what I am doing, but later you will understand' (John 13:7).

2. Be confident in God's covenant love.

Though God has reserved to himself a liberty of afflicting his people, yet he has tied up his own hands by a promise never to take his loving-kindness from them.

Can I look this scripture in the face, with a sad, discontented spirit? 'I will be his father, and he will be my son. When he does wrong, I will punish him with a rod wielded by men, with floggings inflicted by men. But my love will never be taken away from him' (2 Sam. 7:14, 15). O my heart! Do you have reason to be downcast, when God has given you the whole tree, with all the clusters of comfort growing on it, because he decides to blow down a few leaves?

To keep the heart from sinking under afflictions, call to mind that your own Father has the ordering of them. Not a creature moves hand or tongue against you, but by his permission. Suppose the cup is a bitter one, yet it is the cup which your Father had given you to drink, and can you suspect poison to be in that cup which he delivers you? Foolish man, put the case to your own heart: can you find in your heart to give your child what would hurt him? No, you would as soon hurt yourself as him. 'If you, then, though you are evil, know how to give good gifts to your children, how much more will your Father in heaven give good gifts to those who ask him!' (Matt. 7:11).

The very consideration of his nature, a God of love, pity, and tender mercies, or of his relation to you as a Father, Husband, and Friend might be comfort enough, if he had not spoken a word to comfort you in this case. And yet you have his word, too: 'I will not harm you' (Jer. 25:6). You lie too near his heart for him to hurt you, and nothing grieves him more than your groundless and unworthy suspicions of his designs for you.

3. Be convinced that God will never leave you, whatever happens.

God respects you as much in a low as in a high condition, and therefore it need not trouble you so much to be made low. In fact, God manifests more of his love, grace, and tenderness in the time of affliction than prosperity. As God did not at first choose you because you were high, so he will not forsake you because you are low. When providence hath blasted your estates, your summer friends may grow distant, fearing you may be troublesome to them. But will God do so? No, no; 'Never will I leave you; never will I forsake you' (Heb. 13:5). Indeed if adversity and poverty could bar you from access to God, it would be a sad condition, but you may go to God as freely as ever. 'My God (says the church) will hear me' (Mic. 7:7). Poor David, when stripped of all earthly comforts, could yet encourage himself in the Lord his God, and why can't you? Suppose your husband or child had lost all at sea, and should come to you in rags; could you deny the relation, or refuse to look after him? If you would not, much less will God. Why then are you so troubled? Though your condition is changed, your Father's love and care are not changed.

4. Reflect on the fact that your troubles might be the means of real blessings.

And what if by the loss of outward comforts God will preserve your souls from the ruining power of temptation? Surely then, you have little cause to sink your hearts by such sad thoughts about them. Are not these earthly enjoyments the things that make men shrink and warp in times of trial? For the love of these many have forsaken Christ in such an hour; 'he went away sad, for he had great wealth' (Matt. 19:22). And if this is God's design, what have I done in quarrelling with him about it?

We see seamen in a storm throw overboard rich bales of silk and precious things to preserve the vessel and their lives with it, and everyone recognizes they act wisely. We know it is usual for soldiers in a besieged city to tear down or burn the fairest buildings outside the walls, in which the enemy may shelter during the siege, and no one doubts that it is wisely done. Those who have gangrene in their legs or arms willingly stretch them out to be cut off, and not only thank but pay the surgeon for his pains. And must God be complained at for casting overboard what will sink you in a storm, for pulling down that which would advantage your enemy in the siege of temptation, or for cutting off what would endanger your eternal life? O inconsiderate, ungrateful man! Are not the things which you grieve over the very things that have ruined thousands of souls? Well, what Christ is doing in this you currently do not know, but hereafter you may well know.

5. Consider that your problems may be God's answer to your prayers.

It would much help the heart under adversity to consider that God by such humbling providences may be accomplishing that for which you have long prayed and waited. And should you be troubled at that? Have you not many prayers which depend on God, that he would keep you from sin, show you your emptiness and insufficiency, that he would put to death your lusts, so that your heart might never find rest in any enjoyment but Christ? Why now, by such humbling and impoverishing strokes God may be fulfilling your desire. Do you want to be kept from sin? Look, he has blocked your way with thorns. Would you see the emptiness of human efforts? Your own affliction is a fair mirror to discover it, for the vanity of the creature is never so effectively found as in our own experience of it. Would you have your sinful desires put to death? Well now God takes away the food and fuel that maintained them. For as prosperity gave them birth and nourishment, so adversity, when sanctified, is a means to kill them. Would you have your heart rest nowhere but close to the heart of God? What better way can you imagine providence should take to accomplish your desire than by pulling from under your head that soft pillow of earthly delights on which you rested before?

And yet as you fret at this like a little child, do you realize that you are actually trying your Father's patience? If he delays to answer your prayers, you are ready to say he ignores you; if he does what actually answers their purpose, but just not in the way you expected, you quarrel with him for it, as if instead of answering, he were frustrating all your hopes and aims. Is it not enough that God is so gracious to do what you want, must you be so impudent as to expect him to do it in the exact way which you prescribe?

6. Understand that God always works for our best ends.

Again, it may strengthen your heart if you consider that in these troubles God is about that work which, if you were to see its design, your soul would rejoice. We poor creatures are clouded with much ignorance, and are not able to discern how particular providences work towards God's end, and therefore, like Israel in the wilderness, we are often murmuring, because providence leads us in a howling desert, where we are exposed to all sorts of difficulties. And yet, just as God led his children then, he is leading us now by the right way to our city. If you could only see how God, in his secret counsel, has exactly laid the whole plot and design of your salvation, even to the smallest means and circumstances! It is by this way, and by these means, you shall be saved, and by no other.

Could you but discern the admirable harmony of God's dealings, and then of all the conditions in the world, you would choose where you are now, if you had the freedom to make your own choice. Providence is like a strange piece of tapestry, made of a thousand threads. We don't know what to make of each one, but when stitched together, they represent a beautiful history to the eye. Just so, God works all things according to the counsel of his own will, so that his counsel has ordained this as the best way to bring about your salvation. One believer has a proud heart, and so God appoints many humbling providences for him. Another has a worldly heart, so God brings many impoverishing providences for him. If you could only see this, then I need say no more to support the most dejected heart.

7. Acknowledge the foolishness of complaining.

Further, it will bring much comfort to your hearts to consider that by fretting and discontent you do yourselves more injury than all the afflictions you lie under could do. Your own discontent is that which arms your troubles with a sting. It is you that makes your burden heavy, by struggling under it. If you could lie quiet under the hand of God, your condition would be much easier and sweeter than it is. This makes God lay on more strokes, as a father will upon a stubborn child that refuses correction. Suffering is a pill which, when wrapped up in patience and quiet submission, may be easily swallowed; but discontentment chews the pill, and so embitters the soul. God throws away some comfort which he saw would hurt you, and you will throw away your peace after it: he shoots an arrow which sticks in your clothes, and was never intended to hurt, but only to frighten you away from sin, and you will thrust it onward to the piercing of your very hearts, by despondency and discontent.

8. Think of where your sins would condemn you to be, apart from grace.

Lastly, if all this will not do, but your heart (like Rachel's) still refuses to be comforted or quieted, then consider one thing more which, if seriously pondered, will doubtless do the work, and that is: compare the condition you are now in (and with which you are so dissatisfied) with that condition others are, and you deserve to be in. Others are roaring in flames, howling under the scourge of vengeance, and amongst them I deserve to be. O my soul, is this hell? Is my condition as bad as the damned? O what would thousands now in hell give, to change conditions with me! It is a famous instance which Dr Taylor gives us of the Duke of Condé.

'I have read', said he, 'that when the Duke of Condé had entered voluntarily into the hardships of poverty for the sake of Christ, he was one day seen and pitied by a lord of Italy, who out of tenderness wished him to look after himself more. The good duke answered, "Sir, do not be troubled, and do not think that I am ill-provided for, for I send a servant before me, who makes ready my lodgings, and makes sure that I am royally entertained." The lord asked him who his servant was. He answered, "The knowledge of myself, and the consideration of what I deserve for my sins, which is eternal torments. And when with this knowledge I arrive at my lodging, how mean I find it, methinks it is ever better than I deserve."' Why then does the living man complain? And thus the heart may be kept from desponding or repining under adversity.

Motives to keep the heart

If all that has been said by way of inducement is not enough, I have yet some motives to offer you:

1. The studying, observing, and diligently keeping of your own heart will help you to understand the deep mysteries of the faith.

An honest, well-experienced heart is an excellent help to the head. Such a heart will serve for a commentary on a great part of the Scriptures. By means of such a heart you will have a better understanding of divine things than the most learned (but graceless) man ever had, or can have. You will not only have a clearer, but a more profitable grasp of them. A man may discourse with depth and orthodoxy on the nature and effects of faith, the troubles and comforts of conscience, and the sweetness of communion with God, who has never felt the effective and sweet impression of these things upon his own soul. But how dark and dry are his notions compared with those of an experienced Christian!

2. The study and observation of your own heart will powerfully secure you against the dangerous and infecting errors of the times in which you live.

For what do you think is the reason why so many professing Christians have departed from the faith and listened to fables? Why have so many been led away by the error of the wicked? Why have those who have sown corrupt doctrines had such plentiful harvests among us? Is it not because they have met with a race of professors who never knew what belongs to practical godliness and the study and keeping of their hearts?

3. Your care and diligence in keeping your heart will prove one of the best evidences of your sincerity.

I know no external act of religion which truly distinguishes the sound from the unsound professor. It is marvellous how far hypocrites go in all external duties and how plausibly they can order their outward lives, hiding all their indecencies from the observation of the world. But they pay no attention to their hearts. They are not in secret what they appear to be in public. And before this test no hypocrite can stand. They may, indeed, in a fit of terror, or on a deathbed, cry out the wickedness of their hearts. But such complaints are of no worth. No credit in law is to be given to the testimony of one upon the rack, because it may be recognized that his torture will make him say anything to get relief. But if jealousy for ourselves, care and watchfulness are the daily workings and frames of your heart, you have some evidence of your sincerity.

4. How comforting and how profitable would all ordinances and duties be to you, if your heart were faithfully kept.

What real communion you might have with God every time you approach him, if your heart were in a right frame! You might then say with David, 'My meditation of him shall be sweet' (Psa. 104:34

KJV). It is the indisposition of the heart which renders ordinances and secret duties so comfortless to some. They strive to raise their hearts to God, now pressing this argument upon them and then that one, to stir them up; yet they often get nearly through the exercise before their hearts begin to be interested in it, and sometimes they go away no better than they were when they came. But the Christian whose heart is prepared by being constantly kept, enters immediately and whole-heartedly into his duties. He outstrips his sluggish neighbour, gets the first sight of Christ in a sermon, the first seal from Christ in a sacrament, the first communication of grace and love in secret prayer. Now if there be anything valuable and comforting in ordinances and private duties, look to your heart and keep it, I urge you.

5. An acquaintance with your own heart will furnish you a well-spring of needs for prayer.

The man who is diligent in heart-work will be richly supplied with matter in his addresses to God. He will not be confused for a lack of thoughts, and his tongue will not falter for lack of expressions.

6. The most desirable thing in the world, the revival of religion among a people, may be effected by means of what I am urging upon you.

O that I might see the time when professing Christians shall not walk in a vain show, when they shall please themselves no more with a name to live while they are spiritually dead, when they shall be no more a company of frothy, vain people, but when holiness shall shine in their lives and awe the world, and command reverence from all that are around them, and when they shall warm the hearts of those who come near them, and cause it to be said, 'God is truly among them.' And may such a time be expected? Until heart-work becomes the business of professors, I have no hope of seeing a thing so blessed! Does it not grieve you to see how the gospel is despised and trampled underfoot, and the professors of it ridiculed and scorned in the world? Christians, would you recover your credit? Would you obtain an honourable testimony in the consciences of your very enemies? Then keep your hearts.

7. By diligence in keeping our hearts we should prevent the occasions of fatal scandals and stumbling-blocks to the world.

Woe to the world because of offences! Keep your heart faithfully, and you will be prepared for any situation or service to which you may be called. This and this only can properly fit you for usefulness in any station, and with this you can endure prosperity or adversity, you can deny yourself, and turn your hand to any work. Thus Paul turned every circumstance to good account, and made himself so eminently useful. When he preached to others, he provided against being cast away himself. He kept his heart, and everything in which he excelled seems to have had a close connection with his diligence in keeping his heart.

8. If the people of God would diligently keep their hearts, their communion with each other would be unspeakably more inviting and profitable.

It is the fellowship which the people of God have with the Father and with the Son that kindles the desires of others to have communion with them. I tell you, that if saints would be persuaded to spend more time and take more pains about their hearts, there would soon be such a divine excellence in their conversation that others would account it no small privilege to be with or near them. It is the pride, passion, and worldliness of our hearts that has spoiled Christian fellowship. Why is it that when Christians meet they are often jarring and contending? Is it not because their passions are not put to death? Where do their uncharitable criticisms of each other come from, but from their ignorance of themselves? Why are they so rigid and unfeeling toward those who have fallen, if it is not because they do not feel their own weakness and liability to temptation? Why is their discourse so light and unprofitable when they meet, but because their hearts are worldly and vain? But now, if Christians would study their hearts more and keep them better, the beauty and glory of communion would be restored. They would divide no more, contend no more, censure rashly no more. They will feel right one toward another, when each is daily humbled under a sense of the evil of his own heart.

9. Lastly, keep your heart, and then the comforts of the Spirit and the influence of all ordinances will be more fixed and lasting than they now are.

Do the comforts of God seem small to you? Ah, you have reason to be ashamed that the ordinances of God, as to their life-bringing and strengthening ends, should make so light and transient an impression on your heart.

Now, reader, consider well these special benefits of keeping the heart which I have mentioned. Examine their importance. Are they small matters? Is it a small matter to have your understanding assisted, your endangered soul made safe, your sincerity proved, your communion with God sweetened, your heart filled with matter for prayer? Is it a small thing to have the power of godliness, all fatal scandals removed, a fitness to serve Christ obtained, the communion of saints restored to its first glory, and the influence of ordinances abiding in the souls of saints? If these are no common blessings, no ordinary benefits, then surely it is a great and indispensable duty to keep the heart with all diligence.

And now are you inclined to undertake the business of keeping your heart? Are you resolved upon it? I charge you, then, to engage in it earnestly. Away with every cowardly feeling, and make up your mind to encounter difficulties.

Draw your armour from the word of God. Let the word of Christ dwell in you richly, in its commands, its promises, its threatenings. Let it be fixed in your understanding, your memory, your conscience, your affections. You must learn to wield the sword of the Spirit, which is the word of God, if you would defend your heart and conquer your enemies. You must call yourself frequently to an account, examine yourself as in the presence of the all-seeing God, and bring your conscience, as it were, to the bar of judgment. Beware how you plunge yourself into a multiplicity of worldly business, and how you venture at all to indulge your sinful appetites. You must exercise the utmost vigilance to discover and check the first symptoms of departure from God, the least decline of spirituality, or the least indisposition to meditation by yourself, and holy conversation and fellowship with others. These things you must undertake in the strength of Christ, with invincible resolution in the outset. And if you engage in this great work, be assured you shall not spend your strength for nothing: comforts which you never felt or thought of will flow in upon you from every side.

The diligent prosecution of this work will constantly afford you the most powerful zeal towards vigilance and commitment in the life of faith, while it increases your strength and wears out your enemies. And when you have kept your heart with all diligence a little while, when you have fought the battles of this spiritual warfare, gained the ascendancy over the corruptions within, and conquered the enemies without, then God will open the gate of heaven to you, and give you the portion which is promised to those who overcome. Awake then, this moment; get the world under your feet, refuse to long for the things which a man may have, and eternally lose his soul; but bless God that you may have his service here, and the glory hereafter which he appoints to his chosen. 'Now may the God of peace who brought again from the dead our Lord Jesus, the great shepherd of the sheep, by the blood of the eternal covenant, equip you with everything good that you may do his will, working in us that which is pleasing in his sight, through Jesus Christ, to whom be glory forever and ever. Amen' (Heb. 13:20, 21).

10

Trust God in Tough Times

THIS sermon is part of a series based on the text of Isaiah 26:20, which was published under the title *The Righteous Man's Refuge* (1682). Flavel has explained to his readers that, like the people of God in Isaiah's day who were facing Babylonian captivity, they were facing dangerous times too. But God's all-providing grace is available still. Flavel explores the attribute of God's almighty power and encourages us to meditate particularly on this aspect of God's being when life gets hard.

There are three parts to the sermon, in which we see God's power, how it exceeds human expectations, and how it works according to God's will.

How we need sermons such as this! It has been said that the Bible is effectively a treatise on suffering. If this is so, then the preacher's task is to return to the subject of suffering again and again, to teach Christians how to face suffering and how to live trusting in Christ through tough times.

Go, my people, enter your rooms and shut the doors behind you;
hide yourselves for a little while until his wrath has passed by.
—Isaiah 26:20

LET us view our 'rooms', and see how well God has provided for his children in all the distresses that befall them in this world. It is our Father's voice that calls to us, 'Go, my people, enter your rooms.' The room which comes to be opened as a refuge to distressed believers in a stormy day is that most secure and safe attribute of divine power. Let us first enter this room by serious and believing meditation, and see how safe they are whom God hides under its protection, in the worst and most dangerous days.

In opening this attribute, we shall consider it in its own nature and properties, with respect to the promises, and as it is brought into action by providence on the behalf of distressed saints. And then I will give you an encouraging sight of the safe and happy condition of those who take up their lodgings by faith in this attribute of God.

The grace of power: what is God's power?

Let us consider the power of God in itself, and we shall find it represented to us in the Scriptures, in the three aspects of omnipotent power, supreme power, and everlasting power.

1. Omnipotent power

God's is an omnipotent and all-sufficient power, which has no bounds or limits but the pleasure and will of God. 'He does as he pleases with the powers of heaven and the peoples of the earth. No one can hold back his hand or say to him: "What have you done?"' (Dan. 4:35). 'The LORD does whatever pleases him, in the heavens and on the earth, in the seas and all their depths' (Psa. 135:6). Divine pleasure is the only rule according to which divine power exerts itself in the world. We are not therefore to limit and restrain it in our narrow and shallow thoughts, and to think in this, or in that, that the power of God may help or secure us; but to believe that he is able to do exceeding abundantly above all that we can ask or think. Thus Daniel's three friends by faith exalted the power of God above the order and common rule of second causes: 'If we are thrown into the blazing furnace, the God we serve is able to save us from it, and he will rescue us from your hand, O king' (Dan. 3:17). Their faith rested itself upon the omnipotent power of God, and so expected deliverance from it in an extraordinary way. It is true, this is no standing rule for our faith ordinarily to work by, nor do we have ground to expect such miraculous salvations, but yet when extraordinary difficulties press us, and the common ways and means of deliverance are closed against us, we ought by faith to exalt the omnipotency of God, by ascribing its glory to him, and leave ourselves to his good pleasure, without reducing his almighty power, according to the mould of our poor, low thoughts and understanding of it.

The Lord himself directs our faith in difficult cases: '"For my thoughts are not your thoughts, neither are your ways my ways," declares the LORD. "As the heavens are higher than the earth, so are my ways higher than your ways and my thoughts than your thoughts"' (Isa. 55:8, 9). He speaks there of his pardoning mercy, which he will not have his people contract and limit according to their own despondency, misgiving, and unbelieving thoughts, but he wants them to exalt and glorify it, according to its unbounded fullness. As it is in the thoughts of God, the fountain of that mercy, so it ought to be with respect to his power, about which his thoughts and ours do vastly differ. The power of God as we cast it in the mould of our thoughts, is as vastly different and disproportionate from what it is in the thoughts of God its fountain, as the earth is to the heavens, which is but a tiny speck compared with them.

2. Supreme power

The power of God is a supreme and sovereign power, from which all creature-power is derived, and by which it is over-ruled, restrained, and limited at his pleasure. Nebuchadnezzar was a great monarch, he ruled over other kings, yet he held his kingdom from God. It was God that placed not only the crown upon his head, but his head upon his shoulders. 'You, O king, are the king of kings. The God of heaven has given you dominion and power and might and glory' (Dan. 2:37). Hence it follows that no creature can move tongue or hand against any of God's people, but by virtue of a commission or permission from their God, although they do not think so. 'Don't you realize, said Pilate to Christ, 'I have power either to free you or to crucify you?' Proud worm! What an ignorant and insolent boast was this of his own power! And how does Christ spoil and shame it in his answer, 'You would have no power over me if it were not given to you from above' (John 19:10, 11).

Wicked men, like wild horses, would run over and trample underfoot all the people of God in the world, were it not that the bridle of divine providence had a strong curb to restrain them: 'See how each of the princes of Israel who are in you uses his power to shed blood' (Ezek. 22:6). And it was well for God's Israel that their power was not as large as their wills were. This world is a raging and boisterous sea, which sorely tosses the passengers for heaven that sail upon it, but this is their comfort and security: The Lord 'stilled the roaring of the seas, the roaring of their waves, and the turmoil of the nations' (Psa. 65:7). Moral, as well as natural waves, are checked and bounded by divine power: 'Surely your wrath against men brings you praise, and the survivors of your wrath are restrained' (Psa. 76:10).

Not only the power of man, but the power of devils also is under the restraint and limitation of this power. 'The devil will put some of you into prison to test you, and you will suffer persecution for ten days' (Rev. 2:10). Satan would have cast them into their graves and into hell if he could, but it must be only into a prison. He would have kept them in prison till they had died and rotted there, but it must be only for ten days. Oh glorious sovereign power, which thereby keeps the reins of government in its own hand!

3. Everlasting power

The power of God is an everlasting power. Time does not weaken or diminish it, as it does all creature-powers. ' The LORD is the everlasting God, the Creator of the ends of the earth. He will not grow tired or weary, and his understanding no one can fathom' (Isa. 40:28), and 'surely the arm of the LORD is not too short to save' (Isa. 59:1). He has as much power now as ever he had, and can do for his people as much as ever he did. Time will decay the power of the strongest creature, and make him faint and feeble, but the Creator of the ends of the earth will not grow tired. 'But you remain the same, and your years will never end' (Psa. 102:27). In God's working there is no expense of his strength; he is able to do as much for his church now as ever he did, to act over again all the glorious deliverances that ever he wrought for his people from the beginning of the world. He is able to do as much for his church now as he did at the Red Sea, and upon this ground the church builds its plea: 'Awake, awake, put on strength, O arm of the LORD; awake, as in the ancient days, in the generations of old'

(Isa. 51:9). Lord, why should your people in our day not expect as glorious a display of your power as any of them found in former ages?

How does God's power work for us?

Let us view the power of God in the vast extent of its operations, and then you will find it working far above creature-power, creature-expectation and human probability.

1. Above all created power, even on the hearts, thoughts, and minds of men, where no creature has any jurisdiction.

So, God bound up the spirit of Laban, and made it calm towards Jacob (Gen. 31:29). 'He caused them to be pitied by all who held them captive' (Psa. 106:46). The Lord promised Jeremiah, 'I will make your enemies plead with you in times of disaster' (Jer. 15:11). This power of God softens the hearts of the most fierce and cruel enemies, and sweetens the spirits of the most bitter and enraged foes of his people.

2. Above all creature-expectations

God 'is able to do immeasurably more than all we can ask or imagine' (Eph. 3:20). He does so in spiritual matters, as appears by those two famous parables: '"I am no longer worthy to be called your son; make me as one of your hired men." But the father said to his servants, "Quick! Bring the best robe and put it on him. Put a ring on his finger and sandals on his feet"' (Luke 15:19, 22). The prodigal desired to be but as a hired servant, and lo, the fatted calf was killed for him, and music played for him, and the gold ring placed upon his finger. And in Matthew 18:26, 27 the debtor begged for patience, and the creditor forgave the debt. Oh, thinks a poor humbled sinner, if I might have but the least glimpse of hope, how sweet would it be! But God brings him to more than he expects, even the clear shining of assurance.

It is the same in earthly matters, as the church confesses that the Lord *did things they did not expect* (Isa. 64:3). And in both spiritual and earthly matters this power moves in a higher orbit than our thoughts: "'my thoughts are not your thoughts, neither are your ways my ways", declares the LORD. "As the heavens are higher than the earth, so are my ways higher than your ways and my thoughts than your thoughts'" (Isa. 55:8, 9). The earth is but a mere speck compared to the heavens. All its tallest cedars, mountains and pyramids cannot reach them. Isaiah speaks, as was said before, of God's pitying, pardoning, and merciful thoughts, and shows that no creature can think of God as he does of the creature under sin, or under misery. Our thoughts are not his thoughts. We cannot think such thoughts towards others in distress by way of pity, or towards those who sin against us by way of pardon, as God does. Nor can we conceive or comprehend what those thoughts of God towards us are.

3. Above all probabilities and the thoughts of men

This almighty power has brought about deliverance for the people of God when things have been brought to the lowest ebb, and all the means of salvation have been hidden from their eyes. We have different famous instances of this in Scripture, wherein we may observe a remarkable gradation in the working of this almighty power. It is said, 'The LORD had seen how bitterly everyone in Israel, whether slave or free, was suffering; there was no one to help them' (2 Kings 14:26). A deplorable state! How inevitable was their ruin to the eye of sense! Well might it be called a bitter affliction; yet from this immediate power arose for them a sweet and unexpected salvation. And if we look into 2 Corinthians 1:9, 10 we shall find the apostles and choicest Christians of those times giving up themselves as lost men. All ways of escaping were quite out of sight, for Paul says, 'in our hearts we felt the sentence of death'. But though they were sentenced to death, and though they sentenced themselves, this power, which was at work above all their thoughts, reprieved them.

In Ezekiel the people of God are represented as actually dead, as in their graves, and as rotted in their graves, and their very bones dry, like those who are dead, so utterly improbable was their recovery (Ezek. 37:4-7). Yet by the working of this almighty power, which subdues all things to itself, their graves in Babylon were opened, the breath of life came into them, bone came to bone, and there stood up a very great army. It was the working of his power above the thoughts of man's heart which gave the ground to that famous proverb, 'On the mountain of the LORD it will be provided' (Gen. 22:14), and the ground of that famous promise, 'When evening comes, there will be light' (Zech. 14:7). This means that light shall unexpectedly spring up, when all men according to the course and order of nature expect nothing but increasing darkness. How extensive is the power of God in its glorious workings!

God's power, God's promises

Let us view the power of God in its relation to the promises, for so it becomes our sanctuary in the day of trouble. If the power of God is the room, it is the promise of God which is that golden key that opens it. And if we will consult the Scriptures in this matter, we shall find the almighty power of God made over to his people by promise, for many excellent ends and uses in the day of their trouble. It is given,

1. To uphold and support them when their own strength fails

'So do not fear, for I am with you; do not be dismayed, for I am your God. I will strengthen you and help you; I will uphold you with my righteous right hand' (Isa. 41:10). And which of the saints has not felt these everlasting arms underneath their spirits, when afflictions have pressed them above their own strength? So runs the promise to Paul, 'My grace is sufficient for you, for my power is made perfect in weakness' (2 Cor. 12:9), meaning, it is made known in your weakness. Our weakness adds nothing to God's power, it does not make his power perfect, but it puts forth itself more conspicuously in our weakness, as the stars which shine so gloriously in the darkest night.

2. To preserve them in all their dangers, to which they lie exposed in soul and body

You 'are shielded by God's power' (1 Pet. 1:5); kept, as in a garrison. This is their arm every morning: 'O Lord, be gracious to us; we long for you. Be our strength every morning, our salvation in time of distress' (Isa. 33:2). The arm is that limb which is fitted for the defence of the body, and for that end so placed by the God of nature, that it may guard every part above and below it. But it is God's arm that defends us and not our own. This invisible power of God makes the saints the world's wonder, 'I have become like a portent to many, but you are my strong refuge' (Psa. 71:7). To see the poor defenceless creatures preserved in the midst of furious enemies, that is a just matter for wonder; but God being their invisible refuge, that solves the wonder; to this end the power of God is by promise engaged to his people. 'I, the LORD, watch over it; I water it continually. I guard it day and night so that no one may harm it' (Isa. 27:3). And thus they live in the midst of dangers and troubles, as the burning bush (the emblem of the church) did amidst the devouring flames (Exod. 3:3).

3. To deliver them out of their distresses

So runs the promise, '"Because he loves me", says the LORD, "I will rescue him; I will protect him, for he acknowledges my name. He will call upon me, and I will answer him; I will be with him in trouble, I will deliver him and honour him''' (Psa. 91:14, 15). And Jeremiah 30:7 says, 'How awful that day will be! None will be like it. It will be a time of trouble for Jacob, but he will be saved out of it.' It is easy with God to save them out of it. Are they to the eye of sense lost, as hopeless as men in the grave? Yet see Ezekiel 37:12: 'O my people, I am going to open your graves and bring you up from them; I will bring you back to the land of Israel.' And he does whatever he does easily, with a word: 'You are my King and my God, who decrees victories for Jacob' (Psa. 44:4). And it requires no more violent motion to do it, than he who swims in the water uses (Isa. 25:11). A gentle easy motion of the hand does it.

4. As the power of God can deliver them easily, so it can deliver them speedily.

Their deliverance is often brought about by way of surprise: 'In the evening, sudden terror! Before the morning, they are gone!' (Isa. 17:14). So the church prays, 'Restore our fortunes, O LORD, like streams in the Negev' (Psa. 126:4). The southern countries are dry, the streams there come not in a gentle and slow current, but being occasioned by violent sudden spouts of rain, they presently overflow the country, and as soon retire. So speedily can the power of God free his people from their dangers and fears.

5. Yes, such is the excellency of his delivering power, that he can save alone, without any contribution of creature-aids.

'He saw that there was no one, he was appalled that there was no one to intervene; so his own arm worked salvation for him, and his own righteousness sustained him' (Isa. 59:16). We read indeed (Judg. 5:23) of helping the Lord, but that is not to express his need, but their duty; we have continual need of God, but he has no need of us. He uses instruments, but not out of necessity; his arm alone can save us, even if the danger is great, or the visible means of deliverance is so remote.

6. Once more, let us view this room of divine power, as it is contin-
ually opened by the hand of providence, to receive and secure the
people of God in all their dangers.

It is said, 'For the eyes of the LORD range throughout the earth
to strengthen those whose hearts are fully committed to him.
You have done a foolish thing, and from now on you will be
at war' (2 Chron. 16:9). Here you have an excellent account of
God's immediate, universal, and effective providence, as it uses
and applies this divine power for the guard and defence of that
people who are its charge. He doesn't only set angels to watch
for them, but his own eyes guard them, even those seven eyes of
providence mentioned (Zech. 3:9), which never sleep nor slum-
ber. They are said to run continually to and fro, and that not in
this or that particular place only, for the service of some more
eminent and excellent persons, but through the whole earth. It is
an encompassing and surrounding providence which has its eye
upon all whose hearts are upright. All the saints are within the
line of its care and protection. The eye of providence discovers
all their dangers, and its arm defends them, for he shows himself
strong on their behalf.

The secret but almighty effectiveness of providence is also excellently described to us in Ezekiel 1, where the angels are said to have
their hands under their wings, working secretly and indiscernibly,
but very effectively for the saints committed to their charge. Oh
that we could sun ourselves in those strengthening and reviving
beams of divine power, by considering how gloriously they have
broken forth and shone out for the salvation of his people in
all ages. So it did for Israel at the Red Sea (Exod. 15:6), and for
Jehoshaphat in that great danger (2 Chron. 20:12, 15), and so in
the time of Hezekiah (2 Kings 19:3, 7). In fact, in all ages from the
beginning of the world the saints have been sheltered under these
wings of divine power (Isa. 51:9, 10). Thus providence has hung

and adorned this room of divine power with the glorious histories of the church's many preservations by it.

Trusting in God's power in tough times

Having taken a short view of this glorious room of God's power, as it is in itself, and also in relation to his promises and providences, it remains that I urge and persuade all the people of God under their fears and dangers, according to God's gracious invitation, to enter into it, shut their doors, and to behold with delight this glorious attribute working for them in all their difficulties and distresses. Enter into this room of divine power, all you who fear the Lord, and hide yourselves there in those dangerous and distressing days. Let me say to you as the prophet did to the poor distressed Jews, 'Return to your fortress, O prisoners of hope; even now I announce that I will restore twice as much to you' (Zech. 9:12). 'Fortress', they might ask, 'why, where is it? The walls of Jerusalem are in the dust, the temple burnt with fire, Zion a heap; what do you mean by telling us of our fortress?' Why, admit all this, yet there is refuge enough for you in God alone. Christian, are you not able to find a good nourishment for your soul by faith out of the almighty power of God?

The renowned saints of old did so. Abraham, Isaac, and Jacob met with as many difficulties and depths of trouble in their time as ever you did, or shall meet with. And yet, by the exercise of their faith upon this attribute, they lived with great comfort, and why cannot you? 'I appeared', said God, 'to Abraham, to Isaac and to Jacob as God Almighty' (Exod. 6:3). They kept house and feasted by faith upon this name. O that we could do as Abraham did (Rom. 4:21). We have the same attribute, but, alas, we have not such a faith as his was to improve it. It is easy to believe the almighty power of God when life is comfortable, but not so easy to resign ourselves to it, and securely rest upon it, in a storm of adversity. But oh, what peace and rest would our faith procure us by the free use and exercise of it this way!

To assist your faith in this difficulty where we find even the faith of a Moses sometimes stumbled, let me briefly offer you these four following encouragements.

1. Consider how your gracious God has engaged his almighty power by promise and covenant for the security of his people.

God pawned it, as it were, to Abraham, in that famous promise, 'I am God Almighty; walk before me and be blameless' (Gen. 17:1), and 'Do not be afraid, Abram. I am your shield' (Gen. 15:1). Do not say, this was Abraham's peculiar privilege, for if you consult Hosea 12:4 and Hebrews 13:5, 6, you will find that believers in *these* days have as good a title to the promises made in *those* days, as those worthies had to whom they were immediately made.

2. If you are believers, your relation to God strongly engages his power for you, as well as his own promises.

'"Surely they are my people, sons who will not be false to me"; and so he became their Saviour' (Isa. 63:8). Let your wife, child, or friend be in imminent danger, and it shall engage all the power you have to help and deliver them.

3. This glorious power of God is engaged for you by the very malice and wickedness of your enemies, who will be ready to blame the weakness of God's power for the ruin of the saints.

From where those excellent arguments are drawn, 'If you put these people to death all at one time, the nations who have heard this report about you will say, "The LORD was not able to bring these people into the land he promised them on oath; so he slaughtered them in the desert"' (Num. 14:15, 16). And again, you will find the Lord improving this argument for them himself. If they do not plead it for themselves, he will: 'I said I would scatter them and blot out their memory from mankind, but I dreaded the taunt of the enemy, lest the adversary misunderstand and say, "Our hand has triumphed; the LORD has not done all this"' (Deut. 32:26, 27). O see how much you are indebted to the very rage of your enemies for your deliverance from them!

4. To conclude, the very reliance of your souls by faith upon the power of God, your very leaning upon his arm, engages it for your protection.

'You will keep in perfect peace him whose mind is steadfast, because he trusts in you' (Isa. 26:3). Do not puzzle therefore any longer about whether you are qualified, but know that the very acting of your faith on God, the resting of your souls upon him, is that which will engage him for your defence, however weak and defective you are in other respects.

II

Be Encouraged: God Is at Work!

THIS is the first section from Flavel's best-known work, *The Mystery of Providence*, which is a series of sermons on Psalm 57:2. Flavel says, 'There are two ways whereby the blessed God condescends to manifest himself to men, his word, and his works.' It is through the works of providence, in other words, that we see God in his world. Flavel has no desire to explore the doctrine of providence as such, but focuses on the implications of this doctrine for those who respond to the gospel. The key lesson of the text is that it is our duty to observe God's providence in his dealings with us. As we discover his hand on our lives, our faith will be strengthened.

I cry out to God Most High, to God, who fulfils his purpose for me.—Psalm 57:2

Introduction: grace for the cave

THE greatness of God is a glorious and unsearchable mystery: the Lord Most High is terrible, he is a great king over all the earth. The condescension of the Most High God to men is also a profound mystery: 'Though the LORD is on high, he looks upon the lowly, but the proud he knows from afar' (Psa. 138:6). But when both these meet together (as they do in this scripture) they make up a matchless mystery. Here we find the Most High God working all things for a poor distressed creature.

It is the great support and comfort of the saints in all the distresses that befall them here, that there is a wise spirit sitting in all the wheels of motion, and governing the most hostile creatures, and their most wicked designs to blessed and happy issues. And indeed it would be unbearable to live in a world devoid of God and providence.

How deeply we are concerned in this matter will appear by that great instance, which this psalm presents us with. It was composed (as the title notes) by David in prayer, when he hid himself from Saul in the cave. The heading for the psalm says, 'When he fled from Saul into the cave.' Three things are remarkable in the psalm: David's extreme danger; his earnest address to God in that danger; and the arguments he pleads with God in that address.

His extreme danger is shown both in the title and body of the psalm. The title tells us that this psalm was composed by him when he hid himself from Saul in the cave. This cave was in the wilderness of Engedi, among the broken rocks where the wild goats inhabited, an obscure and desolate hole. Yet even there the envy of Saul pursued him (1 Sam. 24:1, 2). And now he had been so long hunted as a partridge upon the mountains that he seems to be enclosed in the net. The place was surrounded with his enemies, having no other way out, and Saul himself was entering into the mouth of this cave, where David's men were hiding. Judge how great a danger and to what a desperate state things were now brought. Well might he say, 'I am in the midst of lions; I lie among ravenous beasts—men whose teeth are spears and arrows, whose tongues are sharp swords' (Psa. 57:4). What hope now remained? What but immediate destruction could be expected?

Yet not even this frightened him out of his faith and duty, but he prays in the very jaws of death, and earnestly addresses himself to God for mercy: 'Have mercy on me, O God, have mercy on me' (verse 1). This excellent psalm was composed by him when there was enough anxiety to distress the best man in the world. The repetition notes both the reality of the danger, and the conviction of David at prayer. Mercy! Mercy! Nothing but mercy, and that exerting itself in an extraordinary way, can now save him from ruin.

The arguments he pleads for obtaining mercy in this distress are very considerable. He pleads his dependence upon God as an argument to move mercy. 'Have mercy on me, my God, have mercy on me, for in you my soul takes refuge. I will take refuge in the shadow of your wings until the disaster has passed' (verse 1). This is his trust and dependence on God, though it be not argumentative in respect of the dignity of the act; yet it is so in respect both of the nature of the object, a compassionate God, who will not expose any who take shelter under his wings; and in respect of the promise, whereby protection is assured to them that fly to him for sanctuary: 'You will keep in perfect peace him whose mind is steadfast, because he trusts in you' (Isa. 26:3). Thus he encourages himself as he reflects on the God to whom he takes himself in prayer. He also pleads former experiences of his help in past distresses as an argument encouraging hope under the present danger: 'I cry out to God Most High, to God, who fulfils his purpose for me' (verse 2).

The duty resolved upon is 'I cry to God'. Crying to God is an expression that not only denotes prayer, but intense and fervent prayer. To cry is to pray in a holy passion; and such are usually speeding prayers (Psa. 18:6 and Heb. 5:7). The encouragements to this resolution are twofold: one is taken from the sovereignty of God; the other, from the experience he had of God's providence.

1. The sovereignty of God

'I cry to God Most High.' Upon this he puts his faith into action whilst in great danger. Saul is high, but God is the Most High; and, without God's permission, he is assured Saul cannot touch him. He had none to help, and even if he had, he knew God must first help the helpers, or they cannot help him. He had no means of defence or escape before him, but the Most High is not limited by means. This is a singular encouragement to faith (Psa. 59:9).

2. The experience of his providence to date

'To God, who vindicates me' (verse 2). The Lord has brought all his doubtful and difficult matters before to the best outcome, and this gives David encouragement, that he will still be gracious, and perfect that which concerns him now, as he speaks, 'The Lord will fulfil his purpose for me; your love, O Lord, endures forever—do not abandon the works of your hands' (Psa. 138:8). And it is a certain truth that all the results and issues of providence are profitable and beneficial to the saints. Payment is the performance of promises. Grace makes the promise, and providence the payment.

For it cannot but be a great encouragement to his faith, that God's providence had never failed him in any of the dangers that he ever met with (and his life was a life of many dangers). He might well hope it would not now fail him, though this were an extraordinary and matchless one.

A powerful, enraged and implacable enemy had driven him into the hole of a rock, and came after him into that hole. Now whilst his soul is among lions, whilst he lies in a cranny of the rock, expecting every moment to be dragged out to death, the reflections he had upon the gracious work of the Most High for him, from the beginning to that moment, support his soul, and inspire hope and life into his prayers: 'I cry to God Most High, to God, who fulfils his purpose for me.'

God's providence and our duty

The doctrine which I set before you is that it is the duty of the saints, especially in times of danger, to reflect upon the workings of providence for them in all the states and through all the stages of their lives.

The church, in all the works of mercy, owns the hand of God; 'Lord, you establish peace for us; all that we have accomplished you have done for us' (Isa. 26:12). And still it has been the godly and constant practice of the saints in all generations to preserve the memory of the more famous and remarkable providences that have befallen them in their times as a precious treasure. Thus Moses, by divine direction, wrote a memorial of that victory obtained over Amalek, as the fruit and answer of prayer, and built there an altar with this inscription, 'Jehovah-Nissi—The Lord is my banner' (Exod. 17:14, 15). Thus Mordecai and Esther took all care to perpetuate the memory of that remarkable deliverance from the plot of Haman: 'These days should be remembered and observed in every generation by every family, and in every province and in every city. And these days of Purim should never cease to be celebrated by the Jews, nor should the memory of them die out among their descendants' (Esther 9:28).

Now there is a twofold reflection upon the providential works of God.

(1) One is *entire and full*, in its whole complex and perfect frame. This blessed sight is reserved for the perfect state: it is on that mountain of God where we shall see both the wilderness and Canaan, the glorious kingdom into which we will come, and the way through which we were led into it. There the saints shall have a delightful view of that beautiful frame, and every part shall be clearly seen to have had its particular use, and as it was connected with the other parts. And we shall see how effectively and orderly they all came to bring about that blessed design of their salvation, according to the promise, 'And we know that all things work together for good to them that love God' (Rom. 8:28 KJV). For it is certain that no ship at sea keeps more exactly by the compass which directs its course than providence does by that promise, which is its Pole Star.

(2) The other is *partial and imperfect* on the way to glory, where we only view it in its single acts, or, at most, in some branches and more observable course of actions.

The difference between these two perspectives is the same as the difference between the sight of the disjointed wheels, and scattered pins of a watch, and the sight of the whole united in one frame, and working in one orderly motion; or between an ignorant spectator's viewing some more observable vessel or joint of a dissected body, and the accurate anatomist's discerning the course of all the veins and arteries of the body, as he follows the several branches of them through the whole, and plainly sees the proper places, figure, and use of each, with their mutual respect to one another.

O how ravishing and delightful a sight is that! To behold, at one view the whole design of providence, and the proper place and use of every single act, which we could not understand in this world. For what Christ said to Peter is as applicable to some providences in which we are now concerned, as it was to that particular action: 'You do not realize now what I am doing, but later you will understand' (John 13:7). All the dark, intricate, puzzling providences at which we were sometimes so confused, and sometimes amazed, which we could neither reconcile with the promise, nor with each other, nay, which we so unjustly censured and bitterly bewailed as if they had fallen out quite cross to our happiness, we shall then see to be to us as the difficult passage through the wilderness was unto Israel, 'a right way to a city where they could settle' (Psa. 107:7).

And though our present views and reflections upon providence are so short and imperfect, in comparison of that in heaven, yet such as it is, under all its present disadvantages, it has so much excellency and sweetness in it, that I may call it a little heaven, or, as Jacob called his Bethel, the gate of heaven. It is certainly a highway of walking with God in this world; and as sweet communion may a soul enjoy with him in his providences, as in any of his ordinances. How often have the hearts of its observers been melted into tears of joy at the beholding of its wise and unexpected productions! How often has it convinced them, upon a sober recollection of the events of their lives, that if the Lord had left them to their own counsels, they had as often been their own tormentors, if not executioners! Into what, and how many fatal mischiefs had they precipitated themselves, if providence had been as short-sighted as they! They have given it their hearty thanks for considering their interest more than their importunity, and not suffering them to perish by their own desires.

The benefits of reflecting on the works of providence are manifold and unspeakable, as in its place we shall show you. I now intend to prove *that the concerns of the saints in this world are conducted by the absolute wisdom and care of special providence.*

God's providential care: eight lessons for Christians

1. God turns nature whichever way he chooses.

How comes it to pass that so many clear mercies and deliverances have befallen the people of God, above the power and against the course of natural causes, to make way for which, there has been an obvious suspension and stop put to the course of nature? It is most evident that no natural effect can exceed the power of its natural cause. Nothing can give to another more than it has in itself, and it is as clear that whatsoever acts naturally, acts necessarily. Fire burns to the uttermost of its power, waters overflow and drown all that they can, lions and other predators, especially when hungry, tear and devour their prey. For arbitrary and rational agents, they also act according to the principles and laws of their natures. And a wicked man, when his heart is fully set in him, and his will stands in a full bent of resolution, will certainly (if he has the power in his hand, and opportunity to execute his conceived evil) give it vent, and perpetrate the wicked devices of his heart, for having once conceived evil, and travailing in pain with it (according to the course of nature) he must bring it forth (Psa. 7:14). But if any of these inanimate, brutal, or rational agents, when there is no natural obstacle, have their power suspended, and that when the effect is near the birth, and the design at the very article of execution, so that though they would, yet cannot hurt, what is the reason you can give for this? And this is exactly what has often been seen where God's interest has been immediately concerned in the danger and evil of the event.

The sea divided itself in its own channel, and made a wall of water on each side to give God's distressed Israel a safe passage, and that not in a calm, but when the waves roared, as it is in Isaiah 51:15. The fire, when blown up to the most intense and vehement flame, had no power to singe one hair of God's faithful witnesses, when at the same instant it had power to destroy their intended executioners at a greater distance (Dan. 3:22). In fact, we find it has some time been sufficient to consume, but not to torment the body; as in that known instance of blessed Bainham,[1] who told his enemies that the flames were to him as a bed of roses. The hungry lions put off their natural fierceness, and became gentle and harmless when Daniel was cast among them for a prey. A similar account is given in early church history of Polycarp, whom the fire would not touch, but stood after the manner of a ship's sail, filled with the wind about him.

Are these things according to the course and law of nature? To what secret and natural cause can they be ascribed? In like manner, we find the vilest and fiercest of wicked men have been withheld by an invisible hand of restraint from injuring the Lord's people. By what secret cause in nature was Jeroboam's hand dried up, and made inflexible at the same instant it was stretched out against the man of God (1 Kings 13:4)? No wild beasts tear and devour their prey more greedily than wicked men would destroy the people of God that dwell among them, were it not for this providential restraint upon them. So the psalmist expresses his case in the words following my text, 'I am in the midst of lions; I lie among ravenous beasts' (Psa. 57:4). The *disciples* were sent forth as sheep in the midst of *wolves* (Matt. 10:16).

It will not help, in this case, to object that those miraculous events depend only upon scripture-testimony, which the atheist is not convinced by: for besides all that may be alleged for the authority of that testimony (which is needless to produce to men that own it), what is it less than every eye sees, or may see at this day? Do we not behold a weak, defenceless handful of men, wonderfully and (except this way) unaccountably preserved from

[1] James Bainham, a martyr of the English Reformation.

ruin in the midst of potent, enraged, and turbulent enemies, who would destroy them but cannot; when as yet, no natural explanation can be given why they cannot?

And what shall we say, when we see events produced in the world for the good of God's chosen, by those very hands and means which were intentionally employed for their ruin? These things are as much against the intentions of their enemies, as they are above their own expectations. Yet such things are no rarities in the world. Was not the envy of Joseph's brothers, the cursed plot of Haman, and the decree procured by the envy of the princes against Daniel, with many more of the like nature, all turned by a secret and strange hand of providence, to their greater advancement and benefit? Their enemies lifted them up to all the honour and preferment they had.

2. God orders all events and atoms for our good.

How is it (if the saints' concerns are not ordered by a special divine providence) that natural causes unite and associate themselves for their relief and benefit, in so strange a manner as they are found to do?

It is undeniably evident that there are marvellous co-incidences of providence, and agreeing as it were to meet and unite themselves to bring about the good of God's chosen. There is a like face of things showing itself in different places at that time when any work for the good of the church is come upon the stage of the world. As when the Messiah came to the temple, then Simeon and Anna were brought there by providence as witnesses to it. So in reformation-work, when the images were pulled down in Holland, one and the same spirit of zeal possessed them in every city and town, so that the work was done in a night. He who carefully reads the history of Joseph's advancement to be lord of Egypt may number in that story twelve remarkable acts or steps of providence, by which he ascended to that honour and authority. If but one of them had failed, in all likelihood the event would have done so, too; but every one fell in its order, exactly keeping its own time and place. So in the church's deliverance from the plot of Haman, we find no less than seven acts of providence concurring strangely to produce it, as if they had all met by appointment and consent to break that snare for them; one thing so aptly suiting with and making way for another, that every heedful observer must needs conclude, this cannot be the effect of *casualty*,[2] but wise *counsel*.

Even as in viewing the complex structure of the human body, the figure, position, and mutual respects of the several members and vessels, have convinced some (and is sufficient to convince all) that it was the effect of divine wisdom and power. In like manner, if the admirable adapting of the means and instruments employed for mercy to the people of God is carefully considered, who can but confess that as there are tools of all sorts and sizes in the shop of providence, so there is a most skilful hand that uses them; and that they could no more produce such effects of themselves, than the axe, saw, or chisel can cut or carve a rude log into a beautiful figure, without the hand of a skilful craftsman.

We find by manifold instances that there certainly are strong combinations and predispositions of persons and things to bring about some issue and design for the benefit of the church, which they themselves never thought of. They hold no intelligence and don't communicate their counsels to each other, yet meet together and work together as if they did. It is as if ten men should all meet together at one place, and in one hour, about one and the same business, and that without any fore-appointment between themselves. Can any question but such a meeting of means and instruments is certainly, though secretly, overruled by some wise invisible agent?

[2] i.e., chance, or chance occurrence.

3. *God protects his people through the most unlikely means.*

If the concerns of God's people are not governed by a special providence, how do we explain that the most apt and powerful means employed to destroy them, are rendered ineffectual, while weak, contemptible means employed for their defence and comfort are crowned with success? This could never be, if things were wholly swayed by the course of nature.

If we judge by that rule, we must conclude the more apt and powerful the means are, the more successful and prosperous they must needs be, and where they are inept, weak, and contemptible, nothing can be expected from them. Thus reason lays it according to the rules of nature; but providence crosses its hands, as Jacob did in blessing the sons of Joseph, and orders quite contrary issues and events.

Such was the mighty power and deep policy used by Pharaoh to destroy God's Israel, that to the eye of reason it was as impossible to survive it, as for crackling thorns to abide unconsumed amidst devouring flames. It is by this sign that their miraculous preservation is expressed (Exod. 3:2). The bush was all in a flame, but was not burnt up. The heathen Roman emperors, who made the world tremble, and subdued the nations under them, have employed all their power and policy against the poor, naked, defenceless church to ruin it, yet could not accomplish it (Rev. 12:3, 4). O the seas of blood that heathen Rome shed in the ten persecutions! Yet the church lives! And when the dragon gave his power to the beast (Rev. 13:2, i.e. the state of Rome became anti-Christian), O what slaughters have been made by the beast in all his dominions! Therefore, the Holy Ghost represents him as drunken with the blood of the saints (Rev. 17:6). And yet all will not do: the gates, i.e. the powers and policies of hell cannot prevail against it.

How manifest is the care and power of providence herein! Had half that power been employed against any other people, it would have certainly swallowed them up immediately, or in the hundredth part of the time worn them out. How soon was the Persian monarchy swallowed up by the Grecian, and that again by the Roman, while Diocletian and Maximinus, in the height of their persecution, found themselves so baffled by providence, that they both resigned the government, and lived as private men. But in this wonderful preservation God makes good his promise: 'Though I completely destroy all the nations among which I scatter you, I will not completely destroy you' (Jer. 30:11), and 'no weapon forged against you will prevail' (Isa. 54:17).

On the contrary, how successful have weak and contemptible means been made for the good of the church! In the first planting of Christianity in the world, by what weak contemptible instruments was it done! Christ did not choose the eloquent orators, or men of authority in the courts of kings and emperors, but twelve poor labourers and fishermen. These were not sent together in a troop, but some to take one country to conquer it, and some another, the most ridiculous course (in appearance) for such a design as could be imagined. And yet in how short a time was the gospel spread, and the churches planted by them in the several kingdoms of the world! This the psalmist foresaw by the spirit of prophecy, when he said, 'From the lips of children and infants you have ordained praise because of your enemies, to silence the foe and the avenger' (Psa. 8:2). At the sound of rams' horns Jericho was delivered into the hands of Israel (see Josh. 6:20). By three hundred men with their jars and lamps, the huge host of Midian was overthrown (Judg. 7:19). The Protestants, besieged in Beziers in France, were delivered by a drunken drummer, who, going to his quarters at midnight, rang the alarm-bell of the town, not knowing what he did, and just then were their enemies making the assault.

And as weak and improbable means have been blessed with success to the church in general, so they have worked for the preservation of its particular members also. A spider, by weaving her web over the mouth of an oven, hid a servant of Christ, Du Moulin, from his enemies, who took refuge there in the bloody Parisian massacre. A hen sustained another many days at the same time, by lodging her egg every day in the place where he had hid himself from the cut-throats. Examples might be easily multiplied in the case, but the truth is too plain and obvious to the observation of all ages to need them. And can we but acknowledge a divine and special providence overruling these matters, when we see the most apt and potent means for the church's ruin frustrated, and the most silly and contemptible means succeed and prosper for its good?

4. Providence rules over persecution.

If all things are governed by the course of nature, and force of natural causes, how then comes it to pass that men are turned out of the way of evil to which they were driving on with full speed? Good men have been engaged in the way to their own ruin, and knew it not; but providence has met them in the way, and preserved them by strange means, the meaning of which they did not understand, until the event discovered it.

Paul lay bound at Caesarea, while the high priest and chief of the Jews made a request to Festus that he might be brought bound to Jerusalem, having laid wait in the way to kill him. But Festus (though ignorant of the plot) refused it, but chose rather to go with him to Caesarea, and judge him there. By this outcome their bloody design was frustrated (Acts 25:3, 4).

How memorable and wonderful these frustrations are that wicked men have met with in the way of perpetrating the evils conceived and intended in their own hearts. Laban and Esau came against Jacob with mischievous purposes (Gen. 31:24), but no sooner did they come to him, but the shackles of restraint were immediately clapped upon them both, so that their hands could not perform their enterprises. Balaam ran greedily for reward to curse Israel; but met with an unexpected check at his very outset, and though that didn't stop him, and he tried every way to do them harm, yet he still found himself fettered by a powerful restraint, that he could in no way shake off (Num. 22:25-38). Saul, the high priest's blood-hound, breathed out threatenings against the church, and went with a bloody commission to Damascus, to bring the poor flock of Christ to the slaughter; but when he came near to the place, he met an unexpected stop in the way, by which the wicked plan was not only diverted, but himself converted to Christ (Acts 9:1-4). Who can but see the finger of God in these things?

5. God can and does repay in this life.

If there is not an overruling providence, ordering all things for the good of God's people, how comes it to pass that the good and evil which is done to them in this world is accordingly repaid into the lives of them who are instrumental in them?

How clear is it to every man's observation that the kindnesses and benefits any have done to the Lord's people, have been rewarded with full measure into their lives! The Hebrew midwives refused to obey Pharaoh's inhuman command, and saved the male children of Israel. For this the Lord dealt well with them, and gave them their own families (Exod. 1:21). The Shunammite was hospitable and careful for Elisha, and God recompensed it with her longed-for enjoyment of a son (2 Kings 4:9, 17, 31). Rahab hid the spies, and was saved from the common destruction for Jericho (Heb. 11:31). Publius, the chief man of the island Melitus, generously received and lodged Paul after his shipwreck, and the Lord speedily repaid him for that kindness, and healed his father, who lay sick with fever and dysentery (Acts 28:7, 8).

In like manner, we find the evils done to God's people have been repaid, by a just retribution, to their enemies. Pharaoh and the Egyptians were cruel enemies to God's Israel, and designed the ruin of their poor innocent babes; and God repaid it, in smiting all the firstborn of Egypt in one night (Exod. 12:29). Haman erected a gallows, fifty cubits high, for good Mordecai; and God so ordered it, that he himself and his ten sons were hanged on it. Indeed, it was fitting that he should eat the fruit of that tree which he himself had planted (Esther 7:10).

Ahithophel plots against David, and gives counsel like an oracle, how to procure his fall. That very counsel, like an overcharged gun, recoils upon himself, and procures his ruin. Seeing his good counsel rejected (good politically, not morally) it was now easy for him to guess at the issue, and so at his own fate (2 Sam. 17:23).

Charles IX most inhumanely made the very canals of Paris stream with Protestant blood, and soon after he died miserably, his blood streaming from all parts of his body. Stephen Gardiner, who burned so many of God's dear servants to ashes, was himself so scorched up by a terrible inflammation, that his very tongue was black, and hung out of his mouth, and in dreadful torment ended his wretched days.

Maximinus, that cruel emperor, who set forth his proclamation for the utter abolishing of the Christian religion, was speedily smitten like Herod with a dreadful judgment. Swarms of lice preyed upon his entrails, and causing such a stench that his physicians could not endure to come near him, and, for refusing it, were slain. Hundreds of like instances might easily be produced, to confirm this observation. And who can but see by these things, that 'truly, there is a God who judges the earth'?

So exact have been the retributions of providence to the enemies of the church, that not only the same persons, but the same members that have been the instruments of wickedness, have been made the subjects of wrath. The same arm which Jeroboam stretched out to smite the prophet, God smites. The emperor Aurelian, when he was ready to subscribe the edict for the persecution of the Christians, had sudden cramp in his knuckles, so that he could not write.

Mr Greenhill, in his exposition upon Ezekiel 11:13, tells his listeners that there was one then present in the congregation, who was an eye-witness of a woman scoffing at another for purity and holy living, who had her tongue stricken immediately with the palsy, and died within two days.

Henry II of France, in a great rage against a Protestant counsellor, committed him to the hands of one of his nobles, to be imprisoned, declaring that he would see him burnt with his own eyes. But mark the righteous providence of God! Within a few days after, the same nobleman, with a lance put into his hands by the king, ran the lance into one of the king's eyes, which was the cause of his death.

Providence has even made the very place of sinning the place of punishment: 'In the place where dogs licked up Naboth's blood, dogs will lick up your blood' (1 Kings 21:19), and it was exactly fulfilled (2 Kings 9:26ff.). Thus Tophet is made a burying place for the Jews, until there is no room to bury, and that was the place where they had offered up their sons to Molech (Jer. 7:31, 32). The story of Nightingale is generally known, which Mr Foxe relates, how he fell out of the pulpit, and broke his neck while he was abusing the text of Scripture, 1 John 1:10. And so the Scriptures are made good by providence, ' If a man digs a pit, he will fall into it; if a man rolls a stone, it will roll back on him' (Prov. 26:27), and 'with the measure you use, it will be measured to you.' (Matt. 7:2).

So what if people say that these things happen anyway, and that many thousands of the church's enemies have died in peace, and their end been like that of other men? We answer with Augustine, that if no sin were punished here, no providence would be believed, and if every sin should be punished here, no judgment would be expected. But so that none may think these events are merely coincidence, we yet further demand,

6. Providence agrees with Scripture.

How is it that they square and agree so exactly with the Scriptures in all particulars? We read in Amos 3:3, 'Do two walk together unless they have agreed to do so?' If two men travel on one road, it is likely they are agreed to go to the same place. Providences and scriptures go all one way: and if they seem at any time to go different or contrary ways, be sure they will meet at the journey's end: there is an agreement between them to do so.

Does God miraculously suspend the power of natural causes? Why, this is no accidental thing, but what harmonizes with the word: 'When you pass through the waters, I will be with you; and when you pass through the rivers, they will not sweep over you. When you walk through the fire, you will not be burned; the flames will not set you ablaze.' (Isa. 43:2).

Do natural causes unite and associate themselves for the good of God's people? Why, this is no more than what is contained in the promises, and is but the fulfilling of that scripture, 'All [things] are yours, for you are of Christ' (1 Cor. 3:22, 23), i.e. the use, benefit, and service of all things are for you, as your need shall require.

Are the most apt and powerful means employed for their ruin frustrated? Who can but see the Scriptures fulfilled in and expounded by such providences? (See Isa. 45:15-17 and 8:7-10, expounded by 2 Kings 18:17ff.)

At any time a rub of providence diverts the course of good men from falling into evil, or wicked men from committing evil: how loudly do such providences proclaim the truth and certainty of the Scriptures, which tell us, 'a man's life is not his own; it is not for man to direct his steps' (Jer. 10:23).

And when you see the evils men have done, or intended to do to the Lord's people, recoiling upon themselves, he is perfectly blind who can't see the harmony such providences bear with these scriptures, Psalm 140:11, 12; 7:14-16; 9:16.

What exact proportions do providences and scriptures hold! Little do men take notice of it. Why did Cyrus, contrary to all rules of state policy, freely dismiss the captives, except to fulfil that scripture, Isaiah 45:13. It was well observed that as God has stretched out the firmament over the natural world, so he has stretched out his word over the rational world. And as the creatures on earth are influenced by those heavenly bodies, so are all creatures in the world influenced by the word, and do infallibly fulfil it when they design to cross it.

7. God moves exactly when he should.

If these things be so, how is it that they fall out in such remarkable nicks and junctures of time, which make them so greatly observable to all that consider them? We find a multitude of providences so timed to the minute, that had they fallen out just a moment sooner or later, we would have missed the significance which we now see in them.

How remarkable to this purpose was the news brought to Saul, that the Philistines had invaded the land, just as he was ready to grasp the prey (1 Sam. 23:27). The angel calls to Abraham, and shows him another sacrifice, just when his hand was giving the fatal stroke to Isaac (Gen. 22:10, 11). A well of water is shown to Hagar just when she had left the child, when she could not bear to see his death (Gen. 21:16-19). Rabshakeh meets with a devastating providence, hearing a rumour that frustrated his plans, just when ready to move against Jerusalem (Isa. 37:7, 8). So when Haman's plot against the Jews was ripe, and all things ready for execution, 'that night the king could not sleep' (Esther 6:1). When the horns are ready to gore Judah, immediately carpenters are prepared to cut them off (Zech. 1:18-21). If these things happen by chance, how is it they observe time so very exactly? As the Scripture says proverbially, 'On the mountain of the Lord it will be provided' (Gen. 22:14).

8. Prayer and providence always serve one another.

Lastly, if these things are mere coincidence, how can it be that they should fall out so immediately after, and with accord to, the prayers of the saints; so that, in many providences, they are able to discern a very clear answer to their prayers, and are sure they have the petitions they asked of him (1 John 5:15)?

Think about when the sea divided itself just upon Israel's cry to heaven (Exod. 14:10); when so signal a victory is given to Asa, immediately upon that heart-cry to heaven, 'Help us, O Lord our God!' (2 Chron. 14:11, 12). Remember when Ahithophel hanged himself, just upon that prayer of distressed David (2 Sam. 15:31), or when Haman fell, and his plot was broken, just upon the fast kept by Mordecai and Esther (Esther 4:16). Abraham's servant prayed for success, and see how it was answered (Gen. 24:45). Peter was cast into prison, and prayer was made for him by the church, and see the event (Acts 12:5-7, 12). I could easily add to these the wonderful examples of the return of prayers which was observed in Luther and Dr Winter in Ireland, and many more; but I judge it needless, because most Christians have a stock of experience of their own, and are well assured that many of the providences that befall them are, and can be no other than, the return of their prayers.

And now who can be dissatisfied in this point who wisely consider these things? Must we not conclude as it is: 'He does not take his eyes off the righteous' (Job 36:7). 'The eyes of the Lord range throughout the earth, to strengthen those whose hearts are fully committed to him' (2 Chron. 16:9). His providences proclaim him to be a God who hears prayers.

12

How to Look for
God's Work in Your Life

THIS is a further extract from the first section of *The Mystery of Providence*, sermons on Psalm 57:2. Flavel's contention is that God is always at work in the world, and especially in his people, and therefore, we have a responsibility to discern his providence.

This is a discipline as well as a delight. So often, we are tempted to shrug our shoulders at the complexities of life, and just hope that God is somewhere and somehow at work. Flavel challenges us to look carefully at life's circumstances in the light of Scripture, so that we can see God's hand.

He gives us seven reasons for doing so, and then shows us ten ways in which providence works in harmony with God's word. Finally, Flavel brings the lessons of providence to bear upon the hearts of both believers and unbelievers, with the aim of producing a response of worship.

I cry out to God Most High, to God, who fulfils his purpose for me.—Psalm 57:2

HAVING proved that the concerns of the people of God are governed by the care of special providence, and given many examples of what effect providence has upon them, we come in the next place to prove it to be the duty of God's people to reflect upon these performances of providence for them at all times, but especially in times of difficulties and troubles.

Why look for God's providence?

1. This is our duty, because God has expressly commanded it, and called his people to make the most serious reflections upon his works, whether of mercy or judgment.

So when that most dreadful of all judgments was executed upon his professing people for their apostasy from God, and God had removed the symbols of his presence from among them, the rest are commanded, 'Go now to the place of Shiloh where I first made a dwelling for my Name, and see what I did to it because of the wickedness of my people Israel' (Jer. 7:12). So it is also with regard to God's mercies: God calls us to consider and to review them: 'Remember your journey from Shittim to Gilgal, that you may know the righteous acts of the Lord' (Mic. 6:5). If you do not reflect upon that signal providence,

my faithfulness will be covered, and your unfaithfulness discovered. So also for God's works of providence regarding his
creation: we are called to consider them, that we may prop
up our faith by those considerations for our own supplies—
consider the birds and lilies (Matt. 6:28).

*2. It is plain that this is our duty, because the neglect of it is
everywhere in Scripture condemned as a sin.*

To be of a heedless, unobservant attitude is very displeasing to
God, and so much appears by that scripture 'O LORD, your
hand is lifted high, but they do not see it' (Isa. 26:11). No, it is
a sin which God threatens and denounces woe against in his
word (Psa. 28:4, 5; Isa. 5:12, 13). God not only threatens, but
smites men with visible judgments for this sin (Job 34:26, 27).

*3. And for this end and purpose it is, that the Holy Spirit has
fixed those notes of attention to the narratives of the works of
providence in Scripture, all of which invite and call men to a
due and clear observation of them.*

So in that great and celebrated work of providence, in delivering Israel out of Egyptian bondage, you find a note of attention
twice fixed to it (Exod. 3:2, 9). So when that daring enemy
Rabshakeh (who put Hezekiah and all the people into such
fear) was defeated by providence, there is a note of attention
prefixed to that providence: 'Listen! I am going to put such a
spirit in him …' (2 Kings 19:7). At the opening of every seal
which contains a remarkable series or branch of providence,
how particularly is attention commanded to every one of
them: 'Come' (Rev. 6:1-7). All these are very useless and super-
fluous additions in Scripture, if no such duty lies upon us (see
Psa. 66:5).

4. Without due observation of the works of providence, no praise can be rendered to God for any of them.

Praise and thanksgiving for mercies depend upon this act of observation of them, and cannot be performed without it. Psalm 107 is full of narratives of God's providential care of men; to his people in difficulties (verses 4-6), to prisoners in their chains (verses 10-12), to men who lie languishing on their sickbeds (verses 17-19), to seamen upon the stormy ocean (verses 23-32), to men in times of famine (verses 33-40). In fact, his providence is displayed in all those changes that fall out in the world, debasing the high, and exalting the low (verses 40, 41). And at every section of the psalm men are still called upon to praise God for each of these providences; but verse 43 shows you what a necessary ingredient to that duty observation is: 'Whoever is wise, let him heed these things, and consider the great love of the LORD.' God must be defrauded of his praise if this duty be neglected.

5. Without this, we lose the usefulness and benefit of all the works of God for us or for others, which would be an unspeakable loss indeed to us.

This is the food our faith lives upon in days of distress. 'It was you who crushed the heads of Leviathan, and gave him as food to the creatures of the desert' (Psa. 74:14), i.e. food to their faith. From providences past, saints used to argue for fresh and new ones to come. So David says, 'The LORD who delivered me from the paw of the lion and the paw of the bear will deliver me from the hand of this Philistine' (1 Sam. 17:37), and Paul says, 'He has delivered us from such a deadly peril, and he will deliver us' (2 Cor. 1:10). If these are forgotten, or not considered, the hands of faith hang down. 'Do you still not understand? Don't you remember …?' (Matt. 16:9).

6. It is a vile slighting of God not to observe what of himself he manifests in his providences.

For in all providences, especially in some, he comes near to us. He does so in his judgments: 'I will come near to you for judgment' (Mal. 3:5). He comes near in mercies also: 'The LORD is near to all who call upon him' (Psa. 145:18). He is also said to visit us by his providence, when he corrects (Hos. 9:7), and when he saves and delivers (Psa. 106:4). These visits of God preserve our spirits, and it is a wonderful condescension in the great God to visit us so often, every morning, and every moment (Job 7:18). But not to take notice of it is a vile and brutish contempt of God (Isa. 1:3; Zeph. 3:2). You would not behave like this towards a man for whom you have any respect. It is the character of the wicked not to regard God's favours (Isa. 26:10), or frowns (Jer. 5:3).

7. In a word, men can never order their addresses to God in prayers suitable to their conditions without due observation of his providences.

Your prayers are to be suitable to your conditions. Sometimes we are called to praise, sometimes to humiliation. In the way of his judgments you are to wait for him (Isa. 26:8), to prepare to meet him (Zeph. 2:1, 2; Amos 4:12). At any one time your business is to turn away his anger, which you see approaching, and then at another time you are called to praise him for mercies received (Isa. 12:1, 2). But then you must first observe them.

How to look for God's providence

Let us next proceed to show in what manner we are to reflect upon the performances of providence for us. And certainly it is not every quick glance, nor every cold mention of, or recognition of, his providences towards you that will pass with God for a discharge of this great duty. No, it is another manner of business than the most of men understand it to be. O that we were but acquainted with this heavenly, spiritual exercise! How sweet would it make our lives! How light would it make our burdens! You live estranged from the pleasure of the Christian life, while you live in the ignorance or neglect of this duty.

Now, to lead you up to this heavenly, sweet, and profitable exercise, I will beg your attention to the following directions.

Lessons for discovering providence

1. Labour to get as full and thorough recognition of the providences of God about you as you are able.

Fill your hearts with the thoughts of him and his ways. If a single act of providence is so wonderful, what would many such be, if they were presented together to the view of the soul? If one star is so beautiful to behold, what is a constellation! Let your reflections, therefore, upon the acts and workings of providence for you, be full.

(i) Let them be as *extensively* full as may be. Search back into all the workings of providence throughout your lives. So did Asaph (Psa. 77:11, 12): 'I will remember the deeds of the LORD; yes, I will remember your miracles of long ago. I will meditate on all your works, and consider all your mighty deeds.' He laboured to bring to mind all the ancient providences of God's mercies many years past, and taste a fresh sweetness in them, by new reflections on them. Let me tell you, there is not such a pleasant history for you to read in all the world, as the history of your own lives, if you would but sit down and record to yourselves from the beginning till now, what God has been to you, and done for you: what signal manifestations and displays of his mercy, faithfulness, and love there have been in all the conditions you have passed through. If your hearts do not melt before you have gone half through that history, they are hard hearts indeed.

(ii) Let them be as *intensively* full as may be. Do not let your thoughts swim like feathers upon the surface of the waters, but sink like lead to the bottom. 'Great are the works of the LORD; they are pondered by all who delight in them' (Psa. 111:2). Not that I think it feasible to sound the depth of providence by our short line. 'Your path led through the sea, your way through the mighty waters, though your footprints were not seen' (Psa. 77:19); but it is our duty to dive as far as we can, and to marvel at the depth when we cannot touch the bottom. It is in viewing providences as it was with Elijah's servant when he looked out for rain (1 Kings 18:44). He went out once, and viewed the heavens, and saw nothing: but the prophet bids him go again and again, and look upon the face of heaven seven times; and when he had done so, the prophet asks him what he saw. 'A cloud as small as a man's hand is rising', and then, keeping his eye upon it intent, he sees the whole face of heaven covered with clouds. So you may look upon some providences once and again, and see little or nothing in them, but look seven times, i.e. meditate often upon them, and you shall see their increasing glory like that increasing cloud.

There are different things to be distinctly pondered and valued in one single providence before you can judge the amount and worth of it. (a) The *seasonableness* of mercy may give it a very great value. When it shall be timed so exactly, and fall out so seasonably as may make it a thousandfold more considerable to you than the same mercy would have been at another time. Thus when our wants are allowed to grow to an extremity, and all visible hopes fail, then to have relief given, wonderfully enhances the price of such a mercy (Isa. 41:17, 18). (b) And then the *peculiar care* and kindness of providence to us is a consideration which exceedingly heightens the mercy in itself, and endears it to us. So, when in general calamities upon the world we are exempted by the favour of providence, covered under its wings, when God shall call to us in evil days, 'Go, my people, enter your rooms', as it is in Isaiah 26:19, 20. When such promises are fulfilled to us in times of need and famine, as in Psalm 33:18-19, when others are abandoned and exposed to misery, and delivered up, but we saved—then how wonderful are such providences (Psa. 91:7, 8)!

(iii) The *introductiveness* of a providence is of special regard and consideration, and by no means to be neglected by us. There are leading providences, which, how slight and trivial they may seem in themselves, yet, in this respect, justly challenge the first rank among providential favours to us; because they usher in a multitude of other mercies, and draw a blessed train of happy consequences after them. Such a providence was that of Jesse's sending David with provisions to his brethren that lay encamped in the army (1 Sam. 17:17). And thus every Christian may furnish himself out of his own stock of experience, if he will but reflect and consider the place where he is, the relations that he has, and the way by which he was led into them.

(iv) The *instruments* employed by providence for you are of a special consideration, and the finger of God is clearly seen by us when we pursue that meditation. For sometimes great mercies shall be conveyed to us by very improbable means, and more probable ones laid aside. A stranger shall be stirred up to do that for you which your near relations in nature had no power or will to do for you. Jonathan, a mere stranger to David, was closer to him and more friendly and useful to him than his own brothers, who despised and slighted him. Ministers have found more kindness and respect from strangers than their own people that are more obliged to them. 'Only in his home town, among his relatives and in his own house is a prophet without honour' (Mark 6:4).

Sometimes God's providence comes by the hands of enemies, as well as strangers. 'The earth helped the woman' (Rev. 12:16). God has bowed the hearts of many wicked men to show great kindness to his people (Acts 27:3). At other times God makes use of instruments for good to his people, who designed nothing but evil and mischief to them. Thus Joseph's brothers were instrumental to his advancement in that very thing wherein they designed his ruin (Gen. 50:20).

(v) The *design* and *scope* of providence must not escape our thorough consideration of what the aim of providence is. And truly this, of all others, is the most warming and melting consideration. You have the general account of the aim of all providences: 'and we know that all things work together for the good of those who love God' (Rom. 8:28). A thousand friendly hands are at work for them to promote and bring about their happiness. O this is enough to sweeten the bitterness of providence to us, that we know it shall turn to our salvation (Phil. 1:19).

(vi) The *respect* and *relation* providence bears to our prayers is of singular consideration, and a most useful sweet meditation. Prayer honours providence, and providence honours prayer. Great notice is taken of this in Scripture (Gen. 24:45; Dan. 9:20; Acts 12:12). You have had the very petitions you asked of him. Providences have borne the very signatures of your prayers upon them. O how wonderful are such mercies!

2. Next, in all your observation of providence have special respect to that word of God which is fulfilled and made good to you thereby.

This is a clear truth, that all providences have relation to the written word. Thus Solomon in his prayer acknowledges that the promises and providences of God went along step by step with his father David all his days, and that his 'hand' (used there for his 'providence') had fulfilled whatever his mouth had spoken (1 Kings 8:24). So Joshua, in like manner, acknowledges, that 'not one thing had failed of all the good things which the Lord had spoken' (Josh. 23:14). He had carefully observed what relation the works of God had to his word. He compared them together, and found an exact harmony. And so may you too, if you will compare them as he did.

This I shall the more insist upon, because our text reads thus, 'I cry out to God Most High, to God who fulfils his purpose for me.' Now, though I see no reason to limit the sense so narrowly, yet it cannot be denied that this is a special part of its meaning. Let us, therefore, in all our reviews of providence, consider what word of God is at any time made good to us by his providences, whether it be of threatening, caution, counsel, or promise. And hereby a twofold excellent advantage will result to us.

(i) Firstly, it will greatly confirm to us the truth of the Scripture, when we shall see its truth so manifest in the events. Certainly, if Scripture has no other seal or witness, this alone would be an unanswerable argument of its divinity. When men shall find in all ages the work of God wrought so exactly according to this model, that we may say, As we have read or heard, so have we seen. O how great a confirmation is here before our eyes!

(ii) Secondly, this will abundantly direct and instruct us in our present duties under all providences. We shall know what we have to do, and how to behave under all changes of conditions. You can learn the voice and errand of the rod only from the word (Psa. 94:12). The word interprets the works of God. Providences in themselves are not a perfect guide. They often puzzle and entangle our thoughts; but bring them to the word, and your duty will be quickly manifested, as in Psalm 73:16, 17: 'till I entered the sanctuary of God; then I understood their final destiny'. And, not only their destiny, but his own duty, to be quiet in an afflicted condition, and not envy their prosperity.

Well then, bring those providences you have passed through, or are now under, to the word; and you will find yourselves surrounded with a marvellous light; and see the truthfulness of the Scriptures in them. I shall therefore here appeal to your consciences whether you have not found these events of providence falling out agreeable in all respects with the word.

Ten ways in which providence and God's word work together

1. The word tells you that it is your wisdom and interest to keep close to its rules and to the duties it prescribes, that the way of holiness and obedience is the wisest way—'this will show your wisdom' (Deut. 4:5-6).

Now let the events of providence speak, whether this is true or not. Certainly it will appear to be so, whether we respect our present comfort or future happiness, both of which we may see daily exposed by departure from duty, and secured by keeping close to it. Let the question be asked of the drunkard, adulterer, or profane swearer, when by sin they have ruined body, soul, estate, and name, whether it be their wisdom to walk in those forbidden paths after their own lusts? Would they not have been better off consulting their own interest and comfort in keeping within the bounds and limits of God's commands? And they cannot but confess, that this their way is their folly. 'What benefit did you reap at that time from the things you are now ashamed of? Those things result in death!' (Rom. 6:21). Does not the providence of God show the truth of the warnings that are written in the experience of all ages (Prov. 23:21, 29, 30; 5:9, 10; Job 31:12)? Those who walk in God's statutes escape all of these woes and miseries. Look upon all the ruined estates and bodies you may everywhere see, and behold the truth of the Scriptures evidently made good in those sad providences.

2. The word tells you that your departure from the way of integrity, to make use of sinful policies, shall never profit you (1 Sam. 12:21; Prov. 3:5).

Let the events of providence speak to this also: ask your own experience, and you shall have a full confirmation of this truth. Did you ever leave the way of integrity to bring about your own designs, and prosper in that way? Certainly God has cursed all the ways of sin, and whoever finds them to thrive with them, his people shall not. Israel would not rely upon the Lord, but trust in the shadow of Egypt, and what advantage had they by this sinful policy? (See Isa. 30:1-5.) David used a great deal of sinful policy to cover his wicked fact—but it did not prosper! (See 2 Sam. 12:12.)

What David gave in his charge to Solomon has been found true in the experience of thousands (1 Chron. 22:12, 13), that the true way to prosperity is to keep close to the rule of the word. And that the true reason why men cannot prosper is their forsaking that rule (2 Chron. 24:20). It is true, that if God has a purpose to destroy a man, he may for a time allow him to succeed and prosper in his sin for his greater hardening (Job 12:6). But it is not so with those whom the Lord loves, as their sinful ways shall never thrive with them.

3. The word prohibits your trust and confidence in the creature, even in the greatest and most powerful among creatures (Psa. 146:3).

It tells us that it is better to trust in the Lord than in them (Psa. 118:8). It forbids our confidence in those creatures most nearly allied and related in the bonds of nature to us (Mic. 7:5), and it curses the man who gives that reliance to the creature which is due to God (Jer. 17:5).

Consult the events of providence in this case, and see whether the word isn't confirmed in them. Did you ever lean upon an Egyptian reed, and did it not break under you, and pierce as well as deceive you? How often has this been evident in our experience? Whatever we have over-loved, idolized, and leaned upon God has from time to time broken, and made us to see the vanity of it, so that we find that the best course to be rid of our comforts is to set our hearts inordinately or immoderately upon them. For our God is a jealous God, and will not part with his glory to another. The world is full of examples of persons deprived of their comforts, husbands, wives, children, estates, etc. upon this account, and by this means. If Jonah is overjoyed in his gourd, a worm is presently prepared to eat it. Hence it is that so many graves are opened for the burying of our idols out of our sight. If David says, 'my mountain shall stand strong, I shall not be moved', the next news he shall hear is of darkness and trouble (Psa. 30:6, 7 KJV). How true and faithful do we find these sayings of God to be! Who cannot but agree and say, 'Your word is truth'?

4. The word assures us that sin is the cause and inlet of afflic-tion and sorrow, and that there is an inseparable connection between them: 'be sure your sin will find you out' (Num. 32:23).

That is, the sad effects and afflictions that follow sin shall find you out: 'If his sons forsake my law and do not follow my statutes, if they violate my decrees and fail to keep my com-mands, I will punish their sin with the rod, their iniquity with flogging' (Psa. 89:30-32).

Enquire now at the mouth of providence, whether this is indeed so, according to the reports of the word. Ask your own experiences, and you shall find that just so providence has ordered it all along your way. When did you grow into a secure, vain, carnal frame, only then to find some rousing, startling providence sent to awaken you? When did you wound your consciences with guilt, and God did not wound you for it, in some other of your beloved enjoyments? So regular is this with God, that from the observations of their own frames and ways, many Christians have anticipated and avoided troubles at hand.

I do not say that God never afflicts his people except for their sin; for he may do it for their trial (1 Pet. 4:12). Nor do I say that God follows every sin with a rod, for who then should stand before him? (Psa. 130:3)? But this I say, that it is God's usual way to visit the sins of his people with rods of affliction, and this is in mercy to their souls. Upon this account it was that the rod of God was upon David, in a long succession of

troubles upon his kingdom and family, after that great sin of
his (2 Sam. 12:10). And if we would carefully search out the
seeds and principles of those miseries under which we or ours
do groan, we should find them to be our own turnings aside
from the Lord (see Jer. 2:19; 4:18). Have not all these cautions
and threatenings of the word been exactly fulfilled by providence in your own experience? Who can but see the infallible
truth of God in all that he has threatened? And no less evident
is the truth of the promises to all that will observe how providence makes them good every day to us. For consider,

*5. How great security God has given to his people in the prom-
ises, that no man shall lose anything by self-denial for his sake.*

He has told us, 'Truly I tell you, no one who has left home or
brothers or sisters or mother or father or children or fields for
me and the gospel will fail to receive a hundred times as much
in this present age: homes, brothers, sisters, mothers, children
and fields—along with persecutions—and in the age to come
eternal life' (Mark 10:29, 30).

Though that vile apostate Julian derided this promise, yet
thousands and ten thousands have experienced it, and at this
day stand ready to set their seal to it. God has made it good
to his people, not only in the spiritual realm, with inward joy
and peace, but in the temporal realm also: instead of natural
relations, who took care for them before, hundreds of Christians shall stand ready to assist and help them, so that though
they have left all for Christ, yet they may say with the apostle,
'having nothing, and yet possessing all things' (2 Cor. 6:10).
O the admirable care and tenderness of providence over those
who, for conscience' sake, have left all, and cast themselves
upon its immediate care! Are there not at this day to be found

many so provided for, even to the envy of their enemies, and their own wonder? Who cannot see the faithfulness of God in the promises, who has but a heart to trust God in them!

6. The word of promise assures us, that whatever wants and difficulties the saints fall into, their God 'will never leave them, nor forsake them' (Heb. 13:5), and that he will be with them in trouble (Psa. 91:15).

Consult the various providences of your life to this point, and I doubt not that you will find the truth of these promises as often confirmed as you have been in trouble. Ask your own hearts, where or when was it that your God forsook you, and left you to sink and perish under your burdens? I doubt not but most of you have been at one time or other plunged in difficulties out of which you could see no way of escape by the eye of reason, difficulties which staggered your faith in the promise, as David's was when he said 'one day I shall be destroyed by the hand of Saul' (1 Sam. 27:1); and yet notwithstanding all, we see him emerge out of that sea of trouble, and the promises made good in every detail to him.

You will observe the same in your own life. Ask your own souls the question, and they will satisfy it: Did God abandon and cast you off in the day of your difficulties? Certainly you must slander your own experience, if you should say so. It is true, there have been some plunges and difficulties you have met with, wherein you could see no way of escape, but concluded you must perish in them. There have been difficulties that have staggered your faith in the promises, and made you doubt whether the fountain of all-sufficiency would let out itself for your relief. And such difficulties have provoked you to murmuring and impatience, and thereby provoked the Lord to forsake you in them; but yet you see he did not. He has either strengthened your back to bear them, or lightened your burden, or opened an unexpected door of escape, according to the promise of 1 Corinthians 10:13, so that the evil which you feared did not come upon you.

7. You read that the word of God is the only support and relief to a gracious soul in the dark day of affliction (Psa. 119:50, 92; 2 Sam. 23:5).

It was written for this very purpose (Rom. 15:4), and no rules of moral prudence or no sensual remedies can do for us what the word can do. And is not this a certain truth, attested by a thousand undeniable experiences? The saints have found their comforts in it, when fainting under the rod. One word of God can do more than ten thousand words of men to relieve a distressed soul. If providence has at any time directed you to such promises which either assure you that the Lord will be with you in trouble (Psa. 91:15) or encourage you from inward peace, to bear cheerfully outward burdens (John 16:33), or satisfy you with God's tenderness and moderation in his dealings with you (Isa. 27:8), or that you shall reap blessed fruits from them (Rom. 8:28) that confirm your security in God, and his love under your afflictions (2 Sam. 7:14), then what real comfort and relief ensue! How light is your burden, compared with what it was before!

8. The word tells us that there is no such way to improve our conditions as to lay them out with a cheerful liberality for God, and that our withholding our hands when God and duty call to distribute, will not be for our advantage (see Prov. 11:24-25; 19:17; Isa. 32:8).

Consult providence now, and you shall find it in all respects according to the report of the word. O how true is the Scripture testimony in it! There are many thousand witnesses now living who can set their seals to both parts of the conviction that what men save (as they count saving) with one hand, providence scatters by another hand. And what they scatter abroad with a liberal hand, and single eye for God, is surely repaid to them, or to theirs. Never did any man lose by distributing for God. He that lends to the poor puts his money to interest to the Lord. Some have observed how providence has doubled all they have laid out for God in ways unexpected to them.

9. The word assures us that the best expedient for a man to settle his own place in the consciences and affections of men, is to direct his ways so as to please the Lord (Prov. 16:7).

And does not providence confirm it? This the three Jews found by experience (Dan. 3:28, 29) and so did Daniel (Dan. 6:20-22). This kept up John's reputation in the conscience of Herod (Mark 6:10). So it fell out when Constantine made that exploratory decree; those who had kept their faith were in favour, and those who changed their religion expelled. Never did any man lose at last by his faithfulness.

10. The written word tells us that the best expedient to inward peace and tranquillity of mind under puzzling and distracting troubles is to commit ourselves and our case to the Lord (Psa. 37:5-7; Prov. 16:3).

And as you have read in the word, so you have found it in your own experience. O what a burden is off your shoulders when you have resigned the case to God! Then providence orders your affairs comfortably for you. The difficulty is soon over when the heart is brought to this.

Thus you see how the Scriptures are fulfilled by providence in these few instances I have given of it. Compare them in all other cases and you shall find the same, for all the lines of providence lead from the Scripture, and return thither again, and begin and end most clearly there.

Put your heart in tune with providence.

Lastly, work up your hearts to this condition, and exercise those affections which the providences of God around you call for (Eccles. 7:14). Be ready to answer the design and purpose of God in all providences. As there are various affections planted in your souls, so are there several graces planted in those affections, and several providences appointed to draw forth and exercise these graces.

When the providences of God are sad and wounding, either upon the church in general, or your families and persons in particular, then it is seasonable for you to exercise godly sorrow and humility of spirit, for in that day and by those providences God calls us to it (Isa. 22:12; Mic. 6:9). Pleasure and natural joy are out of season (Ezek. 21:10). Should we then make mirth? If there is a filial spirit in us we cannot be light and vain, when our Father is angry, and if we possess any real sense of the evil of sin which provokes God's anger, we must be heavy-hearted when God is smiting for it. Also, if we have any awareness of and compassion for the miseries that sin brings upon the world, it will make us say with David, 'I look on the faithless with loathing, for they do not obey your word' (Psa. 119:158). It is sad to consider the miseries that they pull down upon themselves in this world and in the world to come. If there is any concern in us to prevent utter ruin, and stop God in the way of his anger, we know this is the means to do it (Amos 4:12).

However sad and dismal the face of providence is, yet still maintain spiritual joy and comfort in God under all. 'Though there are no cattle in the stalls, yet I will rejoice in the Lord, I will be joyful in God my Saviour' (Hab. 3:17-18).

There are two sorts of comforts, natural and senses-related, divine and spiritual. There is a time when it becomes Christians to exercise both (so Esther 9:22). And there is a time when the former is to be suspended and laid by (Psa. 137:2). But there is no season wherein spiritual joy and comfort in God is unseasonable, as appears by those scriptures (see 1 Thess. 5:16; Phil. 4:4).

This spiritual joy or comfort is nothing else but the cheerfulness of our heart in God, and the sense of our belonging in him, and in his promises. And it is sure that no providence can render this unseasonable to a Christian. Let us suppose the most afflicted and calamitous state a Christian can be incident to, yet, why should sad providences make him lay by his comforts in God, while those are but for a moment, but these are eternal (2 Cor. 4:17)? And why should we lay by our joy in God on the account of sad providences without, when at the very worst and lowest ebb, the saints have infinitely more cause to rejoice than to be cast down? There is more in one of their mercies to comfort them than in all their troubles to cast them down. All your losses are but as the loss of a farthing to a prince (Rom. 8:18).

Why should they be sad, as long as their God is with them in all their troubles? As Christ said, 'Can the friends of the bridegroom be sad, while the bridegroom is with them?' (Matt. 9:15). So say I, can the soul be sad whilst God is with it? Surely that one promise, 'I will be with him in trouble' (Psa. 91:15) should bear you up under all burdens. Let those be cast down who have no God in trouble to turn to.

And why should they be sad as long as no outward work of providence (be it never so sad) can be interpreted as a mark or sign of God's hatred or enmity? 'The righteous and the wicked all share one outcome' (Eccles. 9:2, 3). Indeed, if it were a sign of the Lord's wrath against a man, it would justify our being dejected, but this cannot be so: his heart is full of love whilst the face of providence is full of frowns.

Why should we be cast down under sad providence, whilst we have so great security, that even by the hand of these providences God will do us good, and all these things shall turn to our salvation (Rom. 8:28)? By these God is but killing your lusts, weaning your hearts from a vain world, preventing temptations, and exciting desires for heaven: this is all the hurt they shall do, and shall that sadden us?

Why should we lay by our joy in God when the change of our condition is so near? It is but a little while, and sorrows shall flee away. You shall never suffer more: 'God will wipe away all tears' (Rev. 7:17). Well then, you see there is no reason upon the account of providence to give up your joy and comfort in God. But if you will maintain it under all providences, then be careful to be sure about your security in God. Faith may be separated from comfort, but assurance cannot. Mortify your love for earthly things. This makes providences that deprive and cross us so heavy. Mortify your opinions and loves and you noticeably lighten your affliction. It is a strong affection that makes strong affliction.

Exercise heavenly-mindedness, and keep your hearts upon things eternal, under all the providences with which the Lord exercises you in this world. Noah walked with God, yet met with as sad providences in his day as any man that ever lived since his time (Gen. 6:9). But alas, we find most providences as *stops* rather than as *steps* in our walk with God. If we are under comfortable providences, how sensual, wanton, and worldly do our hearts grow! And if sad providences befall us, how sluggish or distracted are we! This comes to pass partly through the narrowness, but mostly through the deceitfulness of our spirits. Our hearts are narrow, and know not how to manage two businesses of such different natures, as earthly and heavenly matters are, without detriment to one. But certainly such a frame of spirit is attainable that will enable us to keep on in an even and steady course with God whatever befall us. Others have attained it, and why not we? Prosperous providences are for the most part a dangerous state to the soul. The moon never suffers an eclipse but at full; yet Jehoshaphat's grace suffered no eclipse from the fullness of his outward condition, who 'had riches in abundance, and his heart was fully devoted to the ways of the Lord' (2 Chron. 17:5-6). David's life was as full of cares, turmoil and difficulties, as most men we read of, yet how spiritual the temper of his heart was, as that excellent book of Psalms (which was mostly composed amidst those struggles) will acquaint us. The apostles were cast into as great necessities, and suffered as much as ever men did, and yet how raised and heavenly their spirits were amidst all. And certainly, if it were not possible to maintain heavenly-mindedness in such a state and posture of affairs, God would never exercise any of his people with such providences: he would never give you so much of the world to lose your hearts in the love of it, or so little to distract you with the cares of it. If therefore we were more deeply sanctified, and the tendencies of our hearts more heavenward, ardent and vigorous; if we were more mortified to earthly things, and could but keep our due distance from them; our outward conditions would not at this rate draw forth and exercise our inward corruptions, nor would we hazard the loss of so sweet an enjoyment as our fellowship with God is, for the sake of any concerns our bodies have on earth.

In all providences maintain a contented heart with what the Lord allots you, be it more or less of the things of this world. This grace must run parallel with all providences. Learn how to be 'content whatever the circumstances' (Phil. 4:12).

In this duty all men are concerned at all times, and in every state, not only the people of God, but even the unregenerate also. I will therefore address some considerations to both. And first to the unregenerate, to stop their mouths from repining and charging God foolishly when providence crosses them. Let them seriously consider these four things:

(1) *Hell and eternal damnation are the portion of their cup according to the law and gospel threatenings.* Whatever therefore is short of this is to be admired as the fruit of God's stupendous patience and forbearance towards them. Ah poor souls, do you not know that you are men and women condemned to wrath by the plain sentence of the law (John 3:36; 2 Thess. 1:6-7)? And if so, surely there are other matters to exercise your thoughts, desires, fears, and cares about than these. Alas! If you cannot bear a frown of providence, a light cross in these things, how will you bear everlasting burnings! A man that is to lose his head the next day is not very concerned about what bed he lies on, or how his table is furnished the night before.

(2) *Consider, though you are condemned persons, and have no promise to entitle you to any mercy, yet there are very many mercies in your possession at this day.* Are the necessary supports of life nothing? Does not providence minister to you these things, though you daily defy God and provoke him to send you to your own place? But above all, is the gospel and precious

means of salvation nothing, by which you yet are in a capacity of escaping the damnation of hell? O what would the damned say, if they were but put into your condition once more? What! Fret against God, because not everything suits your desires?

(3) *Consider, that if ever you are rescued out of the miserable condition you are in, such cross providences as these you complain of are the most probable means to do it.* Alas! prosperity and success is not the way to save, but destroy you (Prov. 1:32). You must be bound in fetters, and held in cords of affliction, if ever your ear would be opened to instruction (Job 36:8-10). Woe to you, if you go on casually in the way in which you are, and meet with no hardship.

(4) Lastly, *consider that all your troubles under which you complain are pulled down upon your heads by your own sins.* You turn God's mercies into sin, and then fret against God, because he turns your sins into sorrow. Your ways and doings bring these things upon you. Lay your hand therefore upon your mouth, and say, 'Why should any living man complain when punished for his sins?' (Lam. 3:39).

But I must turn to the Lord's people, who have least pretences of all men to be dissatisfied with any of God's providences, and yet are but too frequently found in that temper. And to them I shall offer the following considerations:

(1) *Consider your spiritual mercies and privileges with which the Lord Jesus has invested you, and complain at his providence if you can.* One of these mercies alone has enough in it to sweeten all your troubles in this world. When the apostle considered them, his heart was overwhelmed with astonishment, so that he could not be silent, but in the midst of all his outward troubles cried out, 'Praise be to the God and Father of our Lord Jesus Christ, who has blessed us in the heavenly realms with every spiritual

blessing in Christ' (Eph. 1:3). Anyone who sees such an inheritance settled upon them in Christ can never open their mouths more to complain at God's providence!

(2) *Consider your sins, and that will make you contented with your lot.* Consider what sin deserves from God, and what it requires to mortify and purge it in you. It deserves from God eternal ruin. The merit of hell is in the least vain thought. Every sin forfeits all the mercies you have, and if so, rather wonder your mercies are so many, than that you have no more. Besides, you cannot doubt that your corruptions require all the crosses, wants, and troubles that are upon you, and, it may be a great deal more to mortify and subdue them. Do not you find, after all the rods that have been upon you, a proud heart still, a vain and earthly heart still? O how many bitter potions are necessary to purge out this tough, malignant humour!

(3) *Consider how near you are to the change of your condition.* Have but a little patience, and all will be as well with you as your hearts can desire. It is no small comfort to the saints that this world is the worst place that ever they shall be in: things will be better every day with them. If the traveller has spent all his money, yet it doesn't much trouble him if he knows himself within a few miles of his own home. If there are no candles in the house, we do not make a fuss about it, if we are sure it is almost break of day, for then there will be no use for them. This is your case: 'Your salvation is nearer than when you first believed' (Rom. 13:11).

PART FOUR

THE CHURCH

13

Living in Gospel Unity

IN this sermon Flavel does what he excels in doing—calling Christians to live out the grace of God in Christ in such a way as 'to promote the peace and unity of the churches of Christ, and to prevent their relapse into past follies'. He and his hearers lived in turbulent times. This fact is all the more reason, Flavel explains, to pursue a unity which is deeply attractive to a watching world, and which honours God. In his 'plain' sermon Flavel strives to be practical. He supplies five reasons for pursuing unity, and follows them up with eight directions for developing and enjoying it.

I appeal to you, brothers, in the name of our Lord Jesus Christ, that all of you agree with one another so that there may be no divisions among you, and that you may be perfectly united in mind and thought.—1 Corinthians 1:10

WHEN I consider this healing and uniting text, and the scandalous divisions of the congregations to which I recommend it, I would prefer to comment on it with tears rather than with words. It is just matter of sorrow to think what feeble influences such divine and heartfelt exhortations have upon the minds and hearts of professed Christians. But it is not sorrow, but proper counsels, and convictions obeyed, that must do the work.

The earliest and purest churches of Christ consisted of imperfect members, who were knit together by the same internal bond of the Spirit, and the same external bonds of common profession and common danger, and enjoyed extraordinary helps for uniting, in the presence and doctrines of the apostles among them. They quickly discovered, however, a divisive spirit, dividing both in judgment and affection, to the great injury of faith, and grief of the apostle's spirit. To check and heal this growing evil in the church at Corinth the apostle addresses his heartfelt exhortation to them, and to all future churches of Christ, whom it equally concerns in the words of my text. And so, we must note, the duty exhorted to, and then the arguments enforcing the duty.

Unity an essential, not an option

The duty exhorted to, namely, *unity*—the beauty, strength, and glory, as well as the duty of a church. This unity he describes two ways:

1. *As it excludes its opposite: schism, or division.* All splits and rash separations are contrary to it, and destructive of it: 'I appeal to you, brothers, in the name of our Lord Jesus Christ, that all of you agree with one another so that there may be no divisions among you.'

2. *As it includes all that belongs to it, namely, the harmony and agreement of their judgments, hearts, and language.* (i) That all of you agree with one another in what you say. (ii) That you are perfectly joined together in one mind. And, (iii) in the same judgment. This threefold union in judgment, affection, and language, includes all that belongs to Christian agreement, makes the saints men of one heart and soul, the loveliest sight this world affords (Acts 2:46, 47).

The apostle's three arguments for unity

The arguments enforcing this duty upon them come next under consideration. And these are three: 1. I appeal to you. 2. I appeal to you, brothers. 3. I appeal to you, brothers, in the name of our Lord Jesus Christ.

These arguments are not of equal force and effectiveness: the first is great, the second greater, while the last is the most effective and irresistible of all the rest. But all together should come with such power and irresistible effectiveness upon the judgments, consciences, and hearts of Christians as should perfectly knit them together, and defeat all the designs of Satan, and his agents around them, or of their own temptations within them, to tear apart their affections or communion.

1. And first, he enforces the duty of unity by a solemn, apostolic charge: 'I *appeal* to you.' He had power to command them to this duty, and threaten them for the neglect of it. He had in readiness to revenge all disobedience, and might have shaken that rod over them. Instead he chooses rather to entreat and exhort

them: 'Now I appeal to you, brothers.' Here you have, as it were, the great apostle upon his knees before them, meekly and tenderly entreating them to be at perfect unity among themselves. It is the entreaty of their spiritual father that had given them new birth in Christ. Now I urge you, brothers, I who was the instrument in Christ's hands of your conversion to him; I, who have planted you a gospel church, and assiduously watered you; I urge you all, by the spiritual ties and endearments between you and me, that there may be no divisions among you.

2. Next, he enforces the duty of unity by the nearness of their relation: 'I urge you, *brothers*.' Brotherhood is an endearing thing, and naturally draws affection and unity with it: 'all of you, be like-minded, be sympathetic, love one another, be compassionate and humble' (1 Pet. 3:8). To see an Egyptian smiting an Israelite is no strange sight; but to see one Israelite quarrelling with another is most unnatural and unpleasant. The nearer the relation, the stronger the affection. 'How good and how pleasant it is when brothers dwell together in unity!' (Psa. 133:1).

3. The greatest argument of all is the last: 'in the *name* of our Lord Jesus Christ'. In this name he begs and entreats them to be at perfect unity among themselves. In the former he sweetly insinuated the duty by a loving compulsion, but here he sets it home by a solemn command, 'I appeal you, brothers, in the name of our Lord Jesus Christ.' That is to say, for Christ's sake, or for the love of Christ, by all that Christ has done, suffered, or purchased for you, and as Christ is dear and precious to you, let there be no divisions. If you have any love for Christ, do not grieve him, and obstruct his great design in the world by your scandalous divisions.

In the name of our Lord Jesus Christ, that is, in the authority of Christ; for so his name also signifies (1 Cor. 5:4). And it is as if he had said, If you revere the supreme authority and sovereignty of Christ, which is the fountain out of which so many solemn commands of unity do flow, then see, as you will answer him at the great day, that you are perfectly united in one mind and in one judgment. The point will be this:

Unity amongst believers, especially in particular church relations, is as desirable a mercy, as it is a necessary and indispensable duty.

How desirable a mercy it is, and how necessary a duty. Let the same apostle, who presses it upon the Corinthians in my text, be heard again, enforcing the same duty with the same warmth upon the church at Philippi: 'Therefore if you have any encouragement from being united with Christ, if any comfort from his love, if any common sharing in the Spirit, if any tenderness and compassion, then make my joy complete by being like-minded, having the same love, being one in spirit and of one mind' (Phil. 2:1, 2).

What unity is in the local church?

There is a twofold union, one *mystical*, between Christ and believers, another *moral*, between believers themselves. Faith knits them all to Christ, and then love knits them one to another. Their common relation to Christ their head endears them to each other as fellow-members in the same body. Hence they become glued together by the blood of Christ.

Union with Christ is fundamental to all union among the saints. Perfect union would flow from this their common union with Christ their head, were they not here in an imperfect state, where their corruptions disturb and hinder it. And as soon as they shall attain to complete sanctification, they shall also attain to perfect unity.

How their unity with one another comes from their union with Christ, and how this unity among themselves shall at last arise to its just perfection, we see in John 17:23: 'I in them, and you in me; that they may be brought to complete unity.'

Unity amongst those that do not hold the head is rather a

conspiracy than a gospel unity. Believers and unbelievers may have a political or civil union, but there is no spiritual unity except that which flows from joint membership in Christ. I will not deny, but in particular churches there may be, and still are, some hypocrites who hold communion with the saints and pretend to belong to Christ, the same head with them. But they have no real union with Christ, so neither have they any sincere affection for the saints. These for the most part are they who raise arguments and divisions in the church, as disloyal subjects do in the common-wealth. Of these the apostle speaks: 'They went out from us, but they did not really belong to us. For if they had belonged to us, they would have remained with us; but their going showed that none of them belonged to us' (1 John 2:19).

Sincere Christianity holds fast the soul by a firm bond of life to the truly Christian community; it is there that they reap those spiritual pleasures and advantages which assure their continuing in them. Those who join with the church upon selfish and worldly inducements think little of disowning it; and God permits their divisive spirits to act like that in order to expose their hypocrisy, or (as the text says) 'their going showed that none of them belonged to us'.

It has indeed been said that it is never better with the church than when there are most hypocrites in it. Then you must under-stand it only with respect to the external peace and prosperity of the church: for as to its real spiritual advantage, they add nothing. And therefore it is right for church officers and members to be exceedingly careful (especially in times of liberty and prosperity) how they admit members, as the Jews in Solomon's time were of admitting proselytes. It is said, 'How can two walk together unless they are agreed?' (Amos 3:3). I do not deny that people who differ in some lesser points may and ought to be one in love. But of this I am sure: that when sanctified persons, agreed in judgments and principles, walk together with godly and careful church officers in tender affection, and the exercise of all duties tending to mutual edification—glorifying God with one mouth (Rom. 15:6), and cleaving together with oneness of heart (Acts 2:42)—this is such a church unity as answers Christ's end in the institution of particular churches, and greatly tends to their own comfort, and the spreading of Christianity in the world. Tongue-unity flows from heart-unity, heart-unity in a great measure from head-unity, and all three from union with the Lord Jesus Christ. The divisions of our tongues come mostly from the divisions of our hearts. Were hearts agreed, tongues would quickly be agreed, and then what blessed times might be expected!

The priority and the delight of unity

1. Unity and the glory of God

The manifest glory of God is all the glory we are capable of giving him, and is the very goal of our being, and should be dearer to us than our lives. It is exceedingly advanced by the unity of his people. Hence is the apostle's prayer, 'May the God who gives endurance and encouragement give you a spirit of unity among yourselves as you follow Christ Jesus, so that with one heart and mouth you may glorify the God and Father of our Lord Jesus Christ' (Rom. 15:5, 6). It is highly remarkable that, as the apostle prays for the unity of the saints, he describes that unity for which he prays, 'one mouth and one mind', and also shows how much God would be glorified by such a union.

He also addresses himself to God for it, under these two remarkable titles, the God of endurance and encouragement, and thereby shows us two things:

(1) How great a need and exercise there is of *endurance* in maintaining unity among the saints. They must bear one another's burdens; they must make allowance for mutual infirmities, for the

church here is not an assembly of spirits of just men made perfect. The unity of the saints therefore greatly depends upon the exercise of endurance, one toward another; and this he begs the God of endurance to give them. And to endear this grace of patience to them

(2) he joins with it another title of God, the God of *encouragement*, by which he points them to that abundant encouragement which would result to themselves from such a blessed unity, continued and maintained by the mutual exercises of patience and forbearance one towards another.

And to set home all, he lays before them the pattern and example of Christ: the God of endurance and encouragement, grant you to be like-minded, *according to Christ*. How many thousand infirmities and failures in duty doth Christ find in all his people? Notwithstanding which, he maintains union and communion with them. If they, after his example, shall do so likewise with one another, God will be eminently glorified therein. This will evidence both the truth and excellency of the Christian religion, which so firmly knits the hearts of believers together.

2. *The strength and joy of unity*

The necessity and desirableness of this unity appears further in the deep interest that the comfort and benefit of our souls have in it. A great example of this is in Acts 2:46, 47. Oh what cheerfulness, strength and pleasure did the first Christians reap from the unity of their hearts in the ways and worship of God! It is next to the pleasure and delight of immediate communion with God himself, and the shedding abroad of his love in our hearts by the Holy Ghost. And there is nothing like it which arises from the harmonious exercises of the graces of the saints, in their mutual duties and communion one with another. How their spirits are refreshed by it. What a lively sign is here of heaven! The courts of princes afford no such delights. Whereas on the other side, when schisms have torn churches apart, they go away from each other exasperated, grieved, and wounded, crying out, Oh, that I had a dwelling in the wilderness! Or, oh, that I had the wings of a dove, that I might fly away, and be at rest!

3. The witness of unity

Lastly, the necessity and desirableness of this union further appears with respect to the world, who are drawn to Christ by it, and scared off from religion by the feuds and divisions of professing Christians. The prayer of Christ relates to this, in John 17:23: 'I in them and you in me—so that they may be brought to complete unity. Then the world will know that you sent me and have loved them even as you have loved me.' This, O Father, will be a convincing evidence to the world, of the divinity both of my person and doctrine, and a great ordinance for their conversion to me, when they shall see my people cleaving inseparably to me by faith, and to one another by love. And on the other side, it will be a fatal stumbling-block in the way of their conversion, to observe my followers biting and devouring, rending and tearing one another.

Five reasons why we must pursue unity

Having briefly explored the nature, necessity, and desirableness of unity among all Christians, and especially of those in particular church relationships, I do earnestly and humbly entreat all my brothers in the words of Philippians 2:1-2: 'Therefore if you have any encouragement from being united with Christ, if any comfort from his love, if any fellowship with the Spirit, if any tenderness and compassion, then make my joy complete by being like-minded, having the same love, being one in spirit and purpose.'

He speaks not as one doubting, but as one disputing when he says 'if you have any encouragement from being united with Christ'. And it is as if he had said, I passionately and earnestly entreat you by all that comfort and joy you have found in your mutual communion with Christ and his ordinances, which you have comfortably walked in together, by all that comfort resulting from the mutual exercises and fruits of Christian love; by the unspeakable joys and delights the Spirit of God has poured down upon you, whilst you walked in unity in the ways of your duty; by all the compassion and mercy you have for yourselves, for your brothers, or for the poor carnal world, who are in danger of being destroyed by our divisions; or for me, your minister, whose joy and comfort is bound up in your unity and stability—'then make my joy complete by being like-minded, having the same love, being one in spirit and purpose'.

What heart that has one spark of the love of Christ in it will not yield to such an exhortation as this, enforced by having 'any encouragement from being united with Christ, any comfort from his love'?

More particularly, bear with this word of exhortation from the consideration of the following arguments or motives:

1. God judges disunity.

Reflect upon the recent long and continued troubles you have been under, as the just rebukes of God for your former contentions and follies.

I need not tell you, you are but recently plucked as brands out of the burning, and that the smell of fire is yet upon you. The time lately was, when you got your bread with the peril of your lives; when God handed it to you behind your enemies' backs; when your eyes did not and could not behold your former teachers, except in corners[1] or prisons, when your souls were sorrowful for the solemn assemblies, when you mournfully confessed before the Lord, that these were the just and deserved punishments for your

---

[1] That is, remote or isolated places.

wantonness, barrenness, and provoking animosities. These things were not only the matter of your humble confessions, but the reformation of those evils was what you solemnly promised the Lord when he should again restore you to your liberty. And is the rod no sooner off your backs but you will turn back to the old work again?

Read Ezra 9:6-10, and view the face of this sin in that glass. Have we been so many years in the furnace, and our dross not purged? Do such sharp and long-continued afflictions produce no better effects? It may be said of our troubles, as of the siege of Tyre, 'every head was rubbed bare and every shoulder made raw' (Ezek. 29:18). Some of us went as young men into persecution and trouble, and have come forth old; and, which is worst of all, we bring our old sins forth with us. Either we did confess and bewail these sins in the days of our suffering, or we did not. If we did not, we were past correction, and have defeated the purpose of God's rod. If we did, our confessions and sorrow were either sincere or hypocritical. If sincere, certainly they would effectually caution us, so that we do not return again to folly. 'What has happened to us is a result of our evil deeds and our great guilt, and yet, our God, you have punished us less than our sins deserved and have given us a remnant like this. Shall we then break your commands again?' (Ezra 9:13, 14).

2. We need unity in the face of our enemies.

Consider the common and imminent danger that now threatens us, both from enemies upon our borders, and within our own selves. The Canaanites are in the land; let there be no strife therefore between brothers. Our natural, civil, and spiritual comforts are all shaking and trembling about us. If wicked children fall out and quarrel at a full table, our enemies stand ready to take away the cloth. They are not so far from us and out of sight that God cannot call them in a few hours to end the strife amongst us. We act not only beneath the rules of religion, but of reason also. Brute creatures will drop their hatred in a common danger. Mr Thomas Fuller, in his *History of the Worthies of England*, tells us that when the Bristol Channel overflowed the lower parts of Somerset, it was observed that dogs, hares, cats and rats, swimming to the burrows and hills to preserve their lives, stood quiet during the flood, not offering the least injury one to another. It is a pity that sense should do more with beasts than reason and religion with men.

3. Disunity gets in the way of gospel progress.

Reflect upon the scandal your divisions give to the world, how it hardens and prejudices them against religion and reformation. And thus the souls of men are eternally put in danger by the follies of professing Christians. They are ready enough to make objections against religion, where none are found, and much more to improve them where they are given. Jesus said, 'Woe to the world because of the things that cause people to stumble! Such things must come, but woe to the person through whom they come!' (Matt. 18:7). The offence fixes such prejudices in the hearts of carnal men that some of them will never have good thoughts of religion any more, but utterly distaste and reject those assemblies and ordinances from which their conversion might with greatest probability be expected.

How long and how anxiously have we prayed and waited for such a day of gospel liberty as we now enjoy? It has been one of the sorest afflictions we have grappled with in the days of our persecution, that we could not speak unto the unbelieving world. If we had an opportunity to speak at all, it was for the most part to such as stood in need of edification more than of conversion. God has now, beyond what most of us dreamed of, opened to us a door of liberty to preach, and for all who will, to hear. Some fruits we have already seen, and more we expect. The children are, as it were, coming to the birth, and will you obstruct it? Will you give the gospel a miscarrying womb? Be instruments at once by your contentions, to destroy the souls of men, and break the very hearts of your ministers, whose greatest comfort is bound up in the success of their labours! Brothers, I urge you, read these words as if they were delivered to you upon my bended knees; I urge you for the Lord Jesus Christ's sake, and for the sake of saving the precious immortal souls of men; and for your poor ministers' sake, who have scarce anything besides the fruits of their labours to recompense their long-continued and grievous sufferings, put aside your strife, maintain the unity of the Spirit in the bond of peace. And help and do not hinder us in our hard labours.

What good will our lives do us if we must labour in vain, and spend our strength for nothing? We find it difficult enough to persuade sinners to come to Christ, when no such stumbling-blocks are laid in the way. The counter-pleas of Satan, the unbelief and sensuality of unsanctified nature, are difficulties too great for us to grapple with. But if to these must be added prejudices against religion, from your dividing lusts and scandalous breaches, what hope then remains? If you have no pity for yourselves, pity perishing souls, and pity your poor discouraged ministers. Have a care you don't make us cry out to God against you.

Or if that is a small thing in your eyes, watch out that the blood of souls is not charged to your account in the great day. Are there none in the towns or neighbourhoods where you live? Are you sure there are none that have hopeful inclinations towards religion? Desires and purposes to attend on the same means of grace you sit under, who will charge the occasion of their damnation upon you at the bar of Christ, and say, 'Lord, we had some weak convictions upon our consciences, that we needed a rousing and searching minister. We were convinced that the profane and carnal world where we lived, was not the right path that leads to salvation. We felt in ourselves inclinations to cast off our old companions, and associate with those who lived with more care and holiness, and place ourselves under the most fruitful and advantageous ministry, and accordingly improved opportunities to get acquaintance with them. But when we came nearer to them we found such wrath and envy, such arguing and divisions, such undermining and supplanting each other's reputations, such whisperings and tale-telling, such malicious aggravations and improvements of common failings and infirmities, such covetousness and worldliness, such pride and vanity, as gave us such a disgust and offence at the ways of reformation, that we could never be reconciled to them.'

Beware, I say, how you incur the guilt of such a dreadful charge as this, by giving liberty to such lusts and passions, under a profession of religion, and pretence to reformation.

4. Disunity opposes Jesus Christ.

Consider the opposition of such practices to that solemn and fervent prayer of Jesus Christ, recorded in John 17. It is highly remarkable how, in that prayer which he poured out a little before his death, with such a mighty emotion and fervency of spirit, he insists upon nothing more than unity among his people. He returns to his Father again and again for the obtaining of this one thing. Four times he begs for unity among them, and every time he seems to rise higher and higher, pleading with his Father, (a) That they may be one. (b) That they may be one in us. (c) That they may be one, as you and I are one. And lastly, (d) that they may be made perfect in one. By all this we learn how intent his spirit was upon this one thing.

Brothers, if you would study how to frustrate the design and grieve the heart of your Lord Jesus Christ (to whom you profess love and obedience) you cannot take a quicker way to do it than by breaking the bonds of unity among yourselves. I urge you, therefore, in the name of our Lord Jesus Christ, who so earnestly prayed for the unity of his people, 'that you be perfectly united in mind and thought', as the text says.

5. Unity is essential in the church.

Consider how directly your divisions cross and frustrate the design and end of church fellowship, which is instituted for the improvement of each other's graces, and helping on the mortification of each other's corruptions.

God has distributed various gifts and graces in different degrees amongst his people. The improvement of these gifts and graces to the glory of God and our mutual edification is the very scope and end of particular church fellowship and communion. Every man has his proper gift of God, and the gifts and graces of all are this way made useful and beneficial. Job was exemplary for plainness and patience. Moses was known for his faithfulness and meekness; Josiah for tenderness and a melting spirit; Athanasius was wise and hard-working; Basil heavenly, and of a sweet spirit; Chrysostom laborious and without affectation; Ambrose was resolved and self-controlled. Now the end and use of church-fellowship is to make a rich improvement for all by a regular use and exercise of the gifts and graces found in every one. One must impart his light, and another his warmth. The eye (the knowing man) cannot say to the hand (the active man) I have no need of you. The benefits resulting from spiritual and orderly communion are unspeakable, but whatever the benefits are, they are all cut off by schisms and dissensions. For as faith is the grace by which we receive all from God, so love is the grace by which we share and divide the comfort of all among ourselves. The excellent things of the Spirit are kept in earthen vessels, which death will shortly break, and then we can have no more benefit by them. But these jars and divisions make saints, as it were, dead one to another whilst they are alive.

How lovely, how sweet and desirable it is, to live in the communion of such saints as are described (Mal. 3:16), to hear them freely and humbly to open their hearts and experiences to one another! Some say the art of medicine was found as one person found a herb, and discovered the virtue of it by an accident. He then made others aware of it, and so the physician's skill was perfected, by a collection of those experiments. But woe to us! We are ready to make others aware of each other's failings and infirmities, to the shame and reproach of religion, and to furnish our common enemies with matter of contempt and scorn against us all.

In a word, these schisms and dissensions in the churches of Christ are ominous signs of some sweeping judgment and common disaster approaching us. It is a common observation with shepherds, that when the sheep push one another, a storm speedily ensues. I am sure it is so here. If God does not turn our hearts one towards another, he will come and smite the earth with a curse (Mal. 4:6).

Eight directions for healing of divisions and pursuing unity

In the last place, therefore, give me leave to lay before you some necessary and proper directions and counsels, for the prevention and healing of schisms and divisions amongst the churches of Christ. For it is not complaints and tears, but proper counsels and directions, and those not only prescribed but obeyed that must do the work. When Joshua lay upon his face before the Lord (Josh. 7:6-9), bewailing the sins and miseries of Israel, the Lord said to Joshua, 'Stand up! What are you doing down on your face? Israel has sinned; they have violated my covenant, which I commanded them to keep' (Josh. 7:10, 11). As if he should say, your moans and tears are good and necessary in their place; but speedy action, and vigorous endeavours must be also used, or Israel will perish. So say I, Up, up, go speedily to your duties, as men in earnest. And for your guidance in the paths of duty, I will lay before you the following plain and necessary directions.

1. Take care that the church is converted!

The orderly gathering of local churches is of great influence to the peace and tranquillity of those churches, and therefore it greatly concerns all that are interested therein, especially such as are vested with leadership responsibilities, to take care about who they receive into their communion.

The Scriptures plainly show us that church members ought to be visible saints (1 Cor. 1:2; 2 Cor. 1:1, 2; Acts 2:41 to the end; Eph. 2:7; 1 Thess. 1:2, 3; Rom. 1:7; Col. 1:2). Hence particular churches are called the churches of the saints (1 Cor. 14:33). If admissions are lax and negligent, so much heterogeneous matter fills the church that it can never be quiet. Christians may live together harmoniously, and coalesce in one orderly and comfortable society, as having one and the same head, one Spirit, the same general design and end: but godly and ungodly, spiritual and carnal, are acted by contrary principles, pursue opposite designs, and can never heartily work together.

There is a spirit of discerning, a judgment of discretion in the saints, and it is especially desirable in a more eminent degree, in those that are leaders in the church, to judge of men's fit qualifications for church communion. We all recognize that gross ignorance and profaneness are just bars to men's admission. And to deny this would be to take all power from the church to preserve the purity of God's ordinances, or to cast out notorious offenders. None ought to be admitted into church communion except those who appear to a charitable judgment (comparing their professions and lifestyles) to be Christians indeed, that is, men fearing God, and living for righteousness.

And I do not doubt that some opinions, as well as practices, render men unfit for church membership (Titus 3:10; 2 John 10).

All opinions which overthrow doctrines which must be believed, which the apostle comprehends under the name of faith, and all such opinions as are inconsistent with a holy life, and overthrow the power of godliness, which the apostle teaches under the name of a good conscience (1 Tim. 1:19, 20); whoever shall hold or maintain any such opinions as these, he is either to be kept out, if not admitted, or cast out, if he is in church fellowship.

In receiving men like these, you are effectively receiving spies and troublemakers among you. What a firebrand did Arius prove, not only in the church of Constantinople, but even to the whole world! Men of graceless hearts, and erroneous heads, will give a continual exercise to the patience of sober Christians. I do not deny that men may arise out of the purest churches, speaking perverse things, and yet the officers and members of those churches are blameless in their admission. But if they can be discerned before they are admitted, a little preventative care would be of singular and seasonable use, for the peace of our churches.

2. Be committed to the work God has given you.

Let all officers and members of the church study their duties, and keep themselves within the bounds of their proper places. 'Make it your ambition to lead a quiet life, to mind your own business and to work with your hands' (1 Thess. 4:11). In these words he condemns two vices, which disturb and distract the church of Christ, curiosity in matters which are not our business, and idleness in the duties of our particular callings. Two things I shall drop, by way of caution:

(1) Let it be for a warning to ministers, that they mind their proper work, aim for the peace of the church, impartially conduct their ministry to the saints committed to their charge, not siding with a party. There are few splits in churches in which ministers have not some hand. Jerome made the observation that 'searching the ancient histories I can find none that have more rent the church of God than those who conduct the office of ministers'.

This is a sad charge, and it is too justly laid upon many of that order. Oh what a blessing is a prudent, patient, peaceable minister, to the flock over which he watches!

(2) Let the people keep their places, and study their proper duties. In most congregations there are some idle people who, having little to do at home, are employed in Satan's errands, to run from house to house, carrying tales to exasperate one Christian against another. These the apostle particularly marks and warns the churches about: 'they get into the habit of being idle and going about from house to house. And not only do they become idlers, but also busybodies who talk nonsense, saying things they ought not to' (1 Tim. 5:13). If that one rule of Christ (Matt. 18:15-16) were conscientiously and strictly attended to, to tell a sinning brother his fault privately, then with one or two more, if his stubbornness makes it necessary, and not to expose him to the whole church, and much less to the whole world, without a plain necessity, how many thousand ruptures would be prevented in Christian societies!

3. Watch your tongue.

Let all Christians govern their tongues, and keep them under the command of the law of kindness in their conversation with one another. 'A gentle answer turns away wrath, but a harsh word stirs up anger' (Prov. 15:1). Hard to hard will never do well. How easily did Abigail disarm angry David by a gentle apology! What is more boisterous than the wind? Yet a gentle rain will allay it. It may be strongly presumed, that a meek and gentle answer will more easily allay the passions of a godly man, than of one that is both ungodly, and full of enmity towards us; and yet sometimes it has done the latter.

4. Watch your behaviour.

Respectful behaviour to those that are less favoured than us in gifts or possessions is an excellent way to preserve peace in the church. Proud and superior behaviour towards those who are beneath us in either respect is a frequent occasion of bitterness and animosities. The apostle charges the Corinthians that none of them be puffed up against another, 'for who makes you different from anyone else?' (1 Cor. 4:7). This doesn't destroy the civil differences God has made between one and another. Grace will teach the godly servant to give double honour to a religious master or mistress, the private Christian to a godly magistrate, or minister. It will teach the people to recognize those who labour among them, and are over them in the Lord, and admonish them, and to esteem them very highly in love for their work's sake, and to be at peace among themselves (1 Thess. 5:12, 13). And it will also teach superiors to keep company with men of low degree, and not to think of themselves above what they ought: 'be completely humble and gentle; be patient, bearing with one another in love. Make every effort to keep the unity of the Spirit through the bond of peace' (Eph. 4:2, 3).

5. Remember that unity comes from grace.

This gentle language and respectful behaviour would naturally and constantly flow from the uniting graces of wisdom, humility, and love, were they more exalted in the hearts of Christians. Wisdom would allay those unchristian passions: 'A man of understanding is of an excellent spirit' (Prov. 17:27), so we render it; but the Hebrew signifies a *cool* spirit; 'the wisdom that is from above is peace-loving and considerate' (James 3:17).

Humility takes away the fuel from the fire of strife. Strife only comes from pride (Prov. 13:10). How dearly has pride, especially spiritual pride, cost the churches of Christ! Love is the very cement of societies, the fountain of peace and unity. It thinks no evil (1 Cor. 13), puts the fairest sense upon doubtful words and actions, it endures all things. 'Love me', says Augustine, 'and correct me as you please.' It is an essential grace, bearing the fruits of peace and unity upon it.

6. Prize and practise forgiveness.

Be of a Christlike, forgiving spirit one towards another. 'Get rid of all bitterness, rage and anger, brawling and slander, along with every form of malice. Be kind and compassionate to one another, forgiving each other, just as in Christ God forgave you' (Eph. 4:31, 32). Has your brother offended you? How ready are you also to offend your brother? And, which is infinitely more, how often do you every day grieve and offend Jesus Christ, who yet freely forgives all your offences? Remember, friend, that an unforgiving spirit is a bad sign of an unforgiven person. They that have found mercy, pity, and forgiveness, should of all men in the world be most ready to show it.

7. Fear disunity.

Be deeply affected with the mischievous effects and consequents of schisms and divisions in the societies of the saints, and let nothing beneath a plain necessity divide you from fellowship with each other. Hold it fast till you can hold it no longer without sin. At the fire of your contentions your enemies warm their hands, and say, Aha, so would we have it. Your prayers are obstructed: 'first be reconciled to your brother, and then come and offer your gift' (Matt. 5:24). Edification is hindered; sick bodies do not thrive (Eph. 4:15). God is provoked to remove his gracious presence from among you. 'Be of one mind', says the apostle; 'live in peace, and the God of peace shall be with you' (2 Cor. 13:11). He implies that their arguments would deprive them of his blessed company with them. The glory of your fellowship is clouded: 'If you have bitter envy and strife in your heart, do not boast about it' (James 3:14). Glory not in your church privileges, personal gifts, and achievements. Whatever you think of yourselves, you are not such Christians as you take yourselves for, living in sin so directly contrary to Christianity. The name of Christ is dishonoured. You are taken out of the world, to be a people for his name, that is, for his honour. But there is little credit to the name of Christ from a dividing, wrangling people. The alluring beauty of Christianity, by which the church gains upon the world (Acts 2:46, 47) is sullied and defaced, and thereby (as I noted before) conversion hindered, and a new stone, as it were, rolled over the graves of poor sinners, to keep them down in their lack of repentance. Tremble therefore at the thoughts of divisions and separations.

St Augustine notes three sins severely punished in Scripture: the golden calf, with the sword; Jehoiachim's cutting the sacred roll, with a dreadful captivity; but the schism of Korah and his accomplices, with the earth's opening her mouth and swallowing them up alive.

8. Union with Christ leads to unity with believers.

Let all church members see that they have union with Christ, evidencing itself in daily sweet communion with him. Lines drawn from a circumference come the nearest to one another in the centre. When God intends to make the hearts of men one, he first makes them new: 'I will give them one heart, and I will put a new spirit within you' (Ezek. 11:19). And the more any renewed heart tastes the sweetness of communion with God, by so much does it long for unity and peace with his people.

Our dissatisfaction and bad temper clearly shows that all is not well between God and us. There is nothing so opposite to or abhorred by a soul that enjoys sweet peace and communion with Christ, than to live in sinful friction and contentions with his people. Return therefore to the first spirit of love and unity: bear with one another; forgive one another; put to death your dividing lusts; cherish your uniting graces; 'I urge you, brothers, to watch out for those who cause divisions and put obstacles in your way that are contrary to the teaching you have learned. Keep away from them' (Rom. 16:17). In a word, and that the word of the apostle in the text, 'I appeal to you, brothers, in the name of our Lord Jesus Christ, that all of you agree with one another so that there may be no divisions among you, and that you may be perfectly united in mind and thought' (1 Cor. 1:10).

14

Authentic Gospel Ministry

☞

THIS sermon on Matthew 24:45-47 (Flavel's title is 'The Character of a Complete Evangelical Pastor, Drawn by Christ') was originally prepared for a gathering of West Country pastors in 1691, though Flavel died before the assembly met. Religious freedom had recently been restored following more than twenty years of persecution, bringing new opportunities for gospel ministry. The 'wise and faithful steward' of the text is the model for such ministry.

The minister is to be faithful and wise. He is to be unstinting in his commitment to the good of his people and the glory of God. Flavel's large and generous heart is seen in his urging his fellow-pastors to be kind and committed to one another, as well as to the flocks they serve. He clearly understands the difficulties associated with the minister's calling, but he tenderly exhorts them to faithful service. Before he concludes he points them heavenward, to the place where all wise and faithful servants will receive their reward.

Who then is a faithful and wise servant, who the Lord has made ruler over his household, to give them their food in due season? Blessed is that servant, to whom his Lord, when he comes, shall find so doing. Truly, I say unto you, that he shall make him ruler over all his possessions.—Matthew 24:45-47

THIS great and solemn assembly brings to my mind those words, and with the words, a very real touch of the same affection, with which the church uttered them: "'This place is too small for us; give us more space to live in." Then you will say in your heart, "Who bore me these? I was bereaved and barren; I was exiled and rejected. Who brought these up? I was left all alone, but these—where have they come from?'" (Isa. 49:20, 21). These words are full of holy admiration and wonder at the church's strange and sudden increase, after such a wasting time as these seventy sad years had been to her. This was a miraculous and surprising work of God in the eyes of the people of God.

We have had our wasting time, as well as they. Multitudes of faithful and wise ministers have been swept into their graves by ejections, banishments, imprisonments, and heart-breaking silencings. Where then are all these from whom our eyes behold this day? Who has begotten us, and brought up these? These, where had they been; and out of what secret recesses have they come?

Many thought the days of our prosperity, and opportunities of our service, had been numbered and finished, and that God had no more work (except suffering work) for us. But now above

and beyond the desponding thoughts and unbelieving fears of our
hearts, we are here this day in a numerous assembly, with peace
and liberty, to consult the affairs of Christ's kingdom. Yes, to the
joy of our souls, we see the plumb-lines once more in the hands
of our Zerubbabels. 'Who has despised the day of small things?
For they shall rejoice, and shall see the plumb-line in the hand
of Zerubbabel, with those seven the eyes of the Lord, which run
to and fro through the whole earth' (Zech. 4:10). Our prudent
repairers, co-working with the divine providence, expressed by the
seven eyes, will bring weak and unimpressive beginnings to happy
and blessed results and issues. Shall one now answer the messen-
gers of the churches? God has founded Zion, and the power of his
people shall trust in it.

Ignorance and error have covered the people, and the wall
of discipline is greatly decayed. Our business is to cleanse our
churches, and repair their walls, so that they may become gardens
of delight, and beds of spices, for Christ to walk and take pleasure
in. When I considered the quality and occasion of this assembly,
my thoughts quickly centred themselves on those words of our
Lord, which I have read unto you: 'Who then is a faithful and
wise servant, whom the Lord has made ruler over his household,
to give them their food in due season?'

Not to spend much time about the background of the text,
Christ had been solemnly warning the disciples, and all the Christian world, of his most certain (though secret) coming to judgment. Therefore, he warns them to beware of luxury, idleness, and
security, and the sins of the world, and to be found at his coming
watchful and diligent in their proper places of duty. This exhortation he infers from what common wisdom would teach any servant, especially any steward of a house to do, to whom his Lord has
committed the care of his family. It is agreed by all that the words
have a special and immediate relevance to gospel ministers, the

stewards of Christ's house, or church, to whom Christ, the Lord of the family, has entrusted the care and management of its affairs. And in them we find an evangelical pastor described, and then the reward for those who answer that description.

1. Christ describes an evangelical pastor by two excellent and essential properties, or qualifications, faithful and wise (Matt. 24:45).

Both of these make up the character of a complete gospel minister. For if he is *faithful* he will not deceive others, and if he is *wise*, or prudent, he is not likely to be deceived himself. His prudence does not allow deceivers easily to impose upon him, and his faithfulness will not allow him knowingly to impose upon his people. His prudence will enable him to discern, and his faithfulness oblige him to distribute, wholesome food to his flock. These two therefore, meeting together, make a pastor after God's own heart, according to Jeremiah 3:15.

Both these are found in the form of a question, and this form of speech suggests how difficult it is to find such a servant. These are their properties.

2. Christ shows the reward of those who answer these characteristics.

'Blessed is that servant' (Matt. 24:46). He is certainly blessed by God, whatever his treatment is from men. If he is faithful, all his prudence will not protect him from the hatred and persecution of men, but it is enough that Christ calls and counts him blessed. And those whom he blesses are truly and eternally blessed. Furthermore, Christ says, 'Truly I tell you, he shall make him ruler over all his possessions' (24:47). Here is an allusion to the custom of great kings and generals, who prefer and advance discreet and faithful servants to places of eminent trust, profit, and honour, as Daniel and Joseph were.

Doctrine: *Our Lord Jesus Christ will amply reward the faithful and wise stewards of his house, in the day of their giving an account.*

The pastor-servant

Ministers, in a special sense, are the stewards, or chief servants in Christ's house. So speaks the apostle: 'let a man reckon us as the ministers of Christ, and stewards of the mysteries of God' (1 Cor. 4:1). To them he has committed the ministry of the word and sacraments, which contain the great mysteries of the kingdom of God.

Every believer who has received any talent from God is a steward (and to be sure, the least among us has at least one talent), and will be called to an account for the employment or non-employment of that talent in the audit day. But ministers are stewards in the strict and special sense. Christ distinguishes them from the others, as door-keepers from the rest of the servants (Mark 13:34). Nor may any assume that office, but by order from Christ the master of the family. But this is too obvious to stay longer upon it.

Wanted: faithful servants

Faithfulness is an essential requirement of a steward (1 Cor. 4:2). It is required of a steward that he is found faithful. What ground is there for trust, where there is no truth? Hence is that solemn charge to commit that great trust of the ministry to faithful men (2 Tim. 2:2). And Paul blesses God, who had accounted him faithful, and put him into the ministry (1 Tim. 1:11). This faithfulness, as it relates to God, ourselves, and the flocks committed to us, includes the following five aspects:

1. Ministerial faithfulness includes pure and spiritual aims and intentions for God.

It is not his own, but his master's honour and interest that the servant must design and aim at. Faithfulness will not endure self-ishness, disguised with a pretence of zeal for Christ. It is said of the master workmen of the temple that there was no reckoning made with them of the money collected for that use, because they dealt faithfully, i.e. they had given sufficient proof that they appropri-ated not a penny to themselves, but truly applied it to the public, sacred end and use, to which it was given (2 Kings 22:7). Oh let us all be such faithful master-builders of the house of our God! Let us say, not our interest, but Christ's, not our glory, but his. Pure ends in our service will give abundant comfort at the end of our service.

Let us beware of all tricks and behaviour designed to accom-modate selfish interests under a show of devotion to God. Tim-othy is our pattern in this, of whom Paul says, 'I have no one else like him, who will show genuine concern for your welfare. For everyone looks out for their own interests, not those of Jesus Christ' (Phil. 2:20). Others had the skill to cloak selfish ends under Christ's honour, but Timothy was ignorant of such unfaith-ful tricks and skills.

2. Ministerial faithfulness involves personal sincerity.

So the word means, where it is said of Abraham, that God found his heart faithful, that is, sincere before him (Neh. 9:8). A faith-ful minister is a sincere-hearted minister. And in this let us show ourselves to be the true ministers of Christ. Let this be our rejoic-ing, that 'with integrity and godly sincerity, we have lived in this world' (2 Cor. 1:12). And let us be very careful in this, because no sin is more apt to insinuate itself into our hearts and duties than hypocrisy. We, of all men, are most in danger to be deceived by it. For our work concerns spiritual things, and we are on that account styled 'spiritual' men (Hos. 9:7). But it is plain, from that very place, that a man may be *objectively* a spiritual, and all the while *subjectively* a carnal man. Believe it, brothers, it is easier to declaim, like an orator, against a thousand sins of others, than it is to mortify one sin, like Christians, in ourselves; and to be more industrious in our pulpits, than in our private times; to preach twenty sermons to our people, than one to our own hearts. Believe it, sirs, all our reading, studying, and preaching, is but trifling hypocrisy, till the things read, studied, and preached are felt in some degree upon our own hearts.

3. Ministerial faithfulness includes ministerial diligence.

A slothful cannot be a faithful servant. 'His Lord said to him, Well done, good and faithful servant', etc. (Matt. 25:21). And it continues, 'His Lord answered, and said to him, You wicked and lazy servant' (verse 26). I may say to him who snatches at the ministry, as Henry IV did to his son, who hastily snatched at the crown, He little knows what a heap of cares and toils he snatches at. 'The labours of the ministry will exhaust the very marrow from your bones, hasten old age and death', said Luther. They are fittingly compared to the toil of men in harvest, to the labours of a woman in travail, and to the agonies of soldiers in the dangers of battle. We must watch when others sleep.

And indeed it is not so much the expense of our labours, as the loss of them, that kills us. It is not with us, as with other labourers. They find their work as they leave it, not so with us. Sin and Satan unravel almost all we do, the impressions we make on our people's souls in one sermon, vanish before the next. How many truths have we to study! How many strategies of Satan, and mysteries of corruption, to detect! How many cases of conscience to resolve! We must fight in defence of the truths we preach, as well as study them to paleness, and preach them unto faintness. But well-spent head, heart, lungs, and all; welcome pained breasts, aching backs, and trembling legs, if we can by all but approve ourselves Christ's faithful servants, and hear that joyful voice from his mouth, 'Well done, good and faithful servants.'

4. Ministerial faithfulness includes our lack of favouritism in all the administrations of Christ's house.

He that is partial cannot be faithful. With what extraordinary solemnity does Paul set his exhortation upon Timothy: 'I charge you before God, and the Lord Jesus Christ, and the elect angels, that you observe these things, without preferring one before another, doing nothing by partiality' (1 Tim. 5:21).

Brothers, you will shortly appear before an impartial God, so see that you are impartial stewards. Take the same care, manifest the same love, attend with the same diligence to the poorest and weakest souls that are committed to your care, as you do the rich, the great, and honourable.

Remember all souls are rated at one value in your Master's book, and your Redeemer paid as much for the one as for the other. Civil differences must be civilly acknowledged, but these have no place in our spiritual ministry.

5. Ministerial faithfulness includes constancy and steadfastness.

You cannot be a backsliding or flinching servant: 'Be faithful (i.e. fixed and constant) to death, and I will give you a crown of life' (Rev. 2:10). We look for happiness, as long as God is in heaven, and he expects constancy, as long as we are on earth.

Many of us have cause to bless the Lord, and greatly to rejoice in his goodness this day, who enabled us to be steadfast and unmovable in the trials that have passed over us; and when the great earthquake shook down our liberties, our estates, and made our hearts to shake, yet our resolutions for God and his truth stood firm and unshaken. Our hearts did not turn back, nor did our steps decline, though we were broken in the place of dragons, and covered with the shadow of death. This we wholly owe to him that holds the stars in his right hand. But our warfare is not yet ended. Our faithfulness is not yet faithfulness to the death. We hope it will shortly be called so, as involves our self-denial, sincerity, diligence, impartiality, and constancy.

These are the principal things included in the first qualification of ministerial faithfulness. In the next place let us weigh and value the second qualification in the text—*ministerial prudence*.

Wanted: wise servants

The Lord's servant must not only be faithful, but prudent, discreet, and wise. Faithfulness and honesty make a good Christian, but the addition of prudence to faithfulness makes a good steward. Faithfulness will fix the eye upon the right end, but it is prudence which must direct to the proper means of attaining it.

If we look into Revelation 4:6, 7, we shall there find a wonderful picture of true gospel ministers. They are 'full of eyes'. They have eyes looking before them to God for direction, behind them to the flocks they lead, and within them to their own hearts, lest, after they have preached to others, they themselves become disqualified. They have also six wings. With two they cover their faces, manifesting their deep reverence of God, with two their feet, manifesting the humble sense of their infirmities, and with two they fly with joy in the service of God. They have not only the courage of the lion, the strength of the ox, the loftiness of the eagle, but the face of a man, i.e., prudence and discretion.

The use of prudence to a minister of Christ is unspeakably great. It gives clarity to the mind by freeing it from passions and earthly impressions, enabling it thereby to see what is best to be done. It also enables them to choose the most apt and proper means, and it directs the application of them at the best time, without too much haste, or hazard by too unwise delay.

Prudence will direct the servants of Christ, in their own proper ministerial work, so that it be well done. And it will guide them in their deliberations to the six following proper means and excellent expedients.

Six steps to wise ministry

1. Prudence will direct us to lay a good foundation of knowledge in our people's souls, by catechizing and instructing them in the principles of Christianity, without which we labour in vain.

Unless you have a people who understand God's truth, you will not have a people who evidence grace. St Paul's convictions lay much in this: 'I have lain the foundation as a wise master-builder' (1 Cor. 3:10). And indeed this is the masterpiece of a master-builder: all your excellent sermons will be dashed to pieces upon the rock of your people's ignorance. You can never arrive at a better project to promote and secure the success of your labours than by catechizing.

2. Ministerial prudence shows itself in the choice of such subjects as the needs of our people's souls most require and call for.

A prudent minister will study the souls of his people more than the best human books in his library, and not choose what is easiest for him, but what is most necessary for them. Ministers that are acquainted with the state of their flocks, as they ought to be, will be seldom at a loss in the choice of the next subject. Their people's needs will choose their text for them. The greatest part of our congregations are poor, ignorant, and unregenerate people who know neither their misery nor their remedy. This will direct us to the great doctrines of conviction, regeneration, and faith, and will make us sit thoughtfully in our studies, asking, 'Lord, what course shall we take, and what words shall we use that may best convey the sense of their sin and danger, with the fullness and necessity of Christ, to their hearts?'

Others are withering and decaying in their love, and unsure in their judgments. Prudence will enable the man of God to give to everyone his proper food, or medicine, in due season. This will make us spend more hours in our studies, and set to it with all our might and skill, that thereby we may both save ourselves, and those who hear us.

3. Ministerial wisdom will not only direct us in the choice of our subjects, but also in the language in which we dress and deliver them to our people.

A crucified style best suits the preachers of a crucified Christ. A grave and proper style becomes the lips of Christ's ambassadors. Prudence will neither allow us to be coarse nor showy in our expressions. Prudence will choose words that are solid, rather than florid. After all, a merchant will value a ship by a sound bottom and capacious hold rather than a golden head and stern. Words are but servants to matter. An iron key, fitted to the wards of the lock, is more useful than a golden one that will not open the door to the treasure.

Prudence will cast away a thousand fine words for one that is apt to penetrate the conscience, and reach the heart. Who, in the last age, was ever honoured with more success in his ministry, than blessed Mr [Jeremiah] Burroughs? And who ever excelled him in skill, to bring down the sublime mysteries of the gospel to the smallest capacity?

4. Ministerial prudence will show us of what great use our own affections are for the moving of others, and will therefore advise us that, as ever we expect the truths we preach should operate upon the hearts of others, we first labour to work them in upon our own hearts.

Such a preacher was St Paul. He preached with tears accompanying his words (Phil. 3:18). A hot iron, though blunt, will pierce sooner than a cold one, though sharper.

And why, my brothers, do we think God has commissioned us rather than angels to be his ambassadors? Was it not, among other reasons, for this: because we have been under the same condemnation and misery ourselves, and felt both the terrors and comforts of the Spirit (which angels do not know by experience), and so we might thereby be enabled to treat sinners with more feeling and love, in a way more accommodated to them, and therefore more apt to move and win them?

5. Ministerial prudence will direct the servants of Christ, who highly value and earnestly long for the success of their labours, to be careful, by the care and gravity of their behaviour, to maintain their esteem in the consciences of their people.

In your pulpits you are carrying on a treaty of peace between God and them. And therefore it will not allow you to do anything out of your pulpits to make the breach wider, or hinder the happy close between him and them. The fowler that spreads his net to take the birds will not leave a feather, or make the least noise, to scare the bird he intends to take. Do not let those who aim no higher than a bird be more prudent and cautious than you who are set to catch immortal souls. Remember the words of Solomon, 'He that wins souls is wise' (Prov. 11:30). Prudence will not allow the ministers of Christ to mix with vain company, and take the same liberty they do in vain jests, and idle stories. Nor will it allow, on the other side, a morose reservedness, and discouraging austerity. Temper seriousness with accessible gentleness.

To you that are juniors and candidates for the ministry, I will assume the boldness to address you with one seasonable word of advice, and it is this: watch out for that light and carefree spirit, which is everywhere in this unserious age. It was the charge of God against some ministers of old, that they were light persons (Rev. 2:2) and yet I cannot but think, comparatively speaking, with some of our times, they might pass for grave and serious. The people have eyes to see how we walk, as well as ears to hear what we say. It will be our wisdom and great advantage, to be able to say, as St Paul did, 'The things which you have both heard and seen in me, do' (Phil. 4:9).

6. Ministerial prudence will send you often to your knees, to seek a blessing from God upon your studies and labours, as knowing all your ministerial success entirely depends upon him (1 Cor. 3:7).

Those are the best sermons that are obtained by prayer. Blessed Bradford studied upon his knees. Luther obtained more this way than by all his studies. If an honest farmer could tell his neighbour that the reason why his corn prospered better than his was 'because he soaked the seed in prayer, before he sowed it in the field', we may blush to think how much more precious seed we have sown dry, and not soaked in prayer, and by this neglect have frustrated our own expectations.

So by laying our foundations in the knowledge of principles, choosing our subjects by the people's needs, handling them in appropriate language, working them first upon your own affections, enforcing them by careful living, and soaking this whole seed in prayer, we shall approve ourselves the prudent ministers of Christ.

Serving together in the gospel

Having said thus much of prudence, with respect to our personal involvement in the work of the ministry, I come next to show its great usefulness with respect to others.

As to our brothers and fellow-workers in the Lord, prudence will compel us, that by the firmest union with them we make their gifts and graces as useful as is possible, for the furtherance and advancement of our great and difficult work.

We cannot be ignorant how much Satan has gained, and Christ's cause has lost, by those unhappy divisions and alienations amongst brothers and fellow-labourers in the work of the Lord. Christ has given various glorious ascension-gifts upon them which are only capable of a full improvement in union and partnership with each other. Gifts are improved in us by prayer and study, but the benefits of those gifts are shared among us by love and unity. Love and union bring every man's gifts and graces into the common bank, and instead of monopolies, they drive a free and open trade, to the great enriching of the church.

There is not a greater or more pleasant variety of qualities, smells and colours among the herbs and flowers with which the earth is clothed for the delight and service of men, than there is in the gifts and abilities of ministers, for the use and service of the church. One is a man of action, but not so deep and solid in judgment. Another is grave and solid, but not so ready and forthcoming. One is wary and reserved, another open and plain. One is melancholy and cautious, another cheerful and courageous. When these different gifts and qualities shine together in the church, heavens, what a glorious constellation do they make! And what sweet and good influences do they shed down upon the Lord's heritage! All these ministerial gifts and graces are to be improved for Christ, firstly on our own, and then more publicly, by brotherly union.

When God casts the lot of two or more fellow-labourers in the gospel in the same city, town, or neighbourhood, then what a blessed advantage have they beyond solitary ministers to carry on the work of the Lord cheerfully, vigorously, and successfully! When love causes their hearts to join together, how must their work be facilitated, sweetened, and prospered in their hands! But if friction and jealousies get in amongst them, and if pride, envy or carnal interest dissolve the bond of brotherly love, and instead of planting for Christ, they begin to supplant one another, then no words are able to show what a trail of mischief and sins will now break in among them, to the great dishonour of Christ, and obstruction of the gospel.

I do therefore in the name of Christ, as upon my bended knees, earnestly entreat and implore my brothers, by all the regard they have to the honour of Christ, the souls of their people, their own comfort, or the success of their labours, that no envying or strife, no competitiveness or disrespect, be ever admitted or named among them. I think it is scarcely imaginable that those who have so lately and severely smarted, should fall again into the same follies, for which God has chastised them.

And as prudence directs us into the way of our profit and comfort by this more private improving of our gifts and graces, so we get into a more excellent way by a general union and coalition with all our brothers who are further away from us. It calls upon us to bury and forget henceforth the factious names of distinction, growing out of our different convictions about smaller disciplinary points. How many fervent prayers have been poured out! How many excellent works aimed at unity have been written by those excellent ministers, that are now at perfect unity in heaven! Though they did not reap the blessed fruits of those holy endeavours, yet I hope we and our children shall.

Let us next see, what direction it gives us with respect to our enemies, who endeavour to obstruct and hinder the work of the Lord in our hands. If we are heartily engaged in the service of Christ, we must expect many adversaries, and strong opposition. Men will raise clouds of reproaches, to darken our reputation among the people. They will represent us to them as ignorant and unlearned, quarrelsome, misguided, and overzealous. Prudence, in this case, will restrain us from rendering reproach for reproach, and show to us the best project in the world, for the vindication of our names, and success of our labours; and that is, that we preach the gospel so that the people may feel the power of Christ in our doctrine, and so live, that they may see the beauty of Christ in our lives. And so by preaching and living like this, we shall break down all the prejudices of the world before us. Such doctrine, seconded with such a lifestyle, like the sun in the heavens, will not only break up and scatter all clouds of reproach, but shed down their enlightening and enlivening influences upon the hearts of the people.

I neither do, nor dare suggest and insinuate anything in this discourse, against any party or body of men, being convinced that among those who differ from us there are many learned, pious, and peaceable men, who can heartily rejoice to see the work of Christ carried on by those who do not follow them. But some there are, almost in every place, who are more concerned for a ceremony than for the substance of religion, and for a tile upon the roof, than a stone in the foundation. In this case, ministerial prudence will carefully shun all occasions of exasperation; and if that care is not sufficient to avoid them, it will furnish us with that patience and perseverance which will be sufficient to bear them.

Thus we see the necessity and excellency of ministerial faithfulness and prudence, considered on their own.

Walking with faith and wisdom

Let us now examine faith and wisdom working together in some particular parts of our work, where they shed their shared influences. And these, among some others, are the duties of, (1) Defending truth against error; (2) Reproving offenders, and (3) Dealing with distressed consciences.

1. There is great need for faithfulness and prudence in defending the truths of Christ against the errors of the times.

Our faithfulness indeed will oblige us to do it, but prudence must direct us *how* to do it. The establishment of our people in the truth is the special aim of the institution of the ministry (Eph. 4:11). But without the assistance of both these graces, that aim is never likely to be attained. A faithful minister dares not be silent where the souls of his people are concerned, yet all his endeavours to secure them will be to little purpose if prudence is lacking in the management of that design. Prudence must both time our contentions and regulate the manner of them. It will never suffer us to appear too soon nor too late.

Not too soon, because errors are sometimes best cured by neglect, and in a little time grow weary of themselves; not too late, lest they get a head, and be past retrieve. Hasty contenders, like young falconers, let fly the hawk with her hood on. On the other side, if friendship or ties with those causing trouble stop our mouths too long, we may in a few days be entertained by them (as Thyestes was by his brother Atreus) with the limbs of our own (spiritual) children. Prudence will not allow our pulpits to ring with invectives against false teachers till the more private and gentle methods have been tried in vain, and then neither prudence nor faithfulness will allow a longer delay. But yet when they both advise us to engage, prudence must regulate the manner of the contention, and commands us to urge hard arguments with mild and soft language.

2. Those who teach error are usually hot and passionate, proud and daring persons.

The joint influences of both these graces must be found in all our ministerial reproof. Reprove we must, or we cannot be faithful, and prudently too, or we cannot be successful. He that is silent cannot be innocent, and yet we need to discern whether cowardly silence is more harmful to the reprover, than indiscreet zeal may be to the reproved. Faithfulness is loth to lose the soul of another for failure to reprove. Prudence takes care not to lose it by the ill-management of the reproof. Faithfulness says, it is better to lose the smiles than the souls of men. Prudence says, to save both is best.

Reproving is medicine for the passions, and surgery is no easy or pleasant work. Sick and pained men are wayward and difficult, but prudence will cast fetters upon their passions, and make them lie quietly, whilst faithfulness probes and searches their wounds to the bottom. Prudence can sometimes convey a reproof so effectually and inoffensively that the conscience of the reproved shall feel it, and yet his passions are not awakened by the slightest harmful touch. Faithfulness considers and urges the necessity of the duty, and prudence considers the quality of the person, time, and manner of application. It will reach the sin, and yet (if possible) avoid the offence of the sinner. Above all, prudence advises us to keep ourselves pure from those sins we reprove in others. When we must apply the precious oil of reproof to them, we work it in with the warm, soft, gentle hand of love and compassion, and then the reproof is likely to do good, and the reprover receives thanks for his kindness. 'Let a righteous man strike me—that is a kindness; let him rebuke me—that is oil on my head' (Psa. 141:5)

3. Once more, their joint influences must also meet in all our dealings with distressed consciences.

Conscience is a very tender thing, and when sick and distressed, needs to be handled both carefully and tenderly. The wound must be searched for, says faithfulness, and it must be searched skilfully, says prudence. He that can so search and cure it, deserves that excellent praise of 'one among a thousand' (Job 33:23). It requires a great measure of both of these graces to bring general confused troubles to a good end. To direct a sin-sick soul to Christ, in the true gospel method, to furnish the tempted Christian with proper weapons against Satan's assaults, and teach him how to manage them, to dissolve the doubts, and remove the scruples which are almost in every step of his way to Christ, and so to settle the fluctuating soul in a sweet and sure dependence upon him by faith, these things, I say, require much faithful prudence, and prudent faithfulness.

And thus we see the manifold usefulness of both these graces in the servants and stewards of Christ. Of such I may say, as Christ in the text, Who then is a faithful and wise servant! These servants are so rare, that out of a thousand scarce one man may be found that discharges that office aright. Christ does not have many such servants, yet, blessed be God, there are some.

Faithful, for the reward

Whoever, or wherever such faithful and wise servants are, Christ will abundantly reward them. This brings me to the third matter I promised to speak on, which is the glory prepared for, and promised to such servants of Christ, as laid out, in shining terms, by the prophet Daniel: 'Those who are wise shall shine as the brightness of the firmament, and those who turn many to righteousness, as the stars for ever and ever' (Dan. 12:3). This promise points directly to faithful and wise ministers. What a beautiful sight is the blue canopy of heaven, when it is about to shut its beautiful eyes in a serene evening! And much more, when it is about to open them with a smile or blush, in the dawning of the ruddy morning! And how is that beauty again exceeded by the glory of the stars, where the pleasing light shines! How does one star excel another in glory! Yet even beyond the brightness of the sun itself shall the servants of Christ shine, who by their faithfulness and prudence have turned many to righteousness!

The question about degrees of glory in heaven is not necessary, and it has difficulties. We reject with abhorrence the popish doctrine of different degrees of glory as founded in the diversity of merits. Nor is it questioned among the orthodox whether there be an equality of glory, as to the essentials, but only in respect to the accidentals. Amongst these they place the additional glory and joy of such ministers, whose faithful and prudent labours God has blessed and crowned with the conversion and edification of many souls. And of this the apostle speaks: 'for what is our hope, or joy, or crown of rejoicing? Is it not you, in the presence of our Lord Jesus Christ at his coming? For you are our glory and joy' (1 Thess. 2:19-20). Here we find something very remarkable. He calls his Thessalonian converts, 'his hope, his joy, and his crown of rejoicing'. His hope, that is, the substance of his hope, that they should be saved; his joy, as they had already given him abundant cause of joy, in their conversion to Christ by his ministry; and the 'crown of his rejoicing in the presence of Christ, at his coming'. This is a high strain indeed! The meaning, I suppose, is that the fruit and success of his ministry among them would add to his crown, and redound to his glory in the day of Christ.

O brothers, who would not study and pray, spend and be spent, in the service of such a bountiful Master! Is it not worth all our labours and sufferings, to come with all those souls we instrumentally give birth to for Christ, and all that we built up strengthened, and comforted on the way to heaven, and say, 'Lord, here am I, and the children you have given me'? To hear one spiritual child say, 'Lord, this is the minister by whom I believed, and another, this is he by whom I was edified, established, and comforted; this is the man that resolved my doubts, quickened my dying affections, guided my soul, when wandering from the truth! O blessed be your name, that I ever saw his face, and heard his voice!' What do we think of this, brethren? But far beyond this, what will it be to hear Christ, the Prince of pastors, say in that day, 'Well done, good and faithful servant; you have been faithful over a few things; I will make you ruler over many things: enter into the joy of the Lord' (Matt. 25:21).

We serve a good Master, who is not unrighteous to forget our work and labour of love for his name's sake. He keeps an exact account of all your fervent prayers, of all your instructive and persuasive sermons, and all your sighs, groans, and pantings, with every tear and drop of sweat are placed like marginal notes against your labours in his book, in anticipation of a full reward.

But I have far outrun my own intention, and, I fear, your patience too in the doctrinal part. I consider to whom I speak, and shall be the shorter in the application, which I shall dispatch apace, in three uses.

Three lessons for wise and faithful gospel servants

1. Remember the call of the ministry.

It appears from this that Christ has established an order and government in his house which no one must violate. The church is a well-ordered family, or household, where Christ is the head, Christians are members, ministers are stewards, and the ordinances are food to be served by them. Everyone is to keep his own place and station. Pastors must faithfully feed and govern the flocks of Christ (Acts 20:28). People must know, honour, and obey those who are over them in the Lord (1 Thess. 5:12; Heb. 13:17). The one must not impose, nor the other usurp, but each walk according to the rule of Christ.

This order is the church's beauty (Col. 2:5). We may expect so much of Christ's presence, as we have of his rule and order amongst us, and no more. O that the rules and orders of his house were better known and observed! Then ministers and people would clearly understand what they are to expect from each other in the way of duty, and each person keep his proper station. Ministers must not invade the civil callings of the people, nor the people the sacred calling of the ministry; but all things should move in order.

In the light of this truth we may also read our duty, how we ought to govern ourselves in the ordination of men to the ministry. This office is to be committed to faithful and able men (2 Tim. 2:2) not to novices (1 Tim. 3:6). I know the needs of the churches are great, but we must take no unwise haste to supply their needs. There is less danger in putting an ignorant man in a chemist's shop to prepare medicines for men's bodies than to trust a man who lacks both faithfulness and prudence, with the ministry of Christ's ordinances to men's souls.

Some men are moved by pitifully low ambitions. 'Put me into the priest's office, that I may eat a piece of bread' (1 Sam. 2:36). What men's secret aims are, we cannot know, but their qualifications for that work we may and ought to know. We are solemnly charged to 'lay hands hastily upon no man' (1 Tim. 5:22). Many are useful who will not excel. Weaker gifts, rooted in a gracious heart, will grow by using, but nothing grows without a root. I think the plainest men have done the greatest service in the church of Christ, as tender-eyed Leah brought forth more children than beautiful Rachel. But still, faithfulness and prudence are essential qualifications.

So, if there are such rewards in the hand of Christ for all his faithful and wise servants, then we have no just cause or reason to repent of our choice of this office, whatever sufferings and reproaches it has or yet may expose us to. I believe none of us ever yet felt such dangers, endured such miseries, or sustained such labours, as the apostle says befell him (2 Cor. 11:23-27), and yet he heartily thanks the Lord Jesus Christ who had counted him faithful, and put him into the ministry.

Brothers, we have served a good Master, and have cause to admire his care over us, and bounty to us, whatever we have suffered. Oh, he has been a good God to us! He has covered us in days of danger, made provision for us and ours. Let no one be scared at the reproaches and persecutions that attend the gospel.

2. Beware of dishonouring the ministry and the Master.

This point stands as a reproach to all unfaithful and imprudent ministers, who give their people the chaff for the wheat, and stones for bread, who glory in the title, and live upon the profits, but neither feed the flock nor mind their behaviour. They preach and pray because they must do so, but none are the better for their prayers or preaching. They seem to labour an hour or two in a week, but their labours turn to no account, nor can be expected to turn to any good account, whilst they are neither motivated by faithfulness nor guided by prudence. I shall leave these men to consider the words immediately following my text, which, like a thunder-clap from the mouth of Christ, discharge woes and threatenings upon them: 'suppose that the evil servant shall say in his heart, My Lord delays his coming, and shall begin to abuse his fellow-servants, and to eat and drink with drunkards. The Lord of that servant shall come in a day when he does not expect him, and in an hour that he is not aware of, and shall cut him to pieces, and appoint him his portion with hypocrites, where there shall be weeping, and gnashing of teeth' (verses 48-51). Who can increase their misery more than these words of Christ have done?

But I am principally concerned at this time with our own defects, both in faithfulness and in prudence. Though neither of these, I hope, are totally lacking us, yet our defects and shortcomings may and must greatly humble us. Our wasting of much precious time, our carelessness in so weighty a study as the salvation of our people, our sinful silence, when conscience says reprove, our coldness and dead-heartedness, our shallow and unprofitable conversations, our pride and showing-off with our gifts: all these clearly show that both our brains and hearts need more strength and tenderness.

3. Give yourself fully to the ministry.

Are faithfulness and prudence the essential requisites of the servants and stewards of Christ's house? And will he so amply reward whoever he finds them in? Then let it be our care and study to approve ourselves to him, as he here describes and encourages.

We have a solemn charge given us by Christ: 'I charge you therefore before God, and the Lord Jesus Christ, who shall judge the living and the dead at his appearing, and his kingdom: preach the word; be ready in season and out of season; reprove, rebuke, exhort with all long-suffering and careful instruction' (2 Tim. 4:1, 2). It must be a powerful drug indeed that can so numb and stupify the conscience of a minister, so that he shall not feel the awesome authority of such a charge.

The precious and immortal souls of men are committed to us, souls about which God has concerned his thoughts from eternity, for the purchase of which Christ has shed his own blood, for the winning and bringing of them to himself, he has put you into this office at whose hands he will also require an account of them in the great day.

We have a solemn account on that day to give to Christ. We 'watch for their souls, as those who must give account' (Heb. 13:17). And what can more powerfully excite to faithful diligence in the discharge of duty than the consideration of that day! The apostle has mentioned this (2 Cor. 5:10), and in the light of this awesome appearance before the judgment seat of Christ he says, 'knowing therefore the terror of the Lord, we persuade men' (verse 11).

Brothers, let us beware of committing or of neglecting anything, that may bring us to the terrors of that day. Let our hard work and faithfulness, our constancy and seriousness, compel a testimony from our congregations, as the apostle did from his, 'That we are innocent of the blood of all men' (Acts 20:26).

We have a great opportunity to take for Christ. If we do it, we shall fulfil his charge, and escape the terrors of his judgment in that great day.

We were once young and inexperienced ministers, compared to what we are now. Though we have too many defects and weaknesses still to lament, yet I am persuaded we have not spent so many years among trials, fears, and sufferings in vain. These things, I am persuaded, have greatly improved our acquaintance with God, and our own hearts. It will be as sad as strange, if they have not. God has been training us up in faith, humility, patience, and self-denial in this school of affliction.

Lift up your eyes, and behold the fields: are they not even ready for the harvest? Let farmers rather lose their seed-time and harvest, than we lose so precious a season, so great, so rich an opportunity as this.

I have finished what concerns you, my dear brothers, and fellow-labourers in the Lord's harvest. A word or two remains to be spoken to the people, and I have done.

You have heard what a range of duties lies upon us, and what difficulty is in every part of them. Yet our labours would be light and our pains pleasant, if we could see more fruit and success amongst you. Your barrenness and hard-heartedness, your divisions and instability, cost us more than all our other pains in our studies and pulpits. How easily and sweetly would the plough go, if you would only set both your hands of prayer and obedience to assist us in that work.

The stewards of Christ provide choice dishes for you, even feasts of good things, and serve it into your souls upon the knee of prayer in due season. Take care that you do not despise them, if at any time the dishes are not flavoured exactly as you expect.

The Lord give you hungry appetites, sound digestions, and thriving souls, then you shall be our crown of rejoicing, and we yours in the day of our Lord Jesus Christ. I commend you all to the word of his grace, which is able to build you up, and give you an inheritance among them that are sanctified.

John Flavel in the
Pocket Puritans series

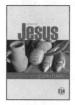 *None But Jesus*

176 pages
ISBN 978 1 84871 407 6

(Quotations from Flavel)

 *Impure Lust*

80 pages
ISBN 978 0 85151 981 4

 *Sinful Speech*

96 pages
ISBN 978 1 84871 017 7

 Binge Drinking

80 pages
ISBN 978 1 84871 015 3

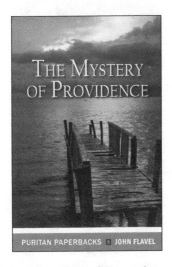

The Mystery of Providence
John Flavel

FIRST published in 1678, this little work is based on the words 'God that performeth all things for me' (Psalm 57:2). It shows us how providence works for us in every stage and experience of our lives. The book is richly illustrated from the lives of believers and from the author's wide reading in church history. There are avenues of spiritual knowledge and experience opened to the Christian in this work which he probably never knew existed.

Puritan Paperback | 224 pages | ISBN 978 0 85151 104 7

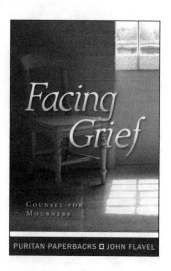

Facing Grief
John Flavel

IN 1674, two years after his second wife's death, John Flavel published *A Token for Mourners*. In it he meditates on the words of Luke 7:13: 'And when the Lord saw her, he had compassion on her, and said unto her, 'Weep not.' From this verse the author helps the reader to think about grief, distinguishing 'moderate' sorrow from 'immoderate'. He spells out what is appropriate for a Christian mourner and what is not. This book is full of Scripture, counsel, warning, and wisdom gained from prayerful reflection on the personal experience of affliction in loss and grief.

Now republished as *Facing Grief: Counsel for Mourners*, this attractive new edition makes Flavel's *Token* accessible once again in the form in which it knew such popularity – a small book, just the right size for carrying, and reading slowly, with meditation, reflection and prayer.

Puritan Paperback | 136 pages | ISBN 978 1 84871 069 6

The Works of John Flavel

in six volumes

THE repeated editions of Flavel's *Works* bear their own witness to his popularity. He was a favourite with Jonathan Edwards and George Whitefield (who ranked him with John Bunyan and Matthew Henry), and, a century later, with such Scottish evangelical leaders as R. M. M'Cheyne and Andrew Bonar. Flavel's complete works had long been unobtainable until we reprinted them in 1968. His six volumes are in themselves a library of the best Puritan divinity and a set will be a life-long treasure to those who possess it. He is one of that small number of evangelical writers who can by their lucidity and simplicity help those at the beginning of the Christian life and at the same time be a strong companion to those who near its end.

6 clothbound volumes | 3,667 pages | ISBN 978 0 85151 060 6